RICHARD ROHR

RICHARD ROHR

Illuminations of His Life and Work

Edited by
ANDREAS EBERT
and
PATRICIA C. BROCKMAN

CROSSROAD · NEW YORK

1993

The Crossroad Publishing Company
370 Lexington Avenue, New York, NY 10017

Printed in the United States of America

Library of Congress Cataloging-in-Publication Data
Richard Rohr : illuminations of his life and work / edited by Andreas
Ebert and Patricia C. Brockman.
 p. cm. ISBN 0-8245-1270-7
 1. Christian life—1960- 2. Rohr, Richard. 3. Church and the
world. 4. Spirituality—Christianity. I. Ebert, Andreas.
BV4501.2.R51167 1993
248.4–dc20
 93-20130
 CIP

To
Richard Rohr, O.F.M.,
through whom his parents, John and Eleanor,
and their German ancestors
have passed on
the gospel message of peace.

Contents

Preface

Celebrating the life of one person in a public way can be a hazardous venture. Only if this person's life has so intersected with our own as to make us know better and touch more intimately our own experience, only then can we be justified in the undertaking. Perhaps Richard Rohr's experience of cancer in 1991 encourages us to linger in our desire to enjoy with him this fiftieth birthday. With this book, its contributors and editors acknowledge what we have found to be true in Richard's life and preaching. In preaching to us, he has preached to himself and walked before us. Together we are one segment of the greater church reality, one moment in the history of the Franciscan experience, one group of people on the universal pilgrimage to uncover some hints of the divine mystery.

Being a public person has placed Richard in roles that others may envy, but that he frequently has accepted with astonishment attended by both joy and pain. From his earliest life with his father and mother, sisters and brother, Richard Rohr learned what has become central to his understanding of God: that he is a son. This has remained crucial to his knowledge of Jesus in relationship to an all-loving God. His theology arises from a childlike marveling at a God who became one with us. Although his role as teacher of persons and founder of communities creates for him the danger of being an archetypal father, he has rejoiced in his leadership, while developing caution about weakening that brotherhood with which both his family of origin and his Franciscan family have blessed him. When, as in all families, misunderstandings have arisen, they have been reconciled by the radical grace that seals the gaps opened by wounding. Thus, anyone who is at all familiar with Richard Rohr knows how closely he has engaged himself in the life and death of Jesus of Nazareth, how deeply he has grasped the biblical experience by choosing to embrace it in lifestyle and in ministry.

Some of those who have helped write this book are famous, others are practically unknown. We all had one thing in common: at some point in our lives Richard Rohr has crossed our paths. The many-sidedness of the book reflects the many different contexts in which Richard lives and by which he is shaped. It is an ecumenical network — European and American, Catholic and Protestant, male and female, young and old, from within the church and without. The variety of authorship gathered to congratulate Richard is a mirror image of the breadth of his heart and mind, which transcends national and denominational boundaries. The collection honors his ability to join together, to synthesize that which in the history of the church has so often been separated: earth and heaven, the world and God, the secular and sacred, the flesh and spirit.

The contributions of this book, therefore, reflect the major gospel themes that Richard Rohr has made the center of his life and ministry. With him we take time to reflect again on the sources and expressions of the spiritual journey: contemplation, living in community, peace, ecumenism, conversion, and social activism. Richard has touched our lives through the power of words and the credibility of his life as a human being, a Franciscan preacher, a counselor, visionary, pray-er, brother, and father.

Nowadays he may say some things differently from the way he did in the early 1970s, when the New Jerusalem Community was just getting off the ground. But readers who aren't frozen in place will notice that any fresh variations return to a basic theme: the love of God as Father, who accepts the world as it is. Richard defines truth from its core and midpoint from whence the light of the Cosmic Christ pours out upon the world. He does not claim to say anything new; in fact, when he speaks one often has the feeling of having known that all along! Believing that God is revealed to everyone who is truly seeking, he is open to the wisdom of nonbiblical religions, yet keeps returning to the incarnation of God in Jesus Christ, to the "folly of the cross" and the mystery of Jesus' death and resurrection, the central mysteries of Christianity. Even when criticizing the church, he still remains true to it.

At an early age Richard read of Francis of Assisi, then met the Franciscan friars at a parish mission. His decision to become a Franciscan flowered so that at age fourteen he left Topeka, Kansas, and went east to Cincinnati to follow in the footsteps of Francis. There Francis's image began to shape Richard's life. He was seized by this Spirit that freed him to develop authentically and creatively.

Some years later at the celebration of Richard's first Mass back in Topeka, a curious event occurred. A woman approached him and declared that this parish church stood in the exact spot where, in 1900, a group of Wesleyans had gathered begging for the gift of the Spirit. Precisely a year later, a "neo-Pentecostal" breakthrough occurred, bursting forth among them with exuberant joy and the gift of tongues. The woman told Richard then that his ordination seventy years later, at this very place, was a promise and sign that God's spirit would now return to the old churches and that he would be an instrument in this movement. At the time he thought the woman overexcited, but shortly later, after his return to Cincinnati, he was assigned to teach adolescents, indicating that his choices were no longer in his hands alone.

The young people he taught and led on retreats were overwhelmed with the gospel message. They gathered around this enthusiastic young priest, hungry for Scripture, increasingly eager for the shared life described there. Their weekly prayer gatherings began with fervent charismatic prayer and expanded from a group of teenagers to, at times, more than a thousand persons of many ages and diverse backgrounds. All the signs and wonders of the early church flourished among the prayers. It eventually became clear that enthusiasm was not enough, and among those followers some desired to live in a closer bond and within the discipleship of Christian community. Thus New Jerusalem came into being, a laboratory-church where many came to commit themselves to the dream of a church that follows and trusts Jesus. This was now no mere ideal, but a palpable reality. Even then Richard said: "For those who have experienced it, you don't need to give any explanations. For those who haven't experienced it, you *can't* give any explanations." Trust prevailed in the midst of the simplest lifestyle. Brothers and sisters shared leadership responsibilities, living together in communal homes of prayer and ministry truly revolutionary for Catholicism in the 1970s. Darkness gave way to liberation as the life of prayer and commitment to the poor opened its members to the Spirit and to one another.

In this context, it was inevitable that Richard's life and that of the community would be led into the political arena. Captured by the vision of Francis's call to prayer in the caves, Richard had first stressed that being precedes action, that to be loved by God, to be the Body of Christ, and to live in just relationships would give rise to all else. He later acknowledged that this was one of the great spiritual misreadings of his life. Indeed, there were many who experienced the love of God in a supportive community who could not spontaneously reach out to feed the poor, or take a public stand for the cause of peace. Like Hans Urs von Balthasar, Richard discovered a second, deeper stage of spirituality: action, that kind of engagement from which meaning and understanding arise. He was arrested in 1983 with a large group of religious leaders, with men and women from New Jerusalem, from around the country, from many walks of life and many religious persuasions. This had a tremendous educational impact on him. Protesting the buildup of nuclear arms, he broke the law against praying publicly in the United States Capitol.

At that time, the picture of Richard — handcuffed and in Franciscan garb — was picked up by the world press and moved him once and for all into the public perception of "leftist." In reality, he discovered in this action itself the Francis who was consistently nonviolent.

At this point a family story took on new value for Richard. His own German ancestors had fled Germany in the eighteenth century when Catherine the Great promised them freedom from military service in Russia. Later, the promise revoked, his family and fellow believers emigrated to the American West, settling on the farmland of western Kansas. In his own protest activities, Richard discovered new pride for these German-Russian Catholic-pacifist ancestors.

As many of the young men and women who had shaped New Jerusalem married and faced the challenge of raising children counter-culturally, Richard's quest for new paths led him ever more deeply into the world of contemplation. What he had discovered in his own action and that of close activist friends led him paradoxically to the hermitage of Thomas Merton. In this holy place Merton's presence guided Richard and transformed him for his calling to Albuquerque, New Mexico. It was in the American Southwest, years before, that Richard had served among the Pueblo Indians of Acoma. He had always remained drawn to this landscape and its spirituality.

And so the new foundation, this next stage of Richard Rohr's life and ministry, is called the Center for Action and Contemplation. Action first! In this scenario community comes into existence as a by-product when people come together because of their hunger for justice and their commitment to take risks. This is Richard's current means to strengthen laypeople in a clerically structured church. In the guest house at CAC, the paths of seekers from around the world cross. Hospitality, autonomy, human dignity, and simplicity are present here as they have been in all those places that shaped Richard's life, qualities that continue to be generated in the environments that he forges.

May these very gifts be the ones that welcome you, dear brother, as you return from the extensive travels that form home for you on your evangelizing trips. We offer these writings to you, Richard, as a gift of appreciation for your life. They are a sign of our love for you. We offer them, also, as a continuing commitment to listen with you to God's word as it is written in each of our hearts. And with these writings we want to give a grateful return to you, to acknowledge your place as son of God, brother, leader, inspirator — growing among us in wisdom and age and (radical) grace!

ANDREAS EBERT AND PAT BROCKMAN

RICHARD ROHR

Brothers

John Quigley

The Franciscan movement evokes stirring, romantic, and perennial tales of the mystery of God's constant unconditional love. By it numerous brothers and sisters have through the ages joined company with Jesus and his band of followers, open to adventure and martyrdom, united in bold courage to become a force for change with global implications. Both as a boy and young man Richard Rohr was caught up in the mythology of Francis, Clare, and their early followers. He has never outgrown this youthful passionate vision. It is as fresh today as it ever was for him, only more radical.

With the twist of a phrase Richard Rohr can turn on lights in a thousand minds. He is perhaps the most influential Catholic preacher in the English-speaking world in the second half of the twentieth century. With translations he is fast becoming very popular in Europe, particularly in the German-speaking countries.

I have known Richard since 1962. At different intervals during the past thirty years we have lived in the same friaries and in the New Jerusalem Community in Ohio, studying or working together. He is an amazing, simple man who has a great passion for speaking about God, "doing" theology in a sensible, practical, and understanding way. He is prophetic, utterly convincing, and seldom satisfied with himself. There have been occasions when the people fascinated by Richard's gifts have asked me if I knew the secrets that contributed to his success as preacher and popular reformer. What does he read? Where did he study? For some it is not an idle curiosity. They want to "crack the code" or learn the secrets in order to be able to preach like Richard.

Richard and I were companions together during a spiral of events and reflections that have profoundly affected our lives: the opening of the Second Vatican Council in October 1962; the ferment, protests, and turmoil of the late 1960s; Graham Greene's identifying Francis of Assisi as the true revolutionary of history; Brother Didier's exhilarating summer school classes on catechetics at Notre Dame University. Together we discovered "doing" systematic theology and learned from the history of the greater church during our classes in Dayton, Ohio. The surprising Pentecostal experiences of the early 1970s, too, the early electric kerygma of Richard's series of talks on themes of Scripture brought us into even deeper brotherhood. Then the sudden blossoming success of the New Jerusalem Community in Cincinnati grew into full-time occupations for us.

Richard founded the New Jerusalem Community in 1971. It became an experiential ecclesial laboratory of discovery and application. Its beginning and development were similar to the beginnings of the greater church, starting with the initial proclamation of the risen and living Jesus, the call to personal conversion and dedication to Jesus Christ, the conviction of God's unconditional everlasting love, and the trust to take a journey on the "flying carpet" of faith. With the formation of a faith community came the responsibilities of pastoring an evergrowing flock, the cost of discipleship, teachings on spiritual family, the discovery of the healing power of God through Christian community, the power of affirmation and listening, decisions to establish Christian households — all leading to a deepened sense of mission. Full-time ministry teams were formed of counselors, evangelists, neighborhood visitors, a renovation crew for our homes. Male and female "coheadship" modeled leadership in our houses and community structures.

There were ongoing dialogues with the archdiocese of Cincinnati, the Episcopalian Church of the Redeemer in Houston, Texas, and the Community of Communities, an activist group of prophetic reform communities in the Anabaptist tradition. There was input from many sources, including the Spiritual Exercises of Ignatius, Jungian psychology, group dynamics, the Enneagram, as well as the "Wild Man" spirituality. All these left an impact on Richard's spirituality and preaching. Formative earlier for Richard had been his experiences as a deacon with the Acoma Pueblo native peoples in Acoma, New Mexico. That experience was to become the seed of his return to the Southwest in 1986 to form the Center for Action and Contemplation in Albuquerque.

Richard and I share many stories, some humorous and some serious. We know each other well. In the seminary we had the same teachers of public speaking. We sat in the same philosophy and theology classes and spent many hundreds of hours recreating together. He was a good student but never known as a "philosopher" or an academic "theologian." During the years that we served as pastors together at New Jerusalem, I was regularly aware of the books that Richard was reading. I also knew the people with whom he was speaking and formulating his constant evergrowing garden of ideas.

Richard constantly reads and observes. He does not write his talks.

He does not labor to craft his insights or phrases. Rather new ideas and observations regularly arise from within where they are stored, hidden in his subconscious or unconscious world. When he is talking or preaching, new and often surprising connections flow forth in an intuitive, unexpected, and free manner. To understand the power and dynamism of Richard's visions and preaching one need study neither different models of ecclesiology, nor the sociologies of North American cultures, nor modern biblical criticism. One need not read Carl Jung, Robert Bly, Dorothy Day, nor Margaret Mead. His theologizing is not a clever rearticulation of what he has read and synthesized. It is his rich community experiments and global experiences together with his many books and conversations that serve as the chief raw material for Richard's theologizing.

Yet even in and of themselves these sources cannot explain Richard's brilliance. He is not merely a clever synthesizer or popularizer of modern research and ideas. In fact, his preaching never remains at a current popular plateau. Rather he is forever impatient to again make one more attempt to talk about the Mystery that is the definite center point in his life. He is like a poet who compulsively, constantly writes, and tears up his drafts, and then tries again to express the poem that is buried in his soul.

There is an underlying base of premises, an integrated worldview that serves as Richard's strong foundation and principle of integration. This clear, powerful foundation is presumed by him. It is a worldview, a world expectation that was sealed within him at a very early age. It continues in his life and propels him into his experiments with profound convictions. That worldview is Franciscan. The mythology begins with Saint Francis and Clare of Assisi, two young people who were profoundly moved by God's incarnation as a human being. They were not romantic, sentimental figurines wrapped in rough brown wool. The insightful revolutionary love of Francis — who believed that he personally was asked by Jesus to "rebuild the church, which had fallen into ruins" — was a great part of the reason Richard left home when he was fourteen years old. He left not to join a military academy or a sports camp. He left home to follow a popular nonviolent crusade, the Franciscans. To understand the inner fire of Richard — and all other Franciscans — you must look at the story of Francis and his followers.

For the past eight hundred years other men and women, inspired by the simple genius and freshness of Francis and Clare, have been developing and popularizing the original Franciscan inspiration. This continual *aggiornamento,* or updating, has had a profound humanizing effect within Christianity, Western civilization, and other cultures. It is not easy to put into a capsule the spirit and gifts of Franciscan thinking. Its hallmarks are simplicity, reverence, fraternity, ecumenism, ecology, interdependence, and dialogue. Its motto and salutation is "Peace and All Good!"

Francis believed that God was nonviolent, the God of Peace. This belief may be a simple presupposition for us today, but at the time when the Christian church was waging a Holy Crusade against its enemies, the Saracens, Francis's interpretation of the gospel life and its demands was revolutionary. Francis saw it from the viewpoint of the poor, especially from the place of the poor, naked, suffering Christ. He had deep devotion to the God who is revealed as nonviolent and poor in the stable of Bethlehem, as abandoned on the cross, and as food in the Eucharist. God's meekness, humility, and poverty led Francis to become "perfected as his Heavenly Father was perfect." Francis identified with the "minores," the lower class within his society, and he passionately pointed to the Incarnation as the living proof of God's love. He frequently cried out in his pain that "Love is not loved!"

The experiences of God's love revealed to Francis our fragile and temporary place within creation. He knew that we share this earth, our loves and work with all of God's creatures, our brothers and sisters. Unlike the monastic life, which strove to domesticate nature and to bring it under control, Francis expected to live lightly on the earth, a burden to neither the earth nor to those who fed and clothed him.

There are many lively legends about Francis and Clare, which serve as the guide and canon for Franciscan tradition. These seminal stories and the insights that arise from them have given impetus to specific themes in Franciscan philosophy and theology. They include the idea that Jesus did not assume flesh to correct Adam and Eve's sin; rather, Jesus would have taken flesh whether we had sinned or not. Love by its very nature wants to be one with its beloved, so our salvation has been announced and realized in an Incarnate God. The suffering and death of Jesus confirms for us how deep and committed is God's love in the Incarnation.

Each individual existence — person, plant, stone, amoeba — is absolutely precious. Each has a certain unique "thisness," which cannot be completely shared or described by another. Each creature of God must attain the full measure of its *own* uniqueness, its "thisness" before the full expression of God's love can be realized in creation.

Simplicity is another Franciscan theme and sign of God's love. We should multiply words, explanations, and actions only when necessary, he tells us. Others may say that we come to understand God by analogies. The Franciscan perspective is that we can have a direct effect and univocal understanding of God by reflecting and understanding our experience of ourselves as human beings. Finally, everything, every Scripture, every law, every action, history itself is to be interpreted in light of the primacy of Love and Christ over all.

It is impossible to describe in a few pages the deep unconscious pools and springs of living water flowing from the Franciscan sources that have nourished, refreshed, and simplified Richard's life. These streams are still flowing and rushing toward the Lord of History, the Love who became one with us and still lives among us. These currents are still and deep, turbulent and pounding, even angry at times, impatient with any obstacle that keeps them from their fulfillment.

Zen Poem

To Honor the Contemplative Teaching of Richard

DANIEL BERRIGAN

"How I long for supernatural powers!"
said the novice mournfully
to the holy one.
"I see a bent old woman
I want to say, Be healed!
I stand before dead men
I long to say, Arise!
Alas, I feel like a dry stick in paradise.
Master, help me, confer on me
supernatural powers!"

The old man shook his head fretfully.
"How long have I been with you," he groaned
"and you know nothing.
How long have you known me
and learned nothing.

"Listen. I have walked the earth
end to end, these eighty years.
Have stood beside
the newborn, the ill, the dying.

"Little could I do,
next to nothing!
the ruse of power
the rush of pride
passing me by.

"I confess to you
never once
have I healed
the ills

or humankind —
never
from their dwellings
summoned the dead.

"We thrive, we sicken
soon, late, under
a stigma of frost or fire.

"And what is soon or late
to you or to me —
but the turn of the wheel
but the way of birth
but the gateway to paradise?

"Supernatural powers!
then you would play God
would spin the thread
and measure the thread
5 years, 40 years, 80 years —
and cut the thread?

"Supernatural powers!
Listen; I have wandered the earth
have stood, withstood
birth, illness, death,
heard the first cry,
dried the last tear —

"Supernatural powers!
I confess to you
sprout without root
root without flower —
I know nothing of supernatural powers.
I have yet to perfect these natural powers!

"To see and not be seduced
to hear and not be deafened
to taste and not be consumed
to touch and not be tricked

"But you —
would you walk water
would you master air
would you swallow fire?

"Go ride with eagles
they will hatch you, nest you
eaglet and airman.

"Go join the circus
tricksters will train you
in deception for dimes.

"Bird man, bag man
spouting fire, moon crawling
at sea forever—
supernatural powers!

"Do you seek miracles?
Go
draw water,
hew wood
break stones!

"I offer a koan;
Enter a dark time
then a red time,
then a green time.

"Endure in the dark time
bleed in the red time
walk free in the green time!

"In the dark time
deceive no one
in the red time
kill no one
in the green time
condemn no one.

"Then you will
behold
the irresistible power
or natural powers—
of height, of joy,
of soul, of non belittling!

"Then
angels and you
will trace
round and round and round—
an inch, a mile,
the earth's vast compass—
a liberated zone
of paradise!"

- 3 -

Forgiveness

WERNER BINDER

Richard, I remember how during our trip to Assisi in 1992 we cele-
brated the Eucharist, standing in a circle around the altar, conscious
of our wounded earth. You broke the bread and said that forgive-
ness meant powerlessness. At that moment it was very quiet, and the
power of the Holy Spirit was in the room.

—

The way to enlightenment, as Jesus Christ taught and teaches, leads
to love and is itself love, which culminates in forgiveness and love of
our enemies.

Jesus did not say: "Go to a quiet place, and ask to be freed from the
chains of your ego, and thus you will become enlightened." Instead
he said, "Forgive even those who persecute you. Love your enemies."

Genuine forgiveness, in which the feelings of injury, rage, and
grief are lived through and felt through, releases and redeems us.

The process of redemption takes place in relation to other people,
to all of creation, and to ourselves. At the same time forgiving love
releases and liberates something in the person who forgives, in the
people who are forgiven, and in the quality of the relationships.

Forgiveness is a process of death and transformation.

To forgive the people who attack us, who threaten our psychic
and physical integrity and our sense of ourselves, is simply impossible
within a basically egocentric attitude. Why?

Forgiveness threatens the ego. The act of deep forgiveness threatens to make the ego break down and disintegrate.

Trapped in compulsive comparisons and judgments, the ego constantly has to justify and validate itself, so that it won't come apart.
It builds itself up on, among other things, the guilt-feelings and mistakes of other people. That is why it's hardly prepared to give away
trumps (power) of its own accord. It never stops insisting that the
other person (the world, fate, or whatever) still owes it something.
In our claims for retribution we hold on tightly to old insults and

disappointed expectations. Resentment binds us to the presumed guilt (the mistakes) of others and is an attempt to bind others to ourselves.

Thus the ego is clinging, oriented to the past, and fixated. . . .

Forgiveness, however, means letting go, means liberation from the entanglements of unhappy bonds. It means giving up false ideals and illusions and facing the question: "What really holds up — what is the foundation of my/our existence?"

This question is stifled in resentment; forgiveness makes it possible to ask it.

Since all true forgiveness means a partial death for the ego, it simultaneously leaves space free for creative and healing power.

Only when we sense or imagine that we are loved beyond and despite all our faults and attempts at manipulation, loved uninterruptedly and unconditionally, will we be ready to sacrifice our power over others. Only then will we be ready to let go of our little ideals and moral notions, which we had hitherto largely misused in order to feel "better" at others' expense.

Forgiving is a process of transformation.

Forms that have become case-hardened (labelings, curses, dismissals) break down in forgiveness. Lots of energy that was tied up by judging is set free. This energy becomes not just fluid and alive again, but transfigured. Fear and stiffness give way to trust, hate turns into love, judging into understanding.

Holy spirit awakens. The moment that we feel the full presence of the love of God in us and we pass on this love in an act of forgiveness, we release imprisoned, split-off power.

This is set free and is regenerated in the fullness of the present moment. It is a miracle. This energy helps to heal the wounds of our planet. Hence a deep-rooted forgiveness (between individual persons and nations) unleashes a surge of regenerative, healing forces not only in the people directly concerned but in the entire cosmos. Even things that lie blocked in the depths of the past can be redeemed.

If we believe in this redeeming power of forgiveness, the possibility opens up for us to take an active part in healing the earth in God's name and in collaboration with the prophets and angels.

Conscious cooperation in this redemptive work, which triggers a good deal of pain and grief, gradually changes our perception: We recognize creation, humanity, and ourselves as incarnate love. We perceive ourselves as matter evolving into light, which comes forth from the integration of darkness and brightness, in other words, from all the contraries of this world.

FORGIVENESS

I was on the point of drowning,
and you pulled me out.
I was gasping for breath,
and you gave me air.
You drew me to land,
and I live
on your compassion,
your forgiveness.

—

Your forgiveness
grew ever more radical,
till you died.

Thus,
when you were risen,
the light grew richer, layer upon layer.
The power of forgiveness pressed deeper into the souls.

—

Forgiving is dying and rising.

—

When I stand in your light
and open my hands
it shatters everything
that separates us,
and when I stop judging,
life begins.

When I feel
that you forgive,
totally,
every cell,
me, because you love me,
at every moment,
then I'd like to make a gift
of what you give me:
Forgiveness, as you forgive me,
wholeheartedly,
from head to toe;
sharing in your work of redemption,
diving into the new dimension,
beyond decency and norms.

Only the crazy
can forgive.

To do that,
what I think I am
must be extinguished,
so I can see in your light:
See, a person,
you and I.

Help me — I'm afraid —
to stand up to this adventure:
to love — not to judge,
to see the distress that leads to despair,
to immerse myself in the night of the unredeemed,
to come before the desperate,
trembling in their convulsions,
to remember you amid the tears,
the way you look at us, smiling,
in your forgiving Yes,
which slowly blossoms on my lips.

Perhaps I live for this smile,
from which healing comes
and the power
that gives birth to the wise
and sudden fulfillment to the frightened.

I sense it:

When I forgive,
all the blockage in the world breaks up
and power is released
to heal the wounds of the nations.

HEALING

Love for the weak and the broken
is what brought me here.
I am the window of your forgiveness,
in which light is refracted into color.

In the pupil of your dark eye
the man of light shone forth.
He is eternally newborn,
here, to proclaim you,
to be you here.

I have come forward
in a twinkling of your loving eye.
Out of the painful contrast
between what you are, my God,
and what we, forgetting you, have made of you,
Christ was born.

Christ is your compassion;

Your grace with us,
who try to bar you from our hearts.
When your compassion touches us,
our grief – for ourselves – turns
into streams of tears,
to water the barren places of the world,
to protect our unborn children, floating in the womb.

Silence and tenderness
are the strength of the wise,
and their vulnerability
is the conduit of their forgiveness.

"How exciting
the violet skin of the wise man,
who is mirrored in his tears
and lays his cheeks
on his knees
to hear the vibration of the world."

I wrote that a few years ago.
Now I think
the wise man walks through the world,
and each of his steps
is a declaration of love to the earth,
which says to him:

His blue breath surrounds me:
the wind.
I am the shimmering-blue embodiment of his tenderness;
the tears of joy and emotion
when he created the world.

I'll sing you the songs of all times,
in which I grew
and made life
and your eyes will burn with pain,
when you see

how beautiful
and how wounded I am.

—

Not I,
you wish to unfold yourself in me,
and as I die,
you will blossom.
Not I,
you will come forth
and your light, your silence will spread out,
as the breeze of the fields,
when the first sunrays
awaken the world.

I am the diamond
that must be polished
so that nothing mars your light.

Let me turn into nothing,
so that you become everything.

I am the door, the eye of the needle,
through which you enter.

Where I once was
has now fallen silent;
the unspeakable silence
around your throne.
Light in the dew of your silence.

The Broken Word

Dreams as Symbols of Transformation in the Christian Community

PATRICIA C. BROCKMAN

"The word is broken into pieces, but I still carry it around; it forms the word WORD."

The WORD is an object, probably made out of wood; it was originally whole, one piece, but over time and through much carrying around it has been broken into many, many pieces. I am a down-to-earth workman. This object is maybe the size of a very small baby, and I carry it with all the love and tenderness with which one would carry a small infant. The miracle is that its being broken into all these pieces doesn't seem to have damaged the original quality; the pieces nest into one another, almost interlock like puzzle pieces. It looks like moss agate or a veined precious stone.

I feel that this is what happens when it is carried around for a long time, this is the nature of the object; as if one could tell that it had been carried a long time, because it is now in many pieces. The value is not decreased, perhaps just the opposite.

It holds together and this is a wonder to me, I don't understand how it does. I am in awe, and I am very happy that I can still carry it and it still remains broken and yet whole at the same time. (Dream 072290 – Barbara G.)

A Community Dream Project

The dream above, named simply "WORD," was one of many collected by the New Jerusalem Community in the time following the loss of their founder, Richard Rohr. In a year given to exploring the possibility of dreams being directed to us as a community of God's people, we gathered our dreams monthly. We held them in reverent – often playful – consideration and asked God to speak again, as in early times, to us as a people. We desired to see if our dreams would reveal God's message to us as dreams did to our scriptural ancestors and through the early days of the church. Collected together the dreams developed patterns that described our life together or gave hints on how we might take action as a community.

My investigations have sought to extend communal symbols of sacrament and ritual to include those of dreams; and by so doing, I have hoped to expand and update the store of symbols within intentional Christian communities.[1] Raising awareness of the power of the unconscious in religious experience invites not only individual persons but also families, religious groups, even nations to rediscover the meaning in dreams for their life.

The opening sentence of the dream states actual words heard within the dream. When in reference to Scripture we use the phrase "break open the Word," we mean to chew on it, to ruminate, to reflect on it in terms of our life experience. We crack it open like a nut that contains rich sweet meat to be digested. As a lay community, New Jerusalem was reflecting in just such a way on the meaning of our life together, feeling deeply our fragility, the awareness that we could fall apart, yet experiencing that — surprisingly — all the pieces were indeed holding together.

In Eucharist, the bread is broken, in its nourishment and sharing an effective symbol of the essence of community life. Yet it is made of the crushed grain of our pain-filled and incomplete lives. In the early days of our intentional Christian community there was a sense of peace, even delight, in acknowledging such weakness and in expecting unconditional love.

The image of the dreamer as workman signified to us the hard work of building community, not a sophisticated work, but one of simple earthy demands. In our "work" we carried our new life tenderly. This was only one of many images of new life: eggs hatching, pregnancy, birth, and crying infants. We were — are — birthing the second stage of community, that necessary and difficult time in every community history when the teachings of the charismatic leader are tested by his or her absence. The dream truly described the community "soul" at that moment.

Dreams As Communal

On what basis can one be justified in claiming that dreams have communal content and reflect the word of God to a community as a group? I have found four sources: the theories of Carl G. Jung regarding the collective psyche; the experiments of Henry Reed; records of tribal dreams among primitive groups; and the history of symbol effectiveness in the Scriptures and Christian communities.

Throughout Jung's study of the structure of the individual psyche, he parallels its nature with that of the collective psyche:

> Inasmuch as there are [individual] differentiations corresponding to race, tribe, and even family, there is also a collective psyche limited to race, tribe, and family over and above the "universal" collective psyche.... We probably get closer to the truth if we think of the conscious and personal psyche resting upon the broad basis of an inherited and universal psychic disposition ... and that our personal psyche bears the same relation to the collective psyche as the individual to society.... *We can now see that the unconscious produces contents which are valid not only for the person concerned, but for others as well.*[2]

Thus, he acknowledges that each depends on the other, the individual carried on the collective and arising out of it, and the collective psyche shaped and transformed by the individuals who make it up.

Henry Reed put this to the test by creating a theoretical community of scattered dreamers who for four years sent to Dr. Reed the dreams they had for the universe, for the nation, or for great events.[3] On the North American continent there is increasing awareness of sensitivity to the native Americans who have shaped our past and have carried the primitive experience into our current cultures. As American peoples we have read about their tribal dreams, have admired them, and have sought to understand their religious experience.[4] Valid as this effort is, we cannot afford to avoid or deny our own "tribal" experiences. The personal spiritual effects of the sacraments as well as our communal conversions are rooted in the triggering effects of symbols that have transformed our lives at key moments. We have known symbols to be effective agents of change in the Christian history.

Learning from Our Experience

In a general sense we learned that the collected dreams of a group give rise to communal themes describing areas of dilemma, growth, and/or feeling, suggesting change or action. The process of collecting communal dreams, of examining their archetypal meaning and subjective implication for the group, heightened insight into our community life. The scriptural experience of God addressing his people through dreams has become a more acceptable reality for us, and therefore a source of increased faith in God's presence among us. As contemporary Christians, dreams have expanded for us the traditional categories of symbols.

Not only "big dreams" but ordinary dreams have multiple levels of meaning, one of which refers to community.[5] The dream is not limited by time; rather, it may refer to the past, suggesting the need for healing or insight, it may describe the present situation, or it may prefigure a future event.

Hermeneutics were applied to the text of dreams to explore the meaning of the symbols, as theological discernment provided a heuristic approach to faith and prayer. These qualitative methods were applied often as play. For example, one of the dreams used the symbol of the community on a treasure hunt. There is much joy in the dream, but mystery surrounds the nature of the treasure they are seeking. It is found in a shopping mall! In this realm of secular life, community members find colorful clothing which, when donned, becomes priestly vestments. Enacting this dream as a ritual, members of the community are struck anew with the realization that they are robed in the priesthood of the people.

In New Jerusalem's quest for God's word in dreams, twenty-eight themes arose throughout the year, six to ten of them becoming particularly emphatic. In some cases, several persons have had almost identical dreams on the same night. A case in point was the dream of a child standing on the edge of a steep precipice with a watchful parent close by. In each dream the parent showed the child how to avoid the danger. Three persons received this dream, and subsequently two others had similar dreams of a dangerous steep slope with muddy water at the foot of the slope. An even later dream indicated that the water was now clear. But in the meantime we addressed a prayer to the Lord using the images of the dream: "Lord, we are standing on the edge of a precipice. Show us what the danger is and how to avoid it." The responding dreams led us to recognize that we were in danger of letting confidence in ourselves as lay leaders within the church fall into the precipice of the unconscious, into unawareness.

Major themes of the dream year included: new life, leadership, ourselves as the church, our masculine and feminine energies, and communion. The theme of children and childhood has been a perduring image from New Jerusalem's earliest history. It appeared regularly in the dreams pointing to the poor whom we serve in ministry, to our own community children, and to our own vulnerable "inner child."

In New Jerusalem's experience community dreams expand the store of the intentional Christian community's traditional symbols beyond those sacraments and rituals with which we are so familiar and from which we draw so much life. To recover and respect the dream is to recover a source of God's word, a word that has been lost and broken in our suspicion of it. To respect it is to honor the God, the source of the dream.

In subsequent explorations of dreams in two traditional religious communities, dreams described communal experiences and opened new questions. The dreams highlighted the current challenge of transition in Catholic religious communities, but in the unique images of each group's collective experience.

Notes

1. Patricia C. Brockman, O.S.U., Ph.D. "Symbols of Transformation in the Intentional Christian Community," unpublished dissertation, The Union Institute, Cincinnati, Ohio, 1992.

2. Carl G. Jung, "The Relation of the Ego to the Unconscious," *Collected Works*, 7:148–49, 178–79.

3. Henry Reed, Ph.D., "The Sundance Experiment: An Introduction," *The Community Dream Journal* 1, no. 1 (1976): 108–41.

4. John G. Neihardt, *Black Elk Speaks* (New York: Pocket Books, 1972).

5. Jeremy Taylor, *Dream Work: Techniques of Discovering the Creative Power in Dreams* (New York: Paulist Press, 1983), 116–42. Taylor lists twenty-five elements common to dreams.

– 5 –

Ministering Communities
Our Answer to Individualism

PIERRE BRUNNER AND CATHERINE BRUNNER-DUBAY

❖

Communities are one of the forms of human connection vitally necessary nowadays for us to move beyond paralyzing and destructive egoism and individualism into greater personalization. They enable us to organize humanity, that is, to turn individuals into an organism. In this context the Pauline image of the Body of Christ takes on a new dimension for us. When human communities center themselves around Christ and let themselves be led by the driving power of love, they inevitably become places of personal freedom (the freedom to be a person) and experiential corporeality (a sense of organic wholesomeness).

If we carry over the image of a ship to our world and the human race, it becomes clear that the success of this "undertaking" can come only from common effort. We, that is, all men and women, rich and poor, the "strong" and the "weak," are in the same boat. We have to acknowledge that we can reach our goal only through connections, relationships, and justice. This gives great importance to precisely those people who are suffering harm from the progress of this world, who can't take part in it, and who continue to be victims of human evolution. Indeed, in all the relatively affluent societies of the West, physically and psychologically sick people, the retarded, the addicted, the unemployed and the homeless, single parents, adolescents looking for meaning and individuals living in isolation all face severe handicaps.

An essential part of the vocation of our ministering community is life together in solidarity with disadvantaged men and women. In ministering communities we share our life with people in difficult situations. This life together, as a contribution to more justice in the face of isolation, exclusion, and pauperization, is fundamentally a question of faith. We believe that we have been assigned the task of being co-workers with God in the completion of the creation. We believe that

22

we have been called to bind ourselves to one another as persons and children of the one God. Ministering communities are our attempt to give a little breathing room to the vision of humanity as the Body of Christ.

The desire and purpose of these communities is to be a place, a home, where we all can find our way to our humanness, where we all can learn to live meaningfully, where each of us can develop in personal freedom.

What does such life in common look like, and how can one experience its value?

In an effort to pass on something of what makes our life so unique and so ordinary, we would like to tell the story of a young man who was a member of our extended family for a year.

> Roger entered the community on November 1. He had just been thrown out of his apartment. Roger was a sensitive, cheerful, witty type, twenty-seven years old.
>
> In one short year of living together we and he learned to feel a mutual appreciation, and he readily made friends. His natural humor and his pointed, pithy sayings had a relaxing and amusing effect on everyday life – he often cracked us up.
>
> His help in running the house was especially noticeable in the kitchen and dining room. He had a special passion for peeling carrots and potatoes, serenely working his way through mountains of them. His creativity in setting the table at mealtime knew no bounds, and everyone who passed by the dining room was struck by his originality.
>
> Roger had been an alcoholic for fifteen years. Around the middle of August his health rapidly deteriorated, so we had to take him to the hospital.
>
> After five weeks of intensive treatment his condition had sufficiently stabilized so that we could bring him home again, although he was very weak and in need of care. He spent his last days in the familiar milieu of his room. He died on September 9, 1991, surrounded by his nearest relatives and all those who had been his family during this year in the Friedensgasse community.

I have tried to capture in a farewell poem what I found moving in our common experience of Roger, what has become important to me, and what I have learned, thanks to Roger.

ROGER

Who knows why a child starts to drink?
Who knows why a young man, just twenty-seven, can die?

You've posed these questions to me
    wordlessly, of course, and yet quite clearly

I've never given an answer
   apart from trying to go a bit of the way with you
Your night has also become mine
   it has made our days brighter
Who knows why a child starts to drink
Who knows why a young man, just twenty-seven, can die?

I've asked myself these questions
   again and again, with speechless pain
And you yourself gave the answer
   so that we go a bit of the way together
You've gone into the final depth of your night
   and I only watched and saw you go
Your night has brought you light
   and made my days brighter.

In everyday life together the group experience should be marked by lively, authentic, and friendly relationships. Mutual respect and appreciation is the way we help one another to acquire a human face.

Once we learn to take up each other's burdens, with all our gifts and limitations, that puts an end to the role of strong and weak, helper and needy, and opens up space for experiencing the unique value of every individual. In ministering communities what's important is how we live, and what's valuable is what we are as a group.

Our communities should be "experimental units" for the evolution of the world and the human race as the expansion of the Body of Christ. And here disadvantaged people have a prophetic function. They make it clear to us that real progress absolutely must bring greater humanity and more justice. Life in such small "experimental units" aimed at relieving distress should sharpen our eye for the worldwide problems of war, injustice, and poverty. It thrusts upon us the responsibility of taking part in the urgently needed efforts for global unity.

Finally, and this is the most important thing, life in common continually leads us to live what's essential, i.e., love. Our sympathy and our feelings of friendliness get exhausted very quickly. They have only a faint capacity for enduring differences and creating unity. "From whom [Christ] the whole body, joined and knit together by every ligament with which it is equipped, as each part is working properly, promotes the body's growth in building itself up in love" (Eph. 4:16).

The starkly heterogeneous make-up of our communities keeps providing plenty of opportunities for irritation. This challenges us to center ourselves anew in Christ through the practice of attentive love.

Attentive love grows out of the equilibrium between love of neighbor and love of self. Love of neighbor is an attitude that tries to see

Christ in others, while love of self wants Christ to unfold with us. This attentive love is a communication that comes forth from the center of each person and turns toward the center of the other, that makes it possible to experience Christ more and more as the center of every encounter.

In an atmosphere of attentive love the differentness of the other and his or her closeness to me not only can cease to be a threat, but can become a special opportunity in which people, in the common process of life, can unfold their individuality by recognizing their capacities and their need for completion. And this experience is the unmistakable sign that we are on the point of organizing ourselves as the Body of Christ.

The Journey

Thomas Buchter

❖

Once we were living
In a paradise of unity
In a garden of one-ness with all
But losing your divinity
We find ourselves
In an endless fall

In contradiction
Life now has taken place
We are wandering here
Through time and space
Reality is divided in me and you
Everything remains
In the world of two

Still in silence and contemplation
We can hear the vocation
To reconcile the "Dia-Balein"
By the work of integration
And out of new wholeness
And healing wounds
The living Christ can arise
Out of our fearful tombs

Rebirth from the paradox
He's the three
The one in us who really can be
And does not need to succeed
This yet unborn invisible child
Of great desire
Finds itself in the world of four
Surrounded with beauty
By water, wind, earth, and fire

Living as a creature
Among God's creation
He moves deep
Into his own incarnation
He starts to perceive
With all five senses
He touches, smells, tastes
Hears and sees
Divine nectar of things
And their mysteries
Open to the transcendent
And endless revelation
No more judging
Only awareness
And observation

While knowing that he's a child of God
And fully human
Again begins the "art of separation"
Led by the spirit
Into the desert of temptation
He faces darkness, evil
And all illusions of this matrix
He has to overcome the enemy
Symbolized by the false "Trinity of Six"
and by denying effectiveness
Rightness and control
He truly worships and trusts
In the living God alone

Then angels come and serve him
'Cause all the heaven knows
This is the son of man
The human powerless king
And seven fruits of the spirit
Are poured out into him
For his ministry
Now he steps back into the world
To give his life for us all
As a mystery

Able to serve and heal
The broken body of this world
He represents the eight
In his true Trinity

Someone laid it down one day
And the eight —
Became infinity

Yet this is not the end
Of this holy way
There's no place in this world
Forever to stay

At the ninth hour
Jesus died
And gave away for us
His life

If your souls one day will be
Empty and virgin again
To receive fully and reflect
The nine faces of Christ
We'll be like children
Who enter the kingdom
Of joy without pain
Rejoicing in the one
Dancing and playing in the warmth
Of the cosmic sun

At the end of the journey
Man is naked and unmasked
Ready to attain
God's consciousness
He has found
The holy grail
And his soul the anima
And as true male
United with beloved Sophia
He will return
Alone and yet all — one
To neverending community
With all the saints
And God — the holy mystery

—

August 1992

Dear Richard,

Like many young men in this time, who are on a search for their own identity as males and seek the spiritual journey to this inner place, your talks have inspired me and led me on a track that seems helpful.

After a men's retreat in Switzerland you gave me the opportunity to spend a few months as an intern at the Center for Action and Contemplation in Albuquerque, where I had time to follow this track more intensely.

I gained new insights and my life started to move. You always encouraged me to trust my own journey and you gave me permission to follow it faithfully — even if it led me into more insecurity and darkness. Deeper experiences with the Enneagram and the connection of the mystical and the political were due to you.

Your humor and spiritual *Gelassenheit* (I know you like this German word) about our weaknesses and traps always made me smile. To take myself honestly but not too seriously and earnestly is what I have learned from you.

On our journey with "Sebil" in May 1992 to Assisi, I wrote this poem for you. Connected with the nine numbers (not necessarily the characters) of the Enneagram, the Kabbala, and some of your talks, it is something like a summary of all my encounters with you.

I'm certainly aware that this poem at my young age can only be a "vision" of a journey, one where I stand right at the beginning. And even though it seems in many of the verses that this is "a loner's heroic way," I know that if I am not to become inflated, this journey can be walked fully only in a community and with the corrective help from others.

Thank you, Richard, for all the encouragement and guidance you gave me for my own journey.

I wish you peace and strength for the coming decade of your life.

Sincerely,
Thomas Buchter

Woe to the Overfed

DOM HELDER CAMARA

✛

> Lord, I pity the hungry,
> but I feel greater pity
> for the overfed,
> who are dying of surfeit and boredom...

I feel pity for the hungry, and I can't get used to seeing how people – God's children – fight over scraps of food in garbage cans.

But how can I dare to say that I feel still greater pity for the overfed, who are dying of surfeit and boredom?

God understands me! People who no longer know what they can do with their money frighten me. Even with pharaonic extravagance they can't manage to shrink their fortunes.

This very day death overtakes them. They have lost all their credit in all the banks on earth, and their checkbooks in their pockets are worthless.

> Lord, I pity
> the homeless,
> the people with no roof over their head.
> But I feel more pity
> for the well-established
> who make the earth
> into a permanent residence...

I pity the homeless, the people without a roof over their heads....

Of course it feels good to come home in the evening after work, to have one's own four walls, to have family members waiting for you, to be able to take baths and enjoy recreation, to eat dinner with your loved ones....

And it must be terrible not to know where you should go, to sleep on the steps of churches, in the entrance ways of large buildings or under bridges, without anything to eat, without family, showers, nothing....

Then how do I have the nerve to say it depresses me even more to meet established and solidly set up people who have completely forgotten that we have no lasting city here and that at any moment the signal for our departure may ring out?

Happy are those who realize that we are on a journey, and that we will find our true eternal home only when we arrive in the Father's eternal world!

Anyone who lives in the light of this faith will do everything possible so that no one goes without a roof over his head or a bed for her tired body.

> Lord, I pity
> those who seek you,
> groping in the dark.
> But I pity more
> those who are self-sufficient,
> who don't need you,
> and take themselves to be super-gods.

I pity those who seek God and think they haven't found him. They grope in the dark. But those who seek the Lord, even if they have the impression that they've failed to find him, can be sure of meeting the Creator and Father.

But, Lord, I am still more concerned about those who are self-sufficient and consider themselves strong and secure, so that they don't need you.

Forgive their irrationality. It's weakness rather than malice. You are too great to have anything to do with pettiness and feelings of revenge. Come forward to meet them... A father is a father, and you are the Father of us all.

Return to Stillness

TEDDY CARNEY

If you live on a California ranch surrounded by oaks randomly placed on the curves of café-au-lait hills, why would you need to go on a retreat? I guess because no corner is spared from cultural madness. Ready for five days of silence, I loaded the pickup with gear and Cora, our white Labrador, and set out for the farthest corner of the ranch. The ascent is so sharp on the last stretches of the road that I needed to lean out the window in order to see beyond the up-tilt of the hood.

A few sheds in the old hunting camp are scattered among a grove of oaks at the bottom of a canyon. I set up sleeping quarters in a small screen house that had been used to hang game, safe from flies and other creatures. I had been to the camp only a couple of times before we bought Les's place, which adjoins ours. Old metal beds with rusted coiled springs hunkered under the trees. Squirrels and mice had had full run for a long time and would attract snakes. In spite of the abandoned feeling of a vacated camp, there was something very touching about the place — an aura of good times, a kind of spell left by men who had come here, shedding their cares, returning to nature, to the primitive camaraderie of the hunt. I kept imagining Les with his endearing little gimp, moving about the camp, poking steaks over the fire, hugging a cup of bourbon, telling stories and laughing, his faded blue shirt pulled tight over his belly. There had been a lot of raucous laughter under these oaks.

After settling my things I set out to the south. The sun was still high. I had hidden my watch in the bottom of the duffel in hopes of getting away from any sense of time. Cora and I were so filled with happiness we almost skipped through the woods and open meadows until we came to a creek. We sat amid rocks in the cool water, listening to flies humming, resting our eyes on marsh marigolds and sedges at the water's edge.

I wondered what it would have been like to have been a Neanderthal woman before we had the power of reflection, before we could watch in our mind's eye what we were doing. How simple it would be to live in the right brain, absorbing nothing more than the fullness of each moment. Surely, our capacity for reflection is our most human gift and, at the same time, our greatest burden. We readily become enslaved by expectations, projections, opinions. Perhaps the most difficult challenge is to come full circle and empty ourselves of rational, reflective thought, to move into a state of contemplation. To the degree that we are able to let go of the chattering monkeys in our heads, let go of our need for control, are we able to reach a level of union with all that exists. As Thomas Aquinas said of his monumental works, they were like chaff in the wind compared to his union with God in meditation.

By the time we reached camp I had a headache. I had drunk some water in the morning, but didn't have a canteen. A sip of cider made me feel worse. Abandoning the idea of fasting on juices for two days, I ate some wafers and dozed. I felt limp. It occurred to me that my energy level was low because I had left behind the things that normally give me energy. I had no one to nurture, nothing to control or organize; no one needed me. I kept asking, "Who am I? Who am I before I was a wife, before I was a mother? Who is the little me made in the image of God?"

I thought about how much of me was dependent upon how I wanted to be seen. My mind meandered over many incidents. It seemed that my most essential needs sprang from the expectations of others that I had internalized. I had carefully constructed patterns of behavior that gave me the energy to fulfill these needs and had assumed the role of the good little girl, who kept the hearth swept. The virtuous woman in Proverbs, who looks well to the ways of her household and eats not the bread of idleness, was my role model.

I smelled the caked earth and rocks cooling in the evening air. The need to know something, even what time it was, overcame me. I dug into the duffel for my watch. It was seven o'clock. Hours of the day had disappeared with no accounting of them. I wasn't sure if I were going to like being here with a headache.

Cora and I would have time for an hour's walk before bed. We climbed the old road pulling occasional beer cans out of the brush and piling them along the side. I needed a detail to focus upon. Details are like possessions, in the same way that opinions are. They are like worry stones that monks carried in a pouch in the Middle Ages, to be pulled out and rubbed and prayed over and worried about. I noticed how the things I fret about are situations I want in some way to control.

Karl Stern developed a theory about anxiety being rooted in the longing to change something over which we had no control, like the weather or the limits of our children. How much of our suffering comes from self-inflicted needs to control the uncontrollable? I imagined opening up my little pouch of worry stones and casting them in the chemiso brush where wild pigs trampled them and rabbits hopped over them.

My headache had become a friendly companion. On the way back I flattened and gathered the beer cans in my shawl. I had kept back a few worry stones, not ready to let go of my need to tidy the landscape. It gave me the energy to get back to camp.

After a cool sponge bath I lay in bed and listened to a Gregorian chant. I had brought a recorder, but had decided to limit its use to a half hour in the evening. The sound of the music released in me a surge of emotion that was startling. I wept at the beauty and perfection of it. I lay in the darkness, feeling very small. I cried over how small I am. Cora waked me with tiny woofs at ten o'clock when the moon came through the trees and transformed the camp. The twigs of the dead branches that stretched over the roof were like a black lace petticoat supporting the foliage above them.

I slept till the sun was visible over the ridge. The headache was faint, but clearly there. We climbed up the road, Cora running ahead, stopping every few minutes to check on me. I had made a walking stick out of the stem of an aloe cactus. It was light with a bulbous protrusion at the base that took hold in the loose dirt. I felt like an old crone out of a fairy tale, with my sun hat, high boots, and loose culottes, stabbing my way up the slopes with my staff.

We climbed and rested, up and up into the vast sky. I kept thanking God for the parched earth, the blue oaks, the dried cucumber vine crawling over gooseberry thickets, the fragrance of the cedar when Cora's tail touched a branch, for my beloved husband and the rest of my family. I kept singing, "O Lord, your love is everlasting!" When we reached the summit we found a shady ledge overlooking the reservoir that was encircled by yellow folded hills like a sapphire. A cottony mist rested between the ridges. Cora sat at my feet while we looked and looked.

On the fourth morning my headache was gone. I felt deeply rested and full of anticipation. Our goal was a hidden spring that I had never seen. Everything was perfect — little circles of cobwebs, like dainty handkerchiefs, appeared to have been dropped along the open slope on ragged oak branches, and a few had fallen askew on the curly leaves of the hackberry. Doves were darting at each other and then gliding on to distant trees. The air smelled sweet and dry.

We made our way along the east fence, climbing across a grassy slope and then into dense brush as we reached the ridge line. The first crescent was thick with ceanothus, cedar, and patches of poison oak. We followed game trails that even a cow could not have penetrated. I had to crouch down, my head bent forward with my sun hat as a means of pushing through the thickets, and a few times crawled on my hands and knees. An arroyo had cut a cliff that rose two hundred feet from the floor of the canyon.

The climb was on an almost vertical path of loose dirt. I could not have made it without my third leg, the aloe staff. As we struggled up the other side, I figured that the next canyon would be our destination. But as we approached the arroyo, I realized it was too narrow and dense. Cora had not had water since we left camp.

While we rested I was aware of how little I had thought about except what was before me on the path, the sound of Cora panting, the heat of the sun pressing on my straw hat, the blister on my hand, the glory of this day. It occurred to me that this hike to find a hidden spring had the same ingredients as a quest out of an old mythical legend. Like Seigfried in the Nibelung, I had to undergo trials, experience heat, thirst, hunger, and exhaustion. I had to struggle through brambles, steer my way through poisonous plants, cross precipitous slopes. Maybe I would never find the spring; perhaps the drought had dried up the pools and the water was reduced to a drip into a mud hole.

What are the lessons of a quest? Is it that we value only what we earn? Is life an ego acquisition of things and experiences that gives us the illusion that we are in control of our destinies? Or does it capture the spirit of humankind in the search for completion, for the life-giving water that will make us whole? Maybe it is all of these things.

My feet were swollen in my boots; I had gone beyond feeling hungry. But the trees were getting bigger, and there it was! A large creek bed leading into a wide canyon lay before us. We quickened our pace as we entered a glen of huge oaks whose branches stretched over the arroyo from either bank. Scattered across the heavy cover of mulch on the forest floor were dots of broken light. To the north was an ancient rock slide, softened by moss and clumps of leggy buckeyes, whose roots had woven through the stones. Thick vines of poison oak reached to the tops of the trees.

I heard a splash. Cora had found the first of numerous pools of black, glistening water, encircled by boulders the size of our chicken house. The air was alive with sound — flies, gnats, and moths, waterbugs scooting across the pools, birds and squirrels scolding us for our intrusion. I took off my clothes and entered the icy waters with black mud oozing through my toes. In the midst of a drought, in land that accustoms itself annually to six months without rainfall, the miracle of live water is like a fantasy. I dried in a shower of sunlight that slanted through the branches and warmed the massive rocks. It was five o'clock when we left the pools. I had been unable to keep the watch in the duffel bag and was finally wearing it. Cora and I sagged into camp at nine o'clock, with just enough light to keep to the road.

When the moon rose at one o'clock, I was still in a state of exhaustion and exhilaration. I thought of the intense sweetness and suffering in life. I felt deeply reconciled to my frequent failure to be my true self, to my frenzy to gain merit and accomplish something, but mostly to the beauty of my life. I wept at the glory of it all and remembered Eliot's lines, " . . . where past and future are gathered. Neither movement from, nor towards, neither ascent nor decline. Except for the point, the still point, there would be no dance, and there in only the dance . . . release from the inner and the outer compulsion, yet surrounded by a grace of sense, a white light still and moving."

How I have searched for a teaching, event, or situation that would transform me, lift me permanently out of my apathy and old familiar patterns that don't work. These days of quiet didn't accomplish any such miracle, but I felt immense gratitude that I am here, now, as a part of an era that is unleashing the human spirit in dimensions never known before. The quantum theory in modern physics has led us to a new sense of being. The whole is not merely a sum of separate parts, but every atom on this earth is intrinsically interrelated with every other atom, joining human, animal, plant, and cosmic life in ways that are validated. Science can eventually guide us toward an understanding of the spirit in every aspect of life. We can get beyond talking about it and begin living it like the Native Americans who feel in their hearts rather than knowing in their heads that the great spirit joins us all. We have new structures of thinking in the implicate order that can move us out of a mechanistic consciousness to the possibility of an evolving, coherent universe, which is very different from the static notion of fixed truths that stem from the Pythagoreans.

Some of us will be pulled kicking and screaming; some of us, like barnacles clinging out of fear to the old systems, will have to be pried loose. But come we will into the new consciousness just as we finally absorbed theories of evolution and psychology.

How could there have ever been a more exciting time to live on this planet?

Empowerment and Spirituality

JOAN D. CHITTISTER

I approach the topic of empowerment and spirituality with a great deal of respect and a certain amount of trepidation. After all, we live in a culture that has seen the dark side of both. Spirituality, clearly, has often been used as an excuse to be humanly irresponsible. And power has too often, God knows, been made a poor substitute for empowerment. The truth is that it is possible to have spirituality and lack power. More: It is also possible to have a power that lacks spirituality.

To be real, spirituality must empower, and power to be holy must be grounded in spirituality. The Talmud says, "Never pray in a room without windows." Never pray, in other words, without one eye on the world around you, or your prayer may become more therapy than energy. And Camus wrote once, "The saints of our time are those who refuse to be either its executioners or its victims." Spirituality, in other words, is not for nothing. Spirituality is not for its own sake. But what is the spirituality of power and what, exactly, is the power of spirituality? How would we recognize them if we saw them? How do we know when they exist and when they do not? And what do they have to say about the use of authority in the church and the world today?

In the pursuit of these answers, I suggest two companions in the process of coming to understand spirituality and empowerment: Moses and the Samaritan woman. One, Moses, had enough power to tame; the other, the Samaritan woman, had insight that impelled. The world of our time and the church of our time may well need both.

Moses knew clearly what power was all about. He had overcome the enemy, brought down plagues on the nation, drawn water from a rock, and parted the very sea. Indeed, Moses was an inspiring figure, a charismatic figure, a powerful figure, who talked to God face to face. Moses could well have been a tyrant, an authoritarian, a dogmatist, a harsh and exacting lawgiver. But Moses clearly had a spirituality of power that forestalled that. Power was from God, Moses knew, to be used for the things of God. He had contemplated the burning bush.

He had heard it on the mountaintop. He had felt it at the Sea of Reeds. And he had held it in his own hands with the prophets of Baal.

But the power was not his, and it was not for hoarding. And he knew it. Power, Moses knew, was given only to be given away — and give it away he did. Moses gave his power to the people themselves. Moses, Scripture says, chose those who were capable and appointed them as heads over the people. Moses didn't have to be the last word on everything, the final word on the work of God, the only word on the will of God. Moses used his power, too, to plead for forgiveness from an angry God: "Pardon the iniquity of this people as you have forgiven them ever since Egypt," Moses insisted in behalf of the weary, faithless band whose impunity tested the power of God. And finally, Moses knew that the power he had belonged to God alone. Over the plains at Rephidim, while the army of Israel resisted the army of Amalek below, Aaron and Hur held up the tired arms of Moses while he prayed with the staff of God in hand that God would see them through the conflict that he was powerless to change. There was no authoritarianism here, no arrogance here, no domination here.

Indeed, in Moses the spirituality of power is a clear one. Power is not meant to keep a people down; power is meant to build a people up. Power is not meant to be punitive; power is meant to challenge. Power is not meant to be consumed by a few. It is meant to energize the people as a whole. Power is to be wielded, Moses taught Aaron, only by those who judge through the "breastplate of decision," through the eyes of Yahweh, through the very heart of God. The very purpose of power, the only proper use of power, is empowerment. And the model is surely one we badly need today.

Power used to target the globe for extinction is certainly ruthless exploitative power. Power used to suppress the national churches in the name of church unity disunifies while it coerces. Power used against Charles Curran, who questioned with love and loyalty, but in support of Archbishop Marcel Lefebvre, who rejected an entire council of the church, has got to be a power gone arbitrary. Power used to rape the environment, to poison the water and pollute the air of this globe is power run amok. Power amassed to protect the church from eleven-year-old altar girls and the erotic feet of women and the use of feminine pronouns is power gone inane. Power used to suppress thinkers in a culture and an era more dominated by questions than by answers is a ruthless use of power that will do more in the end to harm us than the questions ever will.

We are living in a world where power is being misused, in a globe that is seething with the issues of women and hunger and poverty and mass migration and nuclear devastation. We are living in a world where both church and state are writing new laws about flags and liturgical dances and language and dress codes while the world is reeling under a massive burden of pain. An ancient proverb states: "To be properly wicked, you do not have to break the law. Just observe it to the letter."

And we wonder why so few are listening any more. And the deterioration is all around us. These kinds of power are crying for a spirituality that empowers, for a power that pleads, that frees, that gentles, and that cares for the people.

Nurturing power and integrative power, Rollo May insists, are the only hope of our times. We need a government, a people, a church whose vast, massive, overwhelming reservoir of power is used to bring people to life and the world together.

The church that has spoken out against godless communism must, in the name of God, use its power to speak out clearly and strongly against an unholy capitalism that is devoted to stopping refugees at the borders of the wealthiest nation in the world — our own. We need a government, a people, a church, who use their power to build people up rather than to block them out.

The church that says that man is made in the image and likeness of God must soon, if the very power of God is to be credible in it, begin to see God in the image of woman, too.

The arms race and tokenism and propaganda and patriarchy and the concentration on loyalty oaths and the male captivity of the sacraments must give way now to empowerment: to the use of power that works for others and that works with others. Or wasn't that what the Exodus was for? And what Vatican II was all about? Did we misunderstand both the Covenant and the Beatitudes, both Moses' priesthood of the people and the early Christian community, both collegiality and the canonical obligation of the laity — at least according to the new code of canon law — to express our needs and cite our concerns?

And if that's so, what are we saying? Should Luther's questions not have been raised? Should the pope be continuing to free souls only for money? When Innocent III declared England under interdict for having accepted the Magna Carta and limiting the power of a king, which was, he argued (you guessed it), against the natural law — should democracy, therefore, have been forever banned? Has the spirituality of power been reduced to nothing but the trappings of authority? Well, we need prophets now. Let there be no doubt about it. In a modern culture the spirituality of power is crucial to the existence of the planet, and in the modern church it is crucial to the glory of the gospel itself.

To those whose god is system, the criterion for fidelity in times of confusion is seldom only truth. To those who question when the innocent are victimized by an unholy use of power, bureaucrats too seldom preach truth and too often preach obedience. Yet it was a wrong kind of obedience that bred the Inquisition and the cruel crusades. Surely the church deserves a better brand of fidelity than that. And we must remember Moses questioned God.

In times of confusion, to those whose god is system, the criterion for fidelity is too seldom an appeal to values held in common and too often an appeal to unity based on silence. But silence was exacted of Galileo, and without gain. In fact, silence was exacted of Galileo with great loss of power to the church. And we must remember Moses argued with God.

In times of confusion, to those whose god is system, the criterion for fidelity is seldom honest search and too often a limiting brand of orthodoxy. But it was the poorest type of orthodoxy that bred the wars of religion.

In times of confusion, those whose god is system say dissent is unacceptable and so make indifference a virtue. Consequently, to save the whole, we so often feed the system martyrs one at a time — whom we then reclaim centuries later and thereby salve our consciences: a hundred thousand women "witches," Joan of Arc, Mary Ward, Erasmus, Meister Eckhart, Pierre Teilhard de Chardin. And yet, it seems, we have no record that the papacy of the Borgia popes was ever officially condemned. Nor do we know of the dismissal of any hierarchy anywhere that failed to say a word about the gassing of the Jews, or the selling of slaves, or the extermination of the Indians.

System is simply no substitute for the gospel. And power is no substitute for empowerment. Where are you, Moses? We need you now.

Nevertheless, a spirituality of power is not enough. We need also those who refuse to be not only executioners but also victims. It is not enough, in other words, to have leaders with a spirituality of empowerment. We need Christians with an empowering spirituality.

Unlike Moses, our second companion on the road to empowerment and spirituality is quite ordinary — as we are, you and I. She is a woman drawing water from a well in Samaria, a small province on the border of Jerusalem. She has obviously struggled through life, making hard decisions and, as a woman, getting little affirmation from the system. She was full of questions and full of frustration, but she was full, too, of an uncommon sense of the presence of God and her own obligation to respond to it.

In Samaria, we are met head on with a revolution of empowerment. The Samaritans, remember, had once been part of the people of God. But they had been conquered by so many empires that they had been cut off for centuries from the country of Judea and from worship in Jerusalem. As a result, they had gradually developed their own interpretation of the books of Moses, and their religion had become overlaid with many cultures and many faiths.

To the Jews, the Samaritans were impostors. They were simply pagans who pretended to be true believers. The hatred between the two groups had hardened over the centuries. No pious Jew could have any contact whatsoever with Samaritans. Jews did not travel into Samaritan territory. Jews did not talk to Samaritans. Jews would not even touch an article that had been handled by a Samaritan — much like white South Africans treat black South Africans today, and much like white Americans treated black Americans twenty years ago though both called themselves American and both called themselves Christian.

And the even stronger part of the message of the account of the woman at the well is that, in those days no good Jew could speak to a woman in public, not to any woman — not to his daughter, not to his mother, not to his wife. The rabbinic law was very clear on that.

And no good Jew even thought about talking theology with a woman. The Rabbi Eliezer had taught quite clearly, "Better that the Torah be burned than placed in the mouth of a woman." No woman had legal credibility. No woman was permitted to give legal testimony in a court of law. What in heaven's name then would a woman know about messiahs and politics and important things? There is no doubt: Women and Samaritans were outcasts.

The problem of the church today is that Jesus simply did not share that animosity for either. Jesus was traveling through Samaritan territory. The gospel writer John says that Jesus "had to go through Samaria." But that's not true. There was another route then, just as there is now. No, the real truth is that Jesus had to go to those people because they, too, were people attuned to life's great search; because God lived, too, in them; because they were listening and because they, too, were spiritual people, people of deep spirituality; and because no one, no one, has a monopoly on the spirit God.

And there, at that well, in public, Jesus talked to a woman, a Samaritan woman, and asked for a drink out of a Samaritan bucket, and even offered to give her water of his own. And then Jesus had a discussion with this woman about some very deep theological things — about the nature of worship, and the nature of salvation, and the nature of Jesus himself. It is to this woman that Jesus first says in Scripture, "I am the Messiah." It is to a woman far outside the boundaries of any system, far outside the spiritual imaginations of orthodoxy, far outside the seats of power, that Jesus gives the word and the promise and the mission. And this Samaritan, this woman, understood who he was. She went to tell the others, and on her account, the Scripture says, they all believed.

The Samaritan woman was an ordinary woman doing ordinary things who got an extraordinary insight into the fullness of life and was given an extraordinary task in a pagan world and they listened to her. She was a reluctant prophet, an unacceptable evangelist, a powerless figure, an apostle without a portfolio. She wasn't a man — and she was to give the greatest testimony of all time. She wasn't a Jew — and she was to announce the messiah. She was neither politician nor priest, yet she was given the gift of understanding and living water and power and empowerment. And they listened to her.

There's a revolution going on in today's church too. Like the Samaritan woman, people, very ordinary people, are discovering the energy, the insight, and the power that comes with the spiritual life. And as it happens when the Holy Spirit gets out of the chanceries of the world, quite ordinary people are being spiritually empowered to seize some gospel decisions of their own. They've come to some spiritual conclusions that sexism is a sin, that peace is possible, that communism is not all bad, that capitalism is not all good, that authority has limits, and that the Word of God lives too in them.

And they're proclaiming, demanding, and living those things in the name of the gospel of our Lord Jesus Christ. Why? Because Jesus has turned their very ordinary selves and their very ordinary lives into an extraordinary awareness of the presence of God — in them as well as in the powers that be. They have discovered the spirituality that empowers and, like the Samaritan woman, they will not be silenced.

And what the church really needs is more of them to spread the faith instead of the law, to be a sign of hope and contradiction — rather than authority and legalism — in a world that is hungry and ignorant and spending more money and talent and time on the potential destruction of the world and the definition of heresies than on the development of innocent people and the challenge of hard love in a poor, oppressed, groaning, wailing world. With an inner spring welling up inside of them, these spiritually powerful people are the message that God has better plans for us, because when spiritual empowerment and empowering spirituality explode in people, there is simply no holding back what they have come to see. They know with the philosopher Ramana Maharishi, "As you are, so is the world."

They know that they have been sent to do the power of the Beatitudes in a world where two-thirds of the people are deprived of the basics of life; they know that they have been sent to be the sign of the call to gospel commitment in a world that wants controlling power and profit instead; they know that they have been sent to become the Christ figure in a world that says "You get them before they get you" and in a church that says that women are inadequate images of Christ.

They know that they have been sent to turn the world around – one heart at a time.

Some people whose power is threatened by the powerless still ask, "What would a woman know, what would any nobody know, about messiahs, about politics, about nuclear war, about values, about church?" And the answer is the same now as then, the same here as at the well. The spiritually empowered know nothing but Jesus. Nothing but the gospel. Nothing but the power within that comes from an empowering spirituality that is not for our own sakes but for the sake of the other. Most of all, they know they have been sent and that somewhere, someday, someone with a spirituality of power will recognize the power of spirituality and listen to them so that the entire world and the whole church can be empowered – for the sake of the gospel, for the sake of the globe.

And how can we be so sure of all this? Because we have already seen Moses, the liberator, and the Samaritan woman. We have as model Moses, who was brave enough and faithful enough to trust uncertainty to lead to truth and who used his power to create something new, not to control. And we have the model of the Samaritan woman who took power that had not been given to her so that the powerless could have hope.

A folk tale, though, may tell us best. Once upon a time, the priest announced that Jesus Christ himself was coming to church the following Sunday. So the people turned up in large numbers to see him. Everyone expected Jesus to preach, but he only smiled. Everyone offered him hospitality, especially the priest, but he refused. He wanted to spend the night in church. How fitting, everyone thought. But the next morning, by the time the church doors were opened, Jesus had already slipped away. And, to their horror, the priest and the people discovered that their church had been vandalized. Scribbled everywhere on the walls was the single word, "Beware." No part of the church was spared; the doors and windows, the pillars and the pulpit, the altar, even the Bible that rested on the lectern. "Beware," scratched in large letters and in small, in pencil and pen and paint of every color. Wherever the eye rested, one could see the words, "BEWARE, BEWARE, BEWARE, BEWARE, BEWARE . . . " Shocking. Irritating. Confusing. Fascinating. Terrifying. What were they supposed to beware of?

The first impulse of the people was to wipe out every trace of this defilement, this sacrilege. The only thing that stopped them from doing it was the thought that it was Jesus himself who had done this deed. But then that mysterious word, "Beware," began to sink into the minds of the people each time they came to church. They began to beware of the Scriptures so they were able to profit from them without falling into bigotry. They began to beware of the sacraments so they were sanctified without becoming superstitious. The priest began to beware of his power over the people, so he was able to help without controlling. And everyone began to beware of religion that leads the unwary to self-righteousness. They became law-abiding, yet compassionate to the weak. They began to beware of prayer, so it no longer stopped them from becoming self-reliant. They even began to beware of their notions of God, so they were able to recognize God outside the narrow confines of their church. Finally, they inscribed the shocking word over the entrance of their church and, as you drive past at night, you can see it blazing about the church in multicolored neon lights.

The message is a simple one: Beware. Beware of power without spirituality. Beware of any spirituality that does not empower. Beware. Beware. Beware.

Excerpts from
a South African Diary

ANDREAS EBERT

The following is a true story: Some Norwegian friends of mine lived for a while in Bonn. One day Astrid went to the weekly city market. She wanted to buy grapes. Because she's one of the people who boycott the "fruits of apartheid," she asked the woman tending a stand, "Are these grapes from South Africa?" Answer: "Well yes, but you don't have to worry. No nigger ever touched them. They were picked by completely normal white Germans, like you and me...."

Preliminary remark: In 1991 I ran an Enneagram weekend at the Free Protestant Congregation in Aachen. Shortly after that a young teacher named Detlef Hansmann, along with his South African friend Graham Cyster, came to visit me in Celle (northern Germany), so that I could explain the Enneagram to Graham. On the scale set up by South African whites, Graham is a "coloured." He has lived for many years in voluntary exile in England. In the 1970s the situation in South Africa had gotten so tense that he had left the country, fearing that hatred would drive him to murder. He found inner healing at the Christian "Post Green Community." This personal experience of reconciliation planted in his mind the vision of founding a multiracial community in South Africa. For some years now Graham and his wife Dorcas, a (white) American Mennonite, and several other men and women have realized this vision by setting up the Broken Wall Community of Reconciliation near Cape Town. When he left Celle I gave Graham Richard Rohr's Enneagram cassettes and Helen Palmer's book on the same subject (*The Enneagram: Understanding Yourself and the People Around You*).

Graham was so impressed by the cassettes and the book that he invited me to visit his community and other fellowships in South Africa to give lectures and seminars on the Enneagram and on issues of Bible studies. He felt the Enneagram could make a contribution to reconciliation in South Africa because one of the important things it teaches is how to put up with, and even learn to appreciate, polar opposites. In addition I was supposed to have time to travel around making contacts with black and white communities and various "important people."

Friday, July 24

Landed in Cape Town at noon. There wasn't a single black on the jumbo jet. Behind the Hansmanns sat a large family of white South Africans. The wife said they were just returning from a four-week trip to Europe that had cost them 50,000 rands (about $18,000). Unfortunately the family could afford that kind of trip only every other year.

Graham picked us up. On the drive from the airport to the community we passed giant slums with huts made out of cardboard, tin, and old boards. I recalled the area around the airport in Lima, Peru, where I had been five years before. Poverty looks the same everywhere. Women with huge bundles of wood on their heads scuttle along a dangerous highway. Day laborers stand by the side of the road hoping someone will hire them for a few hours.

From the outside the main house of the community looks like a little fortress. Behind the building are two smaller houses and a larger piece of land. I meet the two family dogs and the people who are there: Dorcas, Graham's wife, and the other members of the community.

We had dinner with Lutando, a high school student from Transkei, who has been living in the community for a year. Over the next few years the community wants to take in several students like Lutando to help them graduate. He takes Pastor Martin Wirth, a German friend who is here, and me to the beach. It feels good to walk along the shore, which is lit up by yellow spotlights, and to breathe in the cool, salty breeze. Brightly colored cabanas, fine-grained sand, mussels, restaurants, bars, a mini-golf course. . . . Until recently this beach, we learned, was reserved to whites. Only a few years before when white and black civil rights protesters had bathed together in an act of civil disobedience, they were chased away by police dogs, tear gas, and hippopotamus-hide whips. It is wintertime here now, 62 degrees during the daytime, and practically deserted. The resounding slap of the oncoming waves and their huge crowns of foam in the yellow searchlights invite us to silent contemplation.

Saturday, July 25

To the city in the morning. We are to join in a human chain for peace and democracy. A gigantic crowd of blacks and coloureds, with a few whites mixed in, has gathered. Some are singing and hopping up and down in time with the song – the South African "toye-toye," which I too find so infectious. The discipline of the demonstrators is astonishing. A man with a megaphone points out the line of the march. We are divided into two "strands," which are supposed to march parallel for a while, then split up to the right and left so as to encircle an enormous building complex. ANC monitors in yellow, black, and green uniforms are on duty and tell us to let only ambulances and fire trucks through the "hollow passage." I feel uneasy – this is for real.

We start out "toye-toyeing," now slowly, now spiritedly. By the side of the road curious people watch us; the store windows are barred shut. In front of a hotel uniformed employees greet us with raised fists. Only a few policemen are in sight. By the edge of the highway we see a few trucks with grated windows for armed personnel and attack dogs.

After the march, we head to a shopping center to eat. What a different world. Elegant stores and restaurants – and an incomparably higher percentage of whites. You get the impression that the majority of white South Africa doesn't even pay attention to what's going on outside its doors.

Sunday, July 26

In the morning we attend church services in the little Mennonite parish in the township of Khayelitsha, where Graham is pastor. The people meet in a wretched hut with cardboard walls, old carpets on the floor, a few rickety benches. But the singing! A woman intones a chorus, and the rest pick up the tune and harmonize. They clap hands and move their bodies – this is worship from the gut. After a few hymns they all pray out loud, their voices jangling against one another. Graham's sermon is about the story of the Exodus. He says: "God is a God of history. He is in my personal history; he is present in the history of my family, my tribe, and my people. He hears our cries, and he gets rid of the pharaohs. De Klerk is on the point of becoming the pharaoh who keeps putting off making good on his promises. Buthelezi could be that sort of pharaoh. But God keeps sending leaders whom he has prepared to lead the people to freedom – such as Nelson Mandela. But if these leaders were to begin standing in God's way, God would sweep them aside too." After the sermon the sick come forward. The elders pray for them and lay hands on them. Christianity without a healing ministry is unthinkable in black Africa. After the service the congregation marches singing out of the hut-church. Everybody shakes hands. We whites are welcome too.

After the service I have a conversation with Philly, the "coloured" in whose house we are being put up. He tells me that until he was sixteen he hadn't wanted to be a Christian because he would have had to worship the same God as the whites. "I never decided for God. God decided for me. He grabbed me, and I went down on my knees. With my conversion I lost my hatred for the whites — and I thought it must be the same for them. I was in a mainly white charismatic community. The pastor needed me for the band. But, even though I was single, none of the families ever invited me to dinner. And the pastor invited me only when the conservatives weren't around." Philly quotes the biblical command for man to rule over the animals. "But it doesn't say anywhere that man is allowed to rule over other people. The only way I can explain this is that most whites get converted under false pretenses. Nobody who's really been seized by God can go on treating his brothers the way many whites treat us."

Late in the afternoon another long talk with Graham and Dorcas, prompted by a TV news report: The highest-ranking medical examiner in the country declares for the record that he can no longer be silent about his autopsy findings concerning people who have died while in police custody. In countless cases these individuals did not die a natural death. The police, he says, are completely out of control. Next, the minister of law and order is questioned. He goes into a verbose explanation of how he has already assigned the police (!) to follow up on these charges, though he himself doesn't believe that the police kill anybody. After all, getting arrested is a psychologically exhausting experience that could well lead to a natural death. In addition many arrestees would be likely to commit suicide. . . .

Then the head of the union confederation COSATU and a business representative are questioned about the upcoming general strike. The union leader says that the country isn't going under because of the strike, but because of the failed policies of the illegitimate minority government. The businessman argues that now is the time for "constructive actions" and not the "old methods of confrontation." The strike, he says, will do economic damage to the country and frighten off foreign investors. . . . He doesn't say anything about the economic damage done by apartheid, for example, by the international boycott and the lack of a qualified work force since for decades blacks have been denied access to decent education.

Afterward we learn more about the history of the community and about the difficulties of taking a vision of a common life for all races under one roof and making it plausible, above all to white South Africans. Graham stresses that the gospel isn't an idea, but from the very first means a relationship. All religious revivals have shown that people convert when they experience a new kind of relationship. This sort of structure can show how much hatred and anxiety they bear within themselves, so that they can be healed. Dorcas tells me that she once lived among blacks in Jackson, Mississippi, and that one of the black women she had been with for four years said: "I just can't trust whites." Dorcas says: "At moments like that you can't get defensive and say, 'But I did my best.' When that happens it's important to send a signal to the other person: I sense your hurt, and I stand by you."

Monday, July 27

Afternoon spent reading. Detlef has put together photocopies of all the news reports about South Africa that have come out in the last nine months. One thing is obvious: How quickly the world has rolled out the red carpet for de Klerk, once the first easing up of apartheid occurred. The political and economic establishments were evidently very happy that they finally had an excuse to be back doing business with South Africa. We learn from the TV news that the medical examiner who spoke out yesterday about police violence has already received five death threats.

In the evening Martin and I invite Philly and Beatrice out to dinner at a handsome restaurant. Philly is a union leader of a subdivision in his company, which is a giant synthetic fabric factory. I ask him about the upcoming general strike. He is fighting to make sure that salaries continue to be paid on August 3 and 4, and that his company makes an unequivocal commitment to the workers' demands for real democracy. He and his wife dream of getting their high school diplomas and studying at the university. The community will help them do this. "Without the parish," he says, "I couldn't take a stand and speak the truth without being afraid." Beatrice used to work at the reception desk of a deluxe hotel. She would like to study public relations to become a press secretary or something like that. Philly would like to study theology at the Fuller Seminary in California. He doesn't want to go to a South African school, where they teach the theology of apartheid. I point out to him that Fuller also produces a completely apolitical and individualistic theology. Thereupon he says he could pick up the fundamentals there and study liberation theology afterward. Up till now the academic world has been largely closed to blacks and coloureds, and so their whole educational ideal culminates in the effort to get university degrees.

Although both Philly and Beatrice are "coloured," they consider themselves black. This is quite unusual. As a rule the coloureds have internalized the absurd racial system of the whites, and they distance themselves from the blacks. Philly's father is a Pentecostal preacher. Formerly he was an ANC comrade, but as soon as he became a Christian, he turned apolitical. Philly sees no contradiction between faith and political struggle. On the contrary. But he thinks that many coloureds, including his father, would stand behind de Klerk. With real democracy they would lose their privileges too.

Thursday, July 28

Early this morning I have an appointment at the German Lutheran congregation. The church, parish hall, and kindergarten are centrally located and splendidly equipped by local standards. We are greeted by the pastor and his staff. They speak German here. This is typical of the change of worlds in this country: You go through a door and you find yourself in a completely different atmosphere.

For a long time the German church in Cape Town had been suspended by the Lutheran World Federation because it didn't speak out clearly against apartheid. Recently the suspension was lifted; but, according to Pastor Christian Lehmann, neither of these events particularly shook up his community.

The Cape Town Church has nine parishes with a total of three thousand parishioners. Most of them are Afrikaans-speakers; only St. Martin, the main parish, runs its kindergarten in German. For that reasons its seventy-five places are exclusively occupied by white children.

Pastor Lehmann expresses his anxiety about the general strike set for next week. We ask him what alternatives the blacks have. He has no answer. We want to know how the political situation of the country is judged and discussed in the parish. Pastor Lehmann and the youth pastor, Hans-Walter Reeh, admit that such issues are taboo. If they themselves were to take a public stand in the pulpit, many doors would be shut in their face. They want to provide pastoral care for the frightened whites. The parishioners, Pastor Reeh says, are extremely fearful of giving themselves away. Façades are very important. But behind the façade of intact families things are chaotic. There is a lot of concealed violence; many marriages end in divorce.

We sense the pastors' difficulties in coping with the situation of a shrinking community that wants to preserve its German cultural heritage. Every opening to the multicultural environment harbors the danger of losing identity. A sense of bitterness comes through: Foreign delegations visit only the blacks or at most come to heap abuse on the German pastors.

The parish rooms are locked and equipped with alarms. There seems to be scarcely any commitment to the poor — not even a soup kitchen. Yet the seal of the chapel features the image of its patron, St. Martin of Tours, giving half his cloak to a poor man. At any rate the German Lutherans recently set up a special parish office to build a bridge between the poor (black) and the rich (white) Lutherans, whose churches have yet to be united.

Martin and I notice that this church seems so depressed to us not because it's different from the church at home, but because it's exactly the same. Amid a profound political and social crisis this sort of bourgeois Christianity obviously proves incapable of professing its faith or taking action. The catch phrase one sees in all the travel agencies here, "A whole world in one country," turns out to be true in a totally different sense from the one intended by the advertisers. Like rays of sunlight concentrated in a magnifying glass, the contrasts that tear our world apart can be seen sharply focused in South Africa. Anyone who isn't blind *has* to see them. But nevertheless it seems to be possible to spend your life in one of the many ghettoes of this country — such as the German Lutheran ghetto — without realizing what's going on a few hundred meters from your door. This shocked us because it showed us the situation we're all caught up in. If we in western Germany can't even share with other Germans in the east, if we develop strategies for building bulkheads to protect the wealth of western Europe from the have-nots in the south and east, if we deny the right to vote to people who have been living in our country for decades, because they aren't legally "German" — then this is no different from what happens here in South Africa. Perhaps white South Africa has become the world's scapegoat because we can point the finger at this country and so distract ourselves and others from our own involvement in global exploitation.

Thursday, July 30

At noon to the train station with Martin Wirth to pick up Andreas Richter-Böhne, the second pastor from the "Lorenzer Laden" in Nuremberg, who is arriving from Johannesburg. He is visiting his wife, Ute, there while she does an internship project. We three men want to take a vacation for a few days, so we rent a car. The first day our goal is L'Agulhas, the southernmost point of Africa.

When we arrive it's already dark. In a nearby town we find a restaurant.

We start a conversation with the hostess. She says we can spend the night in her house. Then she tells us about her experiences with coloured and black employees who drink and can't be relied on. She hadn't ever fired anybody, but recently when she asked one of the women why she always came fifteen minutes late, that woman quit immediately, and so did her daughter, who also worked in the restaurant. The hostess keeps insisting that there are also poor whites in South Africa whom nobody cares about, because they have no Nelson

Mandela. She hints how hard it is to live with other people, even (!) in marriage. Sometimes she hates her husband more than anybody, but then you pull yourself together. Once she learns that we are ministers, she throws in a comment about not being a born-again Christian. In reality, she claims, she's just the sort of person a Christian is supposed to be. She always says what she thinks.

We spend the night and after breakfast the hostess waves to us a little sadly, it seems to me, as we drive off. Only later do we realize that we no doubt failed to hear her cries for help because we were so fixated on our own issues.

We take a day trip through breathtaking landscape to the De Hook nature preserve. The first wild animals that we see are ostriches. The way they tear along with their behinds aquiver strikes us as enormously funny. It reminds me of the coquettish ostrich dance in Disney's *Fantasia.* On a lake there are countless flamingoes. As we approach, many of them take flight, their pink feathers rising like a mighty cloud against the brilliant blue sky. We drive toward gigantic sand dunes, which from a distance look like glaciers. We take a walk in the noonday sun through this sandscape till finally we see the ocean. A strong breeze blows the sand in our faces. On the way back we see a herd of zebras by the side of the road; but they too are very shy and flee as soon as we come. The lead stallion covers their retreat. Respect! What a breathtakingly beautiful country!

After a lunch stop at a village with the pretty name of Heidelberg we return to the ocean. It quickly gets dark and rather cool. Martin wants to take a dip, and I don't want to chicken out. It *is* cold, all right, but it's a wild feeling to dive stark naked into the waves — not least of all because even something as simple as skinny-dipping feels like an act of civil disobedience in prudish South Africa.

Monday, August 3

On Saturday we drove back to Cape Town. We went to the theater that night in the harbor district. The musical *Fairy Land* is a review about "District Six," a multicultural area of the city that was leveled by the government to provide housing for whites. It was never built, but at the time the inhabitants were forcibly resettled. The gaiety and vitality of the actors and actresses, their natural wit and agility . . . it's all electrifying. For the first time I'm in a multicultural audience in this country, and I enjoy sitting among the happy, many-colored crowd of people. . . .

On Sunday morning we three Germans go to the German Lutheran worship service at St. Martin's. The liturgy has been prepared in a manner that by Lutheran standards is lively and loving. It's like a piece of our German homeland in South Africa. The readings about the manna in the wilderness and the miraculous multiplication of bread and the sermon text about the sharing of property in the early church all revolve around the theme of balancing out: All the people get enough and are full by sharing with one another. Now that it is just one day before the mass actions and the general strike I feel these texts are quite consoling; and I'm keen to hear the sermon. Without sharing there can be no justice. The pastor speaks about what constitutes a "living community," what God did then and does today. Here he falls into a lament: Fewer people come to church, many members are missing on Sunday. The trend in the parish is downward, not upward. Then the pastor observes that God works at specific times and specific places in a special way, for example, in the Reformation and the revival movements of the eighteenth and nineteenth centuries, for which we should be thankful. Today, for example, God is at work in Eastern Europe and China, even though there isn't much evidence of God's activity in South Africa. The pastor says that we should read the Bible more and that more people should come to the parish discussion groups. He barely touches on the point of the text about the sharing of goods and the balancing of burdens between the rich and the poor. He says that we don't have to copy the early church in everything, since each age has its own forms . . .

I feel like screaming. Andreas and I don't go to the Eucharist. Martin does, but later talks to the pastor at the door and lets him know how staggered he is by the way the sermon was misused to obscure the gospel by leaving out the part that now has such prophetic, pastoral force.

Over coffee after church we have a discussion with some elderly women. We talk about the necessity of meetings between the races. One of the ladies tells us that they were visited once by a German choir that took an interest in the music of the "natives." They set up a joint concert with a South African choir in this very hall. It was "interesting," she says.

After a few more critical questions we are told that you first have to live here for twenty-five years before you can really understand the situation. Only one of the ladies is on our side. She says: "We need a new Reformation. We're sitting on a powder keg while in politics we stick our heads in the sand." An older gentleman with a Tyrolean hat joins us. After a few minutes of heated discussion he rushes away, foaming with rage: "Whenever pastors come here from Germany, something always goes wrong."

That evening Detlef and I fly to Johannesburg. Then we rent a car and drive to see Iwor and Karin. Iwor is a Boer who has worked for some time for "Koinonia," a project of racial reconciliation. Currently he is employed by IGASA, an institute supported by Europeans that offers courses to educate the people in democracy. Iwor has already survived several assassination attempts, and his house has been fired upon.

On Monday morning we go to the Vortrekker Monument near Pretoria. It was erected by the Boers in memory of the great trek in the nineteenth century, when they fled from the English and "civilized" the country. The biblical story of the Exodus has been pressed into service to interpret the Boers' experience as a kind of sacred history — the same tale of the Exodus that liberation movements all over the world invoke today to gloss their own escape from oppression. The monument is obviously a shrine. At the entrance gate there is a sign calling for silence. Women are forbidden to wear short pants, and men can't wear muscle T-shirts. Around the "tower," at whose four corners the heroes of the trek, hewed out of stone, stand guard with fixed bayonets, is a circular wall decorated with the motif of circled wagons. The "laager" is *the* symbol of the Boer trek: from behind it they could fight while taking only a few casualties. Within the "sanctuary" burns an eternal flame: the "light of civilization." Reliefs on the stone wall present the triumphant march of the Boers. In the lower vault is a cenotaph. On December 16 a sunray falls through a little opening in the roof of the monument onto this empty grave, and tradition-conscious Boers renew their deeply religious loyalty oath.

In front of the monument two blacks are working, despite the strike. They tell us that they if they went on strike they'd be booted out. The white media are always talking about "intimidation" directed by the ANC against blacks who are willing to work; they never mention the white masters' efforts at intimidation. We ask the older of the men how much he earns here. He says, "Very little." Then we ask him what he thinks of the monument. "It's only for the whites and the Zulus." He shows us in the brochure we have bought a picture of the relief representing the trekkers making a treaty with the Zulus. "It's the same thing today. The whites pay the Zulus to work with them against all the others." This is an obvious reference to the secret financing of Inkatha, the "freedom party," of the Zulu chief Buthelezi, by the government. The "Inkatha-gate scandal," which recently came to light, has done much to dispel any euphoria about de Klerk on the part of the ANC.

Lunch with Nico Smith. He was once a respected Dutch Reformed theologian until he began to take a stand against apartheid. He became a pastor in a black township and finally won the right to live there with his family. At the same time he founded "Koinonia," a program that brings people of different races together to become personally acquainted. Nico is one of the more radical whites in this country and is widely looked up to. He tells me that last week he was invited with his wife, Nelson Mandela, and a few others to an informal farewell dinner at the German ambassador's. He stresses how wise, statesmanly, and moderate Mandela is. The decades in prison failed to break him. Nico thinks there's no alternative to the general strike. The country must be brought to a halt, so that the white masters finally understand that a sharp turnaround is inevitable and that they can't hold onto power.

Tuesday, August 4

Caesar Molebatsi is one of the key figures of the Christian resistance. He is general secretary of the South African YMCA and one of the cofounders of Concerned Evangelicals, who link evangelization and the struggle for liberation. He beams when we meet at the entrance to Soweto. Wolfgang Vorläner, a common friend from Germany, had sent a flattering letter of recommendation ahead of me. We take a long tour around Soweto. It's very quiet. The general strike is taking a peaceful course. Here and there we see a few stones lying on the road, the remains of barricades to prevent cars from passing through. A few stores have opened. Nobody seems to be "intimidating" the shopowners.

Nobody knows how many people live in Soweto. Is it three million? Four? Five? Many families are crammed together into tiny huts of ten to twelve square meters. The gigantic coal-fired power plant in Soweto feeds the Johannesburg electrical system. Because it lies so close to the city, electrical bills there are very low. But electricity in Soweto is expensive because it has to be transported from far away. Needless to say, the power plant has no filtering system for its smokestacks. Many children in Soweto suffer from chronic coughs and similar environmentally caused diseases.

The city of Soweto has clearly distinguishable quarters. The poorest of the poor live in shacks, wretched handmade huts of corrugated iron, plastic, and cardboard. Scattered between them are the inevitable toilets, which the government providently builds on any site where new slum neighborhoods might crop up. In some places one finds lonely outhouses where huts have yet to arrive. The lower middle class lives in tiny stone houses, each shared by three families. The next category consists of the little one-family houses, for which the tenants must pay around five hundred rands per month. This means that at least four adult family members must work to be able to live here. The interest rates for the poor are so high that they sometimes have to pay eight hundred rands interest to pay off a principal of one hundred rands. There are also a few beautiful and one or two splendid houses in Soweto — not least of all Winnie Mandela's house, which is still no fancier than what any upper-level government official in Germany could afford. Until recently the government used to bus tourists into the better parts of the city to show them how good the blacks had it. This sort of propaganda had to be halted when the busses had rocks thrown at them or were fired upon. Even Mandela's house had to serve for propaganda purposes, as if the president of a free South Africa was supposed to live in a wretched hut, for reasons of credibility. "No African would allow that," said Caesar, "nor would I." He showed me the monument for the first high school student who was shot down by the police in the massacre of 1976. Over two hundred students died then as they protested the plan to introduce Afrikaans as the main language of instruction.

We walk by a spot where only yesterday three people were murdered. I photograph the bullet holes in a window. We pass the enormous "hostels," where hundreds of migrating workers are jammed together and have to share a few showers and toilets. No wonder these places are breeding grounds of violence. Here is Inkatha's stronghold and the source of continual bloodshed. The barracks have a fatal resemblance to the buildings in Dachau or Bergen-Belsen. The inmates could — and still can — travel back to their "homelands" to visit their families only three to four times a year. This is the "pro-family" policy of a conservative white government.

Caesar shows me the layout of the "Youth Alive" ministries, of which he's the leader. This operation tries simultaneously to uphold spiritual life and social consciousness. Despite its modest means the missionary work has been extraordinarily successful. The buildings are very simple. With only a little money to go on committed Christians have gotten superhuman results.

Toward evening I suddenly discover that I have been invited with Ute and her hosts to dine at Frank Chikane's house. The president of the South African Church Council lives in a fine house — surrounded, of course, with a high fence. I feel honored to be sitting across the table from this important man, whose autobiography I have just now been reading. As a Pentecostalist he was thrown out of his church for becoming too political. He was persecuted by the government, continually arrested, horribly tortured, kept going underground, and fled abroad. Finally he returned to South Africa to take an active part in the struggle for liberation. He is the founder and first director of the Institute for Contextual Theology. He was subjected to further persecution and forced again into hiding, until the SACC surprisingly called him to the office of president.

He strikes you as at once youthful and wise. We ask him why he hasn't come out in favor of the strike. He says that as long as the battle lines run between the oppressors and the people, he knows he always has to stand on the side of the people. But this time the battle line runs right through the ranks of the liberation movement. So he can't simply support the ANC demands; instead he has to be ready to take over the role of mediator. Frank tells us about his experience as a child, when the state leveled his parents' house because the lot was supposed to be "used for farming." To this day the land remains untouched. The whole thing was part of their policy of driving the poor from their land into the cities, where cheap labor was needed.

At dinner Frank Chikane casually remarks: "I'm surprised I haven't turned my back on the church and the faith many years ago, after all the trouble the church has caused in this country. I understand everyone who has left the church. And I'm surprised that I'm still in it. God's grace is so amazing..."

As we leave Frank prays with us. In the act of praying I am seized by a strong inner feeling, of the sort I experience – but very rarely – in the presence of a "saint." I have the sense of being unworthy of this encounter. And yet it does me good to experience the nearness of such a person.

In the morning I talk with Caesar about the fact that Germany is spiritually desiccated and that we no longer have any prophets. There's no dialogue between spiritual movements and forces seeking political and social change. And I don't know a single person who's really accepted by both sides. Here in South Africa at the drop of a hat you cite ten names of people who are living from the wellsprings of faith *and* have passed the acid test of politics. Holy envy!

Wednesday, August 5

In the morning along with Ntutu, a young ANC activist, we head to the big demonstration in Pretoria. For the first time in my life I put on a clerical collar. We park the car near the first group of demonstrators and march off. Soon we're running in the toye-toye step, singing and shouting slogans with the others. I had been afraid of taking part in this action. But now that I'm in it I feel great peace. I recall the blockade of NATO headquarters in 1983. Then too my fear had given way to a great sense of peace once I had dared to take the first step "across the border." We three Germans are the only whites to be seen anywhere. The march moves slowly toward the Parliament building. There are only a handful of police in sight. One whole group of them is guarding a flagpole on which the South African flag is waving. At the windows of the office buildings and on roof terraces stand many groups of whites, curious to see the goings-on. Some have fear written all over their faces; others look extremely "cool" and seem to be joking with one another as if this was a carnival parade.

The crowd is so large We can't see the end of it; there must be more than a hundred thousand people (the nightly news will later speak of twenty-five thousand, the police will raise that to as much as seventy thousand — which is typical for the disinformation you get here). We camp around the base of the Parliament building, which is located on a hill. Shortly after two o'clock the "president" arrives. Huge burst of applause. The crowd intones the African national hymn "Nkosi Sikeli iAfrica" (God Bless Africa), which is also sung in church services on Sunday. We hear slogans and battle cries. Mandela speaks like a statesman — he's anything but a populist. These masses could easily be whipped up and stampeded into violence. Mandela speaks calmly, almost softly, about nonviolence, about his vision of a demo-cratic South Africa. He holds out the prospect of all major parties having a share in his government and points out that a freely elected ANC government would protect private property.

Afterward we head back. Again there is singing, skipping, and running. This time there are lots of police and heavily armed soldiers on the side streets. I admire the blacks: After all the injustice that's been done to them, they are still so patient. They don't provoke the police, thus continually proving that the changes they want are peace-ful ones. Finally I see a white marching in front of me. When he turns around, I read on his T-shirt that he belongs to a Jewish student organ-ization. I want to talk to him and tell him how happy I am, as a German alongside a Jew, to demonstrate against racism in South Africa. Then we get separated.

That evening Caesar tells me about his trials as a Christian. He reports about a woman who lived with her husband in a squalid hut. One day Inkatha men came along, went from hut to hut, and shot the men. She begged her husband to hide under the bed. Both began to pray with fervor. The Inkatha people burst into the hut and asked her where her husband was. She said he wasn't there. Then they asked the woman whether she smoked. She said no. But the Inkatha men had smelled the husband's cigarette smoke, went looking for him, found him under the bed, and shot him. "Doesn't God hear the cry of this sort of woman?" Caesar asks. "Aren't we preaching a false image of God when we say that you should pray to God and he'll take care of us? You can understand the ANC people who say, that we shouldn't pray any more, just fight."

Friday, August 7

Yesterday morning Caesar's wife, Chumi, takes me to the Carlton Ho-tel, where I meet Andreas. We go off together to Johannesburg to buy books. In the Methodist bookstore there are all sorts of pious literature from America, and not much else. We ask about liberation theology. The woman at the cash register tells us that they had only a few titles to begin with, and they always go out of print immediately.

In the afternoon we get an invitation to Wolfram Kistner's house. Once again a different world: a very German parsonage with a study and giant bookcase covering an entire wall. Kistner was born in South Africa of German parents (a missionary couple). He wants to talk once again about the get-together that Andreas recently held in Johannesburg to discuss his book *The Unconfessed Guilt*. In it Andreas Richter-Böhne documents the failure of Christian preaching after 1942 to really name and come to terms with the guilt of the Nazi years. "Working off" the past will also be important for white "Christian" South Africa, but less so for the blacks, who set no store by a confession of guilt, but want a new attitude with practical results. Finally Kistner, who shortly has to deliver a lecture on the contribution of theology to the transformation of South Africa, asks us what we think is important in this connection. He himself sees theology as the attempt to formulate for each age what it means to follow Jesus. Thanks to this position Kistner has been imprisoned several times. I say that as "talk about God" theology has to reveal the harm that has been, and still is being, done by the misuse of "God talk." And I believe the church has an urgent need to confront the issues of economic ethics. My friend from Dresden, Peter Meis, had said during the German reunification period that most of all he wanted to study economics. The church, he thought, lacked the technical competence to get mixed up in economic issues, yet these shaped politics more than anything else. Evening: Flight back to Cape Town.

This morning there is a lecture at the Baptist Theological Seminary on the subject of Bible study. First there is a prayer service; after hymns and a reading from Scripture the teacher allows students to offer "testimony." A white tells how during the strike he was in a township as a "monitor," to make sure that the agreements were kept. While he was there it was if scales had fallen from his eyes. He saw how many lies the media had been telling about what goes on in the townships. He had gone there in fear and trembling, in view of the violence he expected to find. In reality he discovered peace-loving people in great distress. A black student reports that on Wednesday for the first time he took part in a protest march and "toye-toyed." He had always thought it was a sin to do this sort of thing. So he was happy to meet so many Christians. Furthermore during the march he had sensed the nearness of God in a quite special way.

At this point a lively discussion ensues, in which George Molebatsi, Caesar's nephew, takes a prominent part and presents his grievances as a black – until a white teacher orders him to be silent, since he's "spreading hatred," which is out of place in this school. I defend George, maintaining that *I* hadn't heard any hatred. In the course of the arguments several coloureds and whites leave the hall.

In my lecture I put special emphasis on the way race, gender, and economic situation mark our understanding of, and our access to, the Bible. I make a case for becoming aware of our own "glasses." Only in dialogue with others, who have different kinds of glasses on, can we be spared from falling victim to our own blind spots.

The subsequent Bible study of the "rich young man" (following Walter Wink's method) becomes very lively. It's evident that the students' own economic background is mirrored in their remarks. For example, a black observes that the young man in the gospel story probably asks how he can "inherit" eternal life because he's already quite familiar with "inheritances." Surely, this student claims, he's inherited all his wealth.

In the end three of the black students come up to me. One of them — the "toye-toyer" — embraces me and gives me his address. George Molebatsi says: "This is the kind of white theology we can use!" I encourage the students not to let up and tell them how much I admire the patience of the blacks in the face of their centuries-old history of oppression. One of the students is speechless. He says that I'm the first white he ever heard calling the blacks "patient." We talk about "unity" at the college. I tell him I see two kinds of unity. First, there's reconciled unity, which comes about when you take conflict and opposition seriously and confront them. Then there is the harmony that consists of "spraying whipped cream on shit." This is greeted with a huge outburst of laughter.

Thursday, August 11

On Sunday I'm to preach in the community of Khayelitsha. For my text I've chosen Luke 4, Jesus' inauguration of his ministry in Nazareth. One of the elders translates my speech sentence by sentence. I tell them that this could be a "year of grace" for South Africa, when everything that Jesus promised will be realized: when prisoners are released, the oppressed set free, the poor have the gospel preached to them. I tell them about my experiences in Pretoria and in the Baptist seminary, and above all about the student who went on his first march and had such a clear sense of God's nearness. I add that the text also contains a promise for the oppressors: The blind shall see. And I cite as an example the white student at the Baptist seminary who felt the scales falling from his eyes when he was a strike observer in the township.

In the evening I do an introduction to the Enneagram for the community. The group gets into it very well, and there's a lot of laughter. Beatrice has the great aha-experience that she is a NINE. The people from the community say there is a great deal of NINE-energy among the blacks: laziness, resignation, repressed power. Only in the young can one see unchecked EIGHT-energy. And white South Africa is full of SIX anxiety. That's probably the reason why the Germans are so popular here.

Wednesday, August 19

Last Thursday evening I began the Enneagram workshop with the Anglicans. Only one coloured was there, a priest from the parish. John Freeth plays the part of official greeter. John is an Englishman, the chief pastor of a large parish with five churches and two thousand worshipers each Sunday. He has long been active in the liberation movement. Only recently have his wounds healed – the seventeen welts from the whipping he got when he took part in the action mentioned earlier, when blacks and whites together took over the "white" beach.

The seminar goes splendidly. You get the impression that white South Africa too is famished and longing for hopeful input from outside. John Freeth tells me how disappointed he was when not long ago Jim Wallis had to cancel a trip to Cape Town because of illness.

I stress the political implications of "reconciliation work on ourselves," which the Enneagram offers, and I say, among other things: "Nowadays many people in the Western world are turning to some form of spirituality. One of the reasons for this has to be that the condition of our planet has become so threatened that some people think they can escape this frightening reality by 'communing with themselves.' Certain kinds of spirituality – whether decked out as Christian or esoteric – prevents people from looking the facts in the eye, and in this way stabilizes the status quo. There is a cheap form of 'reconciliation' that abandons the world's misery to its own devices. Even the Enneagram can be misused in this way . . . I hope that in this seminar I can speak to men and women who aren't running away from the difficult issues facing South Africa today, but who are seeking strength and wisdom in their struggle for a new, just South Africa."

I'm glad to be back home. The four weeks have taken a heavy physical and mental toll. The trip has confronted me with many of my own fears, with my fear of oppression and foreign rule, of violence, sickness, and death. But amid the danger, at the march in Pretoria, I experienced great strength and inner peace. God is on the side of the poor. A pair of verses from Isaiah keeps running through my head:

"Is it [i.e., "the fast that I choose"] not to share your bread with the hungry and bring the homeless into your house; when you see the naked, cover him, and not to hide yourself from your own flesh? Then shall your light break forth like the dawn, and your healing shall spring up speedily . . . " (Isa. 58:7–8). My healing, our healing in the West, can spring up only when we learn to share our bread with the poor.

– 11 –

Suggestions for More Excitement

On Dealing with Inner-City Churches

Felix Felix

Why don't we simply leave the inner-city churches empty – as museums of an obsolete culture, for example? Or maybe we could turn them into mosques or department stores (a kind of consumers' temple). Anyhow, we could definitely find *some* sort of useful purpose that's more meaningful than simply closing them during the week and opening them briefly on Sunday morning for the fifty or so parishioners that are left. Of course, classical concerts still draw well, and then there are always the tourists and Christmas. Isn't that enough?

Jesus

But there's one problem: The churches invoke Jesus of Nazareth. That would create difficulties with closing them and leaving them empty, or with the department store idea, etc. Maybe the best solution, after all, would be the mosque. But locking up just won't do, since Jesus himself opened things up, access to God at any rate, since he tried to let people get at what the scribes and Pharisees had locked up tight, and since he wanted to throw open the kingdom of heaven to the simple folk, the ordinary mortals, wresting it from the pretensions of the pious: "Woe to you, scribes and Pharisees, hypocrites! For you lock people out of the kingdom of heaven. For you do not go in yourselves, and when others are going in, you stop them" (Matt. 23:13).

The Ordinary Mortals

Well, we don't lock up the kingdom of heaven, just the churches. We'd let them come if they wanted. They'd be cordially welcome. Only they no longer come, they don't want to believe any more, they want to sleep late.

But who strays into the inner city on Sunday morning between ten and eleven? From Monday to Friday, of course, they would already be there on the job. Wednesday afternoon you might be out shopping or strolling. Friday night at eleven you might be just getting out of the theater. At night someone might be sitting on the church steps nursing a bottle of wine or waiting for a dealer. But then the church would naturally be closed. Otherwise things could get messy.

Are we really concerned about these people, the ones who live in the city, the ordinary mortals? Isn't our horizon limited to "our" parishioners, to the remaining souls who put envelopes in the collection basket? Needless to say, they're the ones who pay our bills and, as such, they have a special right to "their" church and "their" pastor. But neither the church nor the pastor belong to them, any more than the parishioners belong to us. We all belong to Somebody Else. We are under orders from Jesus Christ. He's the one who asks: "Why do you call me 'Lord, Lord,' and do not do what I tell you?" (Luke 6:46).

The Gospel

The other day I attended the installation of a pastor colleague of mine. The church was packed. The gospel was preached, but I had the impression that it barely got to the rear pews. It seemed to be good news for all the people present, for all those who had gotten up that morning and had come to church. People outside its walls weren't mentioned, never brought up, had no place either in the liturgy or the sermon. They never appeared; the city never appeared, the world never appeared.

Paul Had a Completely Different View of It

Therefore just as one man's trespass led to condemnation for all, so one man's act of righteousness leads to justification and life for all. For just as by the one man's disobedience the many were made sinners, so by the one man's obedience the many will be made righteous. (Rom. 5:18–19)

For the creation waits with eager longing for the revealing of the children of God; . . . the creation itself will be set free from its bondage to decay and will obtain the freedom of the glory of the children of God. We know that the whole creation has been groaning in labor pains till now, and not only the creation, but we ourselves, who have the first fruits of the Spirit, groan inwardly, while we wait for adoption, the redemption of our bodies. (Rom. 8:19, 21–23)

Who of us still lives, thinks, and preaches against the backdrop of this universal horizon? Are our theological discussions and our sermons on Mission Sunday the only occasions when we still talk about God's saving will for all men and women and for creation?

This boundless horizon of the Bible seems to have become irrelevant for our cities. We've fallen back on other ideas of salvation. True, our gospel still reaches the farthest pew, but not the tramps in front of the church door, nor the night owls and the people who work in the area, nor the passers-by during the week. The cross of Jesus is threatening to degenerate into an insignia for the enrolled members of the club.

The Sheep

At Christmastime a colleague of mine at an inner-city church in Zurich simply opened up the church door. He had already set up inside a makeshift stall with three sheep, two goats, and a donkey. The animals munched peacefully away, stank, and gave warmth.

And every day people came: mothers with children and school classes and tramps and business people. They petted the sheep and sat quietly in the choir area in front of the assembled figures of the crèche, painted, or wrote something in it, or tried out one of the recorders that were available there.

You should have seen the eyes of these people. They had a gleam in them like Christmas. And the guestbook overflowed with gratitude:

"They've closed our youth center, but here's a place that's opening up. Thanks!"

"After forty years I'm back again in this church. I was baptized here, but since then I've never had an occasion to return here. You have opened the church to me! Heartfelt thanks."

And I was overwhelmed by a great sadness: How simple and unassuming everything was. The door stood open and there was a reason to look in. There was something to experience and the possibility of silence. Someone was there to listen to a few words or to say something. Nothing more. For the moment there was quite enough. But this church was the exception and not the rule. The other inner-city churches were closed to keep everything neat and orderly or were opened temporarily just for the tour buses.

> To what then will I compare the people of this generation, and what are they like? They are like children sitting in the marketplace and calling to one another, "We played the flute for you (wedding songs), and you did not dance; we wailed, and you did not weep." (Luke 7:31–32)

My colleague, by the way, hadn't fallen prey to some skilled PR-advisor. He simply enjoyed doing something like this for once. In his youth he himself had often herded sheep.

Hope

Imagine how it would be if all the pastors, the church's co-workers, and the parishioners worked out of enjoyment, if they stopped practicing self-censorship, but gave their creativity free rein, and if in the process they were thinking not just about parish councils, parishioners, and pastors, but about Jesus and Paul and the people in the city, the ordinary mortals. Then things might get to the point that our churches would really become "a place of truth and freedom, of justice and peace," as we pray in our liturgies.

For a few years now there have been hopeful attempts in some European cities to open inner-city churches and to make them accessible to the men and women in the city. They are becoming places of prayer but also of encounter, spaces for God but also for people, meeting points for discussion but also places of life and festivity. It's called "expanded use" when once again the churches of the city are the scene of what they were once built for: human life.

The virtue of hospitality is once more being put into practice, and boundaries overcome: Modern art is shown (e.g., at St. Peter's in Cologne). There are thematic exhibits or displays of the churches' own artistic treasures (e.g., the Domkerk in Utrecht). Writers are invited to preach (St. Peter's in Lübeck or the Leonhardskirche in Basel). Theater people and dancers are offered space, or there are concerts of contemporary music (the Passionskirche in Berlin). There are bold encounters with contemporary religious feelings (at St. James in London) or with present-day themes such as AIDS (at the Mozes en Aäronkerk in Amsterdam). Other churches are opening their doors for passersby (as the inner-city Catholic churches of Paris have been doing for years now) or for people in distress (St. Martin-in-the-Fields, London; Pauluskerk, Rotterdam).

Action

Once when I told a friend that I spent twelve hours preparing the Sunday worship service, he said: It'd be better if you spent less time on it and went on three more visits.

Maybe it would be even better to receive visits sometimes. To sit in the church, unlock the doors, and invite people in, start conversations and listen, be attentive and take things in. Set up a bank of candles and a coffee machine. Show pictures and watch a dance. Wipe away a tear and cry together. Listen to someone read or recount a dream.

If we listened to those who come around, the people in need and the homeless, the strollers and vagabonds, the artists and dancers, the writers and esoteric types, the children and the aged, then perhaps we'd get a new understanding of Jesus and the gospel. And the reign of heaven would open for us too. Then our gospel wouldn't stop at the last pews (maybe we should have long since ripped out those hard-backed benches), but would reach our city — and ourselves.

> I thank you, Father, Lord of heaven and earth, because you have hidden these things from the wise and intelligent and have revealed them to infants. (Luke 10:21).

Opening our churches to these "infants" and ordinary mortals would be more than just exciting.

12

Creation Spirituality and the Recovery of the Spiritual Warrior

MATTHEW FOX

✠

I remember attending a Mass on Ascension Thursday three years ago in Chartres Cathedral and how enfeebled all the priests on the altar were. The bishop who presided preached entirely on sickness and ill health, ignoring hundreds of young persons who were present who had hiked on a pilgrimage from Paris for three days to be there. I turned to a young man who was with me and asked: "Is there any room in this church for someone who is healthy?" It is telling how timid and wimpy religion has become in the West.

It has not always been so. In the Scriptures there is much celebration of the warrior archetype. The prophet, for example, is told that his destiny is "to tear up and knock down, to destroy and to overthrow, to build and to plant" (Jer. 1:10). Aquinas says that the first act of the saints is "the work of justice" and this takes "the strength of divine power." He invokes the prophet Jeremiah who says, "The Lord is with me like a brave warrior" (Jer. 20:11). In the Scriptures the messiah is pictured as a warrior as in this passage from Wisdom literature that was traditionally utilized by Christians in the Christmas liturgy:

> When peaceful silence lay over all,
> and night had run the half of her swift course,
> down from the heavens, from the royal throne, leapt your all-
>   powerful Word;
> Into the heart of a doomed land the stern warrior leapt.
>
> (Wisd. 18:14f.)

Jesus, then, is represented as a "stern warrior" and a cosmic one who dares to enter the very heart of a "doomed land" in order to restore it.

In the church in Latin America today there is much warriorhood — just as there was in the church of the martyrs at the beginning of the

Christian era. Is now the time — when earth yearns and humankind yearns for the end of war — to take back the archetype of the spiritual warrior from the Pentagon and bastions of militarism?

Greenpeace has done this; can people of faith also do it? How do we do this? And who are the warriors? Warriors are those who are alert, who concentrate, who contemplate, who center themselves fully. If the warriors are not well grounded, they may die. The warriors are those who face death. The warriors are also those who are committed to a goal that is larger than the individual ego.

Perhaps religion in the West is timid because it, like the rest of our culture, tends to shield us from death and demonic forces. (Consider the sanitizing of our latest war in the Gulf and the lack of the presence of the 150,000 Iraqi dead ones.) The spiritual warrior who struggles with internal wars is distinct from the soldier, who takes orders externally. I propose that all four paths of creation spirituality require of the pathmaker a consciousness of the spiritual warrior.

The Via Positiva

To befriend the beauty in life — to see it in the simplest of gifts and the most universal, even in the gift of existence itself, takes concentration. It takes a willingness to stand toe to toe with beauty. Beauty can terrorize us, for it is so much bigger than we often feel we are, and beauty includes terror. As the poet Rainer Maria Rilke puts it:

For beauty is nothing
but the beginning of terror, which we still are just able to endure,
and we are so awed because it serenely disdains
to annihilate us. Every angel is terrifying.

Thus beauty requires a big heart or courage.

We must become *hunters of beauty,* alert and fully present to its mystery. We need to seek it out, both within us and around us. We need to respect it lest it swallow us up. It takes strength to engage beauty, to be vulnerable to it, to be fully present to it. It takes a kind of single-mindedness that the warriors also demand of themselves. As Thomas Aquinas puts it, "To be incapable of receiving love's gift is a mark of great weakness. To be able to sustain it is a mark of great strength." Yes! To undergo the wonder of the Via Positiva takes a kind of warrior strength. A great emptying is often required to be so receptive, for as Aquinas says of the divine gifts, "The gift is infinite on the part of the giver."

For some time I have asked myself why Western religion has tended to keep quiet the good news of our divinity, our being sons and daughters of the Divine One, and I have come to conclude that deep down we are *afraid of our divinity.* With divinity and with being royal persons responsibilities accrue. "Better guilt than responsibility," Ernest Becker wrote. It takes strength to accept the truth of our royal personhood and to live out of that vocation.

The warrior has faced death and is therefore aware that life is precious and fleeting and ought not be wasted. This is a truth that comes to us in the Via Positiva and that we take to the Via Positiva: To taste life now, before it is too late. "Taste and see that God is good," says the psalmist. Warriors have so committed themselves to the truth and beauty of what they have tasted that they are willing to lay down their lives if need be for the truth they have tasted. "Greater love than this no one has, than to lay down their life for a friend," as Jesus puts it. The Via Positiva sees one through even the event of death itself.

The Via Negativa

The spiritual warrior has descended into the depths of fear, of loss of life, of separation from the beloved. The spiritual warrior has imbibed darkness and even nothingness. The dark night of the soul is no stranger to the spiritual warrior. Saint John of the Cross, who wrote so eloquently of the dark night of the soul, also turned it into a "happy night," a night of "luck" and "good fortune," a night for escape or liberation. Interestingly, he did not formulate his naming of the dark night from an armchair but from a prison cell, indeed a torture chamber, into which his religious brothers had thrown him. Why had they done this? Because he had, in the tradition of the prophets and urged on by the commands of his mentor, Teresa of Avila, dared to call for a reform and renewal of his order in sixteenth-century Spain. John of the Cross was a warrior, a prophetic voice in a dark time in Spanish Catholicism. He paid the price for it; he challenged not only his order but indirectly the Spanish Inquisition. But it is his *spiritual* warriorship, his poetry and mystical music, that we most deeply remember. Having spent half a year in a cell that was the size of a closet, tortured regularly by his brothers, abused in the refectory, forbidden to say Mass, beaten regularly, he had tasted of the dark night. His daring escape, on a night when the moon was dark, was a heroic effort to move beyond the Via Negativa, to let go of his imprisonment. It was a radical creative act. The warrior, to survive, must indeed be resourceful and daring.

Part of the Via Negativa is letting go. Spiritual warriors know about letting go: letting go of comforts and of security, of images that worked in the past, of relationships that worked but may not have served. Spiritual warriors know of the emptying that accompanies deep letting go. Nothingness is no stranger to spiritual warriors. It sometimes becomes their food and drink.

Via Creativa

It takes a spiritual warrior to be creative. This is so not only because one needs to drink deeply of the Via Positiva and the Via Negativa in life in order to birth oneself and to birth truth for others, but also because it takes concentration, presence, being with one's images honestly in order to create. It takes courage to create. *The Courage to Create* is the title of one of Rollo May's important books, a title that he adapted from Paul Tillich's *The Courage to Be.* Path One in the creation spiritual journey might be understood as the path of the "courage to be"; Path Two is the "courage to be not" — to be empty, to let go, to surrender; Path Three requires "the courage to create." In creating we bring new life into the world, we disturb the status quo, we pronounce our belief in what is new, our hope in a future. In creating we put our best self and most intimate inner self forward for all to see and be touched by, and also to be criticized, dismissed, and even trivialized.

In Path Three spiritual warriors stand up and offer their gifts to the community. Here the fight is engaged, the demons are exorcised, the dueling parties are put on display. Creativity arises from a deep awareness that life requires not only life of us, but *our* life. If we do not give back what is our unique gift and expression of life's mystery and truth, no one will do it for us. Responsibility to express the inner self in a particular time and place in history is what flows from spiritual warriors in the Via Creativa. Here the warriors have embraced their shadow and their images of all kinds and have recycled the enemy into a friend, often by way of playing with the enemy. This befriending of the enemy and the realization that all our images are allies of some kind — if only as food and nourishment for the people — this befriending takes concentration, skill, commitment, and singleness of purpose. It takes a warrior.

Via Transformativa

Of all the paths of creation spirituality, the Fourth Path is perhaps most readily evident as a path of a spiritual warrior. The prophet, as Rabbi Heschel says, "interferes." But to interfere with the powers and principalities within oneself and within one's culture (and usually they are strikingly the same) takes a warrior's strength and courage, skill and concentration. And the prophet's willingness to face down death. The prophet is not born of moral outrage and anger alone but of all three paths that precede the Via Transformativa. In each of these paths, as we have seen, spiritual warriors are exercised and undergo disciplines that prepare them for the battles of social transformation, battles that are waged not with artillery and rage but with the untried power of imagination (the Via Creativa). It is in the arena of moral imagination and spiritual creativity that the prophet is most armed for the battles that ensue.

Transformation does not come easily. People and institutions do not relinquish power and privilege cheerfully. Paradigm shifts *are* resisted. But spiritual warriors who are prophets have learned their need for mysticism, for their own spiritual nourishment, and the previous three paths of the journey are a kind of logistics or supply line to the prophet in the field of battle. The prophet is truly the "mystic in action," as William Hocking put it. This does not mean that Paths One to Three do not include action — only that Path Four represents the full field of action to the prophet, the authentic and full expression of compassion that has been learned in the previous journeying but finds its richest expression in the struggle for justice and the struggle for celebration. True spiritual warriors are no fanatics; such persons abhor death and power-trips in all their forms. True spiritual warriors have learned the lessons of the Negativa so deeply that they are ready to let go at any time, of anything, not only of life but of a preoccupation with death, not only of irresponsibility but also of responsibility, not only of the child but also of the adult. Authentic spiritual warriors are capable of becoming children again, celebrative again. They are ready to lay down arms in favor of the weapons of love, delight, play, and surprise. True spiritual warriors have not killed the *puer, puella,* or child inside but have left ample room for the child to become prophet, to interfere, to make moist again, and to call us back to ecstasy and celebration. True spiritual warriors know that fighting is only one dimension to living and that living always takes precedence for it is a goal as well as the way; and fighting is only a means to defend living. True spiritual warriors, like true prophets, work themselves out of being needed. They return to their origins, their childlike wishes to play freely in the universe again.

If the warrior archetype comes to play in every one of the Four Paths of the creation spiritual journey, then we would expect to see a lot of warriors among the practitioners of creation spirituality. Do we have a right to call Francis of Assisi a warrior? And Thomas Aquinas, who fought to bring cosmology back to faith life? And Meister Eckhart, who taught the peasants and the women Beguines how they were all "royal persons" and cosmic Christs? And how about Gandhi, who took on the British empire with a smile and a determined strategy? And Martin Luther King, Jr., who faced down centuries of racial discrimination? And what about the holy women of our ancestry — Dorothy Day and Sojourner Truth? Harriet Tubman and Adrienne Rich? Mechtild of Magdeburg and Julian of Norwich? Teresa of Avila and Catherine of Siena? Consider these words of warriorhood written by Hildegard of Bingen to her sisters in the twelfth century: "When you oppose the devil like a strong warrior opposes his enemy, then God is delighted with your struggle and wishes you to call upon the Godself constantly in all hours in your distress. Become strong, therefore, and be comforted because this is necessary for you."

If warriorhood is an integral dimension to all four paths, then prayer is the making of a warrior; it is the opening and strengthening of the heart, the making of a large heart (courage and magnanimity). We cannot truly live without it.

13

The Norwegian Retreat Movement as an Ecumenical Force

KNUT GRØNVIK

On April 11, 1814, after losing control of Paris, Napoleon Bonaparte abdicated. That same day some 112 Norwegian men got together to draft and pass the constitution of the Kingdom of Norway. By this time the country had been subject to Denmark for more than four hundred years. But the King of Denmark had sided with the rebel from Corsica, and in the grand political chaos prevailing just before and after the fall of Napoleon a power vacuum was created that the Norwegian ruling class alertly exploited.

Five weeks later, on May 17, Norway's constitution was passed and signed. This day became the Norwegian national holiday, and even though the country was united with Sweden for the next ninety years, that didn't halt the influence of the new constitution on the development of modern democratic Norway.

Not for Jews and Jesuits

For its day the Norwegian constitution of 1814 was thoroughly progressive. Naturally it harked back to the French model, but in most matters it was more liberal and democratic than any of its contemporaries. With one exception: it did not guarantee freedom of religion. Article 2 declared that "the Evangelical-Lutheran religion remains the public state religion." And then comes something altogether incredible to our way of thinking: "Jesuits and monastic orders are not allowed. Furthermore Jews are forbidden to enter the Kingdom."

Needless to say this article has long since been revised, and nowadays it expressly establishes the freedom to exercise one's religion. The struggle for the rights of the Jews was won by 1851. But it took another hundred years before the clause about the Jesuits and monastic orders was stricken. That didn't happen till 1956, and to this day Lutheran Christianity has been and still is Norway's "official" religion.

The Jesuit paragraph, to be sure, was never actually put into practice. The Roman Catholic Church was admitted into this country in 1843, and a handful of Catholic orders gained a foothold by the end of the nineteenth century. Nevertheless the paragraph has an eloquence all its own and shows just how absent Catholicism had been from Norway since the Reformation, and how prejudices and ignorance have shaped the views of the Norwegian people and Norwegian Christians toward Catholics.

Even today the Roman Catholic Church comprises no more than a bare 1 percent of the Norwegian population. This number is on the increase, though mainly because of immigration. Typically, the largest Catholic parish in Oslo counts believers from some fifty nations. In the final analysis the largest religious community on earth is a foreign body here, a marginal phenomenon. By contrast, more than 90 percent of the population are members of the established Lutheran Church. No wonder that Catholics barely appear on the religious horizon of Norwegian Christians.

Ignatius as a Model

But enough of this. We now turn to a small, wretched farmstead in the Otta valley at the foot of the Jotunheimen range (highest point 8100 feet). At around the same time as the notorious Jesuit paragraph was being struck from the constitution a group of young Christian preachers and leaders was gathering here. In the early 1950s – which was late by European standards, but far ahead of their time from the Norwegian perspective – they were in the process of laying the foundation for the Norwegian retreat movement. Today the place is called Sandom Retreat Center. And, as if by an irony of fate, we find that one of their most important sources of inspiration was the "forbidden" Ignatius Loyola.

Most of the group's members come from the Norwegian Mission Union, an independent church with its roots in a "great awakening" that took place around the turn of the century. Ever since the period between the two world wars it has been stamped by the revivals centering around Scandinavia's most important preacher, the Finnish-Swedish Frank Mangs. Currently the tone of this group is set by Edin Lövås. Lövås began his career as a revival preacher in his twenties. "I was like a stretched steel spring" is his own commentary on this period. This had to come to grief, and one day, in the middle of a series of meetings, he couldn't bring himself to climb into the pulpit. His energies were spent. And his faith as well?

"My prayer life was weak," Lövås tells us, "when I was alone, but strong at the big public occasions. And while Christ grew fainter and continually faded into the background, I myself had become the center of my service." Burned out, the young preacher took refuge in a lonely farm, where he was the guest of a simple, God-fearing family. Week after week he roamed through the outdoors or sat alone in his room, where he read nothing except the four gospels. He was looking for a new and deeper experience of Jesus. Until he found it.

"I read very slowly and put myself into the stories about Jesus. In this way I made the Jesus meditation my own. I had once read an article about Ignatius that made a deep impression on me," Lövås recalls. "It talked about involving all the senses in reading the Bible." As his crisis grew more intense, he began to collect and devour everything he could find about Christian mysticism or instructions from the old masters of spirituality for deepening one's religious life. At that time on the farm he also had one of the three great mystical experiences of his life, in which he was completely overwhelmed by the nearness and greatness of Jesus.

In the period that followed he continued the theoretical elaboration of his experiences, read more about Ignatius, and wrote his first book, *Spiritual Exercises for a Disciple of Christ*. He shared his experiences with friends and colleagues and discovered that they were all struggling with an arid, dismal prayer life. This led to the idea of going into seclusion to pray – and Sandom, the farmstead near the mountains, was the place they chose.

Dangerous "Catholicizing" Tendencies

But it soon became obvious that it's not enough to leave the city. "As brothers in an independent church we had little feeling for firm daily rhythms or liturgical prayer. But we soon realized that we needed it. We set up a chapel in the stable and met five times a day for prayer. Gradually we developed our own liturgy. It was based on texts from the Bible, but it left room for free and spontaneous prayer," Lövås recalls. "So we started doing genuine exercises, unbeknownst to ourselves."

Only later did the little group of "free church" preachers make contact with Protestant and Catholic retreat houses in Europe. These meetings inspired them to press the development of their retreat work. This was necessary because of the strong resistance in the Mission Union against "Catholicizing tendencies." So strong in fact that for many years Lövås had to shift his work as a preacher to Sweden, where he wouldn't be accused of "Catholic tendencies." In addition the Catholic Church had always had closer ties with the Swedes and so their fear of Catholics was less acute.

Thus the Norwegian ecumenical retreat movement had a difficult birth. But it *was* born. The work at Sandom went on at a snail's pace, and in the 1960s, after internal conflict, it had a breakdown. For a few years the center remained closed, before operations could be resumed again — with support from the outside, from Sweden, of course. The dream of founding a resident community in Sandom for giving retreats to visitors has been alive from the outset, but up until the present all such efforts had failed.

Nevertheless the retreat movement kept going, and nowadays interest in, and openness to, meditation, Christian mysticism, and a deeper spirituality are greater than ever. Besides Sandom there is now Thomas Farm and Lia Farm, which are likewise available for retreats all through the year. Additional retreat houses are being set up at various points in the country. Sandom is the primordial cell of a spiritual movement whose arrival here was long overdue.

Over the last twenty-five years Norwegians have shown increased willingness to admit that "something good could can come even from Catholics." Sandom transmitted something of the best that Catholic tradition had to offer, namely, meditative and contemplative spirituality. And in the Jesuit tradition we recognize the source of the stress on a personal relationship with Jesus Christ himself as the key to meditation. A few other forces, e.g., "Church Renewal," which is dominated by the established church and its theologians, and a little Lutheran nuns' convent, have also contributed to this new openness. It's probably no accident that this all took place in the post–Vatican II era, when for its part the Catholic Church has taken on a more open-minded stance.

Even for Pastors and Bishops

"When we began giving retreats, the message of the resurrection was practically never heard in Norwegian preaching, which is gloomy and totally dominated by the Cross," comments Lövås, now an older man. "By contrast we centered our spiritual life and our preaching around the presence of the risen and ascended Jesus Christ here and now, everywhere and with everyone."

In the early 1970s when the Jesus movement reached Norway, the Sandom group was one of the few that could lend theological and experiential depth to the powerful sense that "Jesus lives today!" During the 1970s the prominent "Jesus People" community in Norway, the group "Guds Fred" (God's Peace) had something like a season ticket for retreat places in Sandom. Today the stress on Jesus' resurrection has once again become "socially acceptable" in the life of Norwegian Christians, and Sandom deserves a sizeable share of the credit for this.

But Sandom's growing importance for the development of Christian life in Norway is based above all on the fact that over the years thousands of people have encountered the risen Lord within the framework of a retreat and with the help of meditation on Jesus. Here both well-known Christian leaders and simple laypeople from the most varied parishes and circles have found their way together to a renewed and renewing fellowship around the Master. When attention is focused on Christ himself, differences between Christians become less important — even when such powerful impulses stem from a Catholic milieu.

A recently retired bishop, Ole Nordhaug, is one of the people who keep coming back to the Sandom Retreat Center. He himself used to invite his pastors for retreat days there. Today he spends a great deal of his time as a pensioner working for the retreat movement. When he was still active as bishop, he invited Edin Lövås to lead a three-day retreat for the whole Norwegian college of bishops. What a distance separates the young revivalist preacher from an independent Norwegian church and the wise old man, whom the Lutheran bishops have invited to introduce them to Ignatian spirituality — as if that were the most natural thing in the world!

Today, in the autumn of 1992, more than forty years since the little group of preachers gathered at Sandom for the first time, the movement has taken one further step. The Pastors Association of the Norwegian Church wants to incorporate "Retreat Spirituality and Theology" into its continuing education program. The Practical Theological Seminary of the Parish Faculty, Norway's largest institution for training clergy, has added retreat days at Sandom as an obligatory part of the training. In other words, the Lutheran Church in Norway is quite seriously caught up in the process of discovering a spirituality that other European countries had taken as a matter of course, literally for centuries.

Norway's Most Inclusive Ecumenical Forum

Since 1988 the Norwegian retreat movement has been publishing its own little journal called *Over Alt* (Everywhere). To emphasize the ecumenical orientation and the Church Universal roots of prayer, the Jesus meditation, and Christian mysticism in the church as a whole, *Over Alt* has put together an editorial board of unusual breadth. On it sits a Greek Orthodox "pope," together with a Roman Catholic sister, laypeople from several independent churches, a Lutheran theologian and – as always – a pastor of the Norwegian Mission Union.

This is without a doubt the most inclusive ecumenical forum in Norway today. And that at a time when so many – fruitless – efforts continue to be made at setting up a Norwegian ecumenical council in which Catholics are welcome.

14

Building Peace

RAYMOND G. HUNTHAUSEN

Recently, before a talk at Pacific Lutheran University, I had the pleasure of dining in the home of two Lutheran pastors. We were joined by, among others, their two young and lively daughters. As I passed down the hall of the house, I noticed a sign on the door of the bedroom that the daughters share. There, in the bold, if imprecise, hand of a child, was this warning: "All who enter this room must agree not to fight." Though I had no design on their territory, I thought this was a sensible treaty. I signed on.

In times like these, we need to return to the straightforward hopefulness and faith manifest in the simple declaration of these children. "Agree not to fight." This is no slogan. This is no empty platitude. This is a clear statement of the deep aspirations of all humanity.

Children around the world know instinctively that "to fight" is not good. I believe that beneath our adult sophistication, down at the bottom of our hearts, we know it too.

I know that many will say that the Persian Gulf War was different. That it was just. That aggression was halted. That Kuwait was liberated. That a brutal dictator was taught a lesson.

I am happy and relieved that our troops returned home so soon and with so few losses. I share their joy. I can understand their pride and their sense of accomplishment.

But do these emotions of joy, pride, and accomplishment make this a good war?

The weight of evidence could lead us to a quite different conclusion: 100,000 to 150,000 dead, Kuwait in shambles, the Persian Gulf fouled with millions of barrels of oil, and Iraq embroiled in civil conflict while disease and hunger stalk the land.

Here at home, I see our democracy weakened by the failure of the mass media to withstand blatant manipulation. I see our national capacity, and will, to meet pressing social needs undermined. The results of this war, I believe, tell us that we must find another way to solve international problems.

George Washington, in his farewell address to the nation nearly two hundred years ago, set out the principles of a sound foreign policy.

"Observe good faith and justice toward all nations," Washington said. "Cultivate peace and harmony with all. Religion and morality enjoin this conduct."

"It will be worthy of a free, enlightened and great nation," Washington continued, "to give to humankind the magnanimous and novel example of a people always guided by an exalted justice and benevolence."

"A people always guided by an exalted justice and benevolence." Those are Washington's words, not mine. But it is my privilege as an American to apply them. In this war, I ask, were we "a people always guided by an exalted justice and benevolence?"

Patriotism demands that we take responsibility for the public good. Patriotism sometimes demands that we speak out against popular actions for the sake of what is just and benevolent. But true patriotism never demands we say "my country, right or wrong."

Our hope for peace is one of the longest and deepest of American political traditions. Our country's founders envisioned a foreign policy that would be impartial, evenhanded, and peace-loving. They spoke of being free of foreign entanglements and maintaining only a small military to defend our shores.

Yet two centuries later we find ourselves as the only remaining imperial power, as the world's policeman.

What happened to the vision of our nation's founders? What happened to our essential founding belief that human nature is good? That society is perfectible? That humankind desires peace, not war?

I believe that those essential beliefs and desires are still with us. But all too often they are overshadowed by our preoccupation with security, strength, control, and power.

Our deep-seated fears generate in us an irrational and fatal attraction to power. But power, rather than securing our relationships, destroys their mutuality and undermines their stability. The very presence of power risks its use and therefore threatens our lives.

We buy handguns to feel secure and strong but end up killing more fellow citizens than any other nation in the world. We sell weapons to other nations to insure their security and then find ourselves and others slaughtered by the weapons we have sold. We double our prison population to keep criminals off the streets but crime reaches record levels. We resort to 1.5 million abortions annually rather than adequately address problems such as teen pregnancy and the feminization of poverty.

The point is that power, control, security, strength, all the words we use to justify our wars against social problems and foreign nations, lack the ideals that George Washington articulated two hundred years ago: good faith, justice, harmony, peace.

I believe that peace starts simply and humbly in the hearts of each of us. It starts at home — simple things such as listening respectfully to those who disagree with you or teaching children not to hit when they're angry. Such actions, so seemingly small and insignificant, are the actions that become the social context that frames our lives. If we live peace, we will have peace.

I am reminded of a visit that Pope John Paul II once made to a supreme patriarch of Buddhism in Thailand. Protocol required that the two men be together in a room and, for a half hour, make no conversation. Instead, they were to gaze benevolently at each other.

Think about that for a moment: gazing benevolently. Seeing someone not out of curiosity or hate or indifference but with benevolence and love. What if George Bush and Saddam Hussein, who made war without ever talking to each other, had met each other with benevolent gazes?

From the home, we must take peace to the community, to the nation, and to the world beyond. If we are to change our national focus from making war to making peace, it seems to me that we must address our actions to three key issues:

1. our continuing export of arms;

2. our need to change from military spending to domestic spending;

3. the culture of violence that is so pervasive in our country today.

There can be no sure peace until developed nations stop providing the rest of the world with the instruments of war. Saddam Hussein was a threat to us and our allies because we armed him. He had the ability to invade Kuwait because we armed him. We then opted for war, rather than economic sanctions, because we feared the weapons we had sold him.

Our guns killed the six Jesuit priests and two laywomen in El Salvador a year ago. Our guns arm the Khmer Rouge in Cambodia and the Islamic fundamentalists in Afghanistan. Our guns allow guerrilla groups to terrorize, maim, and kill in Mozambique, Namibia, and Angola.

Even as we fought in the Persian Gulf, our government was drawing up proposals to send $20 billion in arms to the Middle East. Congress is considering new, more sophisticated arms for Israel, Egypt, Turkey, and Saudi Arabia. Is this the road to peace in the Middle East? Will Patriot missiles bring Israel to the bargaining table? Will F-16 fighter jets cause Saudi Arabia to share its wealth or improve human rights?

Selling arms to other countries means, of course, that we have to maintain a weapons capability that exceeds that of our customers. So we spend fantastic sums on our military. The Congressional Budget Office figured that our military spending would grow by a minimum of $40 billion in the next five years. If that happens, we will continue to rob the poor, the ill, the unemployed, the homeless, the suffering. We will do great damage to our economy, our environment, our future.

In the past decade, we increased military spending by 50 percent. The gap between rich and poor in this country is wider now than at any time in our history. Average real hourly earnings in the United States have fallen by 16 percent since 1974. Because we invest half of our research and development dollars in military technology, we deprive ourselves of the resources for building a genuine peacetime economy.

The $3 trillion we spent on the military in the last decade could have fed the world's hungry, housed our homeless, and educated all our children. It could have rebuilt our economic infrastructure. Sadly, it did not.

If we are to stop trafficking in arms and shift from military to domestic spending, we will need to end our willingness to use violence to resolve problems. Our willingness to use weapons so readily, I believe, is the taproot of violence in our society.

To build weapons of mass destruction, we needed to convince ourselves that violence or the threat of violence is an effective, even desirable tool of foreign policy. This we have done. From learned papers to comic books, we have created a national philosophy of glorifying weapons and condoning violence.

As a result, violence and the threat of violence have become common ways of dealing with complex social problems. For example:

- Murder is now the leading cause of death among young males in the United States.

- Reported cases of child abuse have doubled every other year over the past decade.

- Some 100,000 rapes were reported nationwide last year.

- And in our own state, violent crimes committed by youths have tripled in the past ten years.

We find ourselves caught up in a whirlwind of violence of our own making. The philosophy of justified violence squanders our national resources, misdirects our lives, and tramples on our basic instincts toward peace.

Ultimately, the peace movement must wrestle with the whirlwind. As I said, the process must start here, in our hearts and in our homes.

Mother Teresa, I am told, is the most widely admired person in the world. She has no office, no title, no retinue of advisors. She lives in poverty. She is old and sick. She ministers to the dying who die anyway. How do we explain this paradox?

Questioned about her life, Mother Teresa said, "We are not asked to do great things; we are asked to do small things with great love."

We are asked to do small things with great love. This is the insight we need to carry with us. This is the hope for the renewal of the peace movement. This is the antidote to the imperial illusions and pretensions that have caused our country to stray from the course set by our founders.

After all is said and done, I believe that all the weapons we have built and all the troops we have sent will count for less than a pair of caring hands.

– 15 –

Confession and Resistance

A Conversation

INGE KANITZ AND JOACHIM KANITZ

✖

Inge (b. 1911) and Joachim (b. 1910) Kanitz are German "witnesses to an era." In 1981 they gave an interview to students from the Albert Schweitzer Gymnasium about their critical view of the "Confessing Church" and about people such as Dietrich Bonhoeffer and Martin Niemöller, with whom they had close ties. In 1983 Richard Rohr, Jim Wallis, and Andreas Ebert were guests in their house. Since these days the couple are very frail, they gave us permission to reprint excerpts from the 1981 interview.

—

Joachim Kanitz: I passed my university qualifying exam in 1928 and then went to Erlangen and Bonn as a student of theology. At the time Karl Barth was teaching in Bonn. Actually I didn't have a proper understanding of him as a theologian until one evening when he gave a speech on his development as a religious socialist.

In the period before Hitler, in that world of many competing parties and high unemployment, all of us students were politically motivated. I came from a consciously German nationalist home, but, thanks to Barth, I became somewhat more inclined to socialism and actually noticed rather early on what the brownshirts were bringing with them.

In 1931 a young man appeared in Barth's seminary; he was Dietrich Bonhoeffer, still very young, but already very sharp. He struck us as an especially good theologian. I was glad to hear that he was going to Berlin as a Privat-Dozent. I was happy about Bonhoeffer's work as a teacher because for my exam I had to go to the University of Berlin, where many of the professors were high-and-dry pedants.

In the summer of 1932 I was sent by Dietrich Bonhoeffer, whom I had come to appreciate in Berlin, as a representative to the World Federation for the Ministry to Students in New York. While there I wanted to report about the situation of the students in Berlin. At that time the elections for the Reichstag had just taken place, and in contrast to the previous election the Nazis had suffered deep losses. We all felt that Hitler was finished. Of course we had no idea of what would replace him. But then in 1933 Hitler came to power after all. . . .

On January 30, 1933, the day Hitler seized power, I was one of the people in Berlin clenching their fists in their pockets. We were full of rage, but it was impotent rage. Then came all the events and laws that Hitler used to solidify his power and get rid of his political opponents. Afterward it became clear to me that the dismantling of democracy had already begun with the brutal hounding of socialists and communists and with the introduction of the so-called Aryan paragraphs. On March 21, 1933, Hitler, the criminal, received the Prussian inheritance, so to speak, from the hands of Hindenburg. And General Superintendent Dibellius, another Prussian, gave him the church's blessing at a worship service in the Nikolaikirche, which Hindenburg attended along with the Protestant members of Parliament. Perhaps it wasn't as clear to us then as it is today what a perversion the whole thing was. But I know I felt that this political development was horrible.

Then came my exam, at a time when the government was launching its first attacks on the church. Niemöller became famous for his proclamation of the Young Reformers Movement, which took a stand against the "German Christians."

Q: What was the Young Reformers Movement?

JK: That was the name taken by theologians of the most varied background who rejected the theology and church politics of the "German Christians." The church was absolutely unprepared for what happened. We had in the church and in the pastorate a preponderance of supporters of the German nationalist wing. These people were conservative, anticommunist (of course), and at bottom antidemocratic as well. The revolution of 1918 had never been accepted by my father and many others like him. My father was loyal to the kaiser till the end. Many people saw Hitler as an upstart.

Among the pastors and, as a matter of fact, in the whole bourgeois German world, people had never understood what democracy and socialism meant. This explains why it was possible to have the sort of assaults on the church that soon followed: Members of the church leadership were dismissed, and parish council elections were grossly manipulated in 1933, when German Christians, wearing brown uniforms, chased people out of the voting places. With few exceptions, the German Christian candidates were victorious everywhere — but only because of the pressure from above. At that point Hitler thought that with the help of the German Christians he could turn the church into a compliant tool. The Young Reformers had stood up in opposition to this. Later, after the Barmen Confession-Synod in May 1934, they joined with other groups in calling themselves the "Confessing Church."

In 1934 Martin Niemöller write his book *From a U-Boat to the Pulpit.* In the book's Afterword Niemöller (in 1934!) said it was the church's responsibility to preach the Word of God so that "the mighty work of uniting and uplifting the *Volk,* which has begun among us, may acquire an unshakable foundation and lasting stability!" And a theologian whose books were widely read at the time, Friedrich Gogarten, declared in 1933: "If a nation that has gotten out of shape as badly as ours has is to be gotten back into shape, then it first must be put in uniform." Well, that soon occurred. Gogarten was a man who had begun as a supporter of Karl Barth. So you can imagine the condition the church's resistance was in at the beginning of the Third Reich....

Here in Dahlem there was a man working with Niemöller as an assistant preacher named Franz Hildebrandt. He was a "half Jew" and Bonhoeffer's best friend. The two were the same age. Hildebrandt saw from the start what was heading our way. He realized that our main opponents weren't the German Christians. They were basically a ridiculous outfit, and they had gone so outrageously far that they had made themselves completely impossible. It so happened that Hildebrandt and I were on hand when Niemöller was preparing a sermon. We started discussing who our real enemy was, who was actually attacking us. Wasn't it Hitler himself? Wasn't it our responsibility to commit ourselves not just to the church and to the Christians who were now being dismissed and treated unfairly, but to the Jews — their persecution had already begun by then — and to the communists? As he himself admitted, Niemöller was far too late in recognizing this.

One of those who did realize it from the very first and who also talked publicly about it was Bonhoeffer. That was why within the Confessing Church he was always considered a bit of an outsider and a difficult person. In fact, this was for two reasons. At the synod held in the fall of 1934 at Berlin-Dahlem, the Confessing Church declared: "We are the church. The churches bearing the imprint of the German Christians have separated themselves from the true church by their teachings, their actions, and the measures they have taken. We assert the claim to being the true church because we have the authentic church leadership, etc." Bonhoeffer took this basic decision of the Dahlem Synod quite seriously and even formulated the principle: "Whoever knowingly parts with the Confessing Church in Germany parts with salvation." The second reason why Bonhoeffer was an outsider within the Confessing Church is clear from the following story: In 1935 a colleague of Bonhoeffer's who was interested in the liturgy supposedly asked him whether it was all right for him to get deeply involved in the church's liturgical renewal in such troubled times. To this Bonhoeffer replied: "The only people entitled to sing Gregorian chant are the ones who also shout for the Jews."

—

I would like to mention here something that happened in 1935. March 17 of that year was "Heroes Memorial Day," as it was called. On that day many people used to go to church. And now — by exception, I'm afraid — the Confessing Church had the courage to make a public statement. It didn't simply talk about the pastors who had been arrested, but singled out the transgression of God's commandments in public life, including the First Commandment, which had indeed been violated most of all.

This statement from the Confessing Synod of the Old Prussian Union, which had met in Dahlem on March 4 and 5, was supposed to be read from pulpits all over Prussia. Naturally the Gestapo had gotten wind of the plan to take a public stand. So every pastor in the Confessing Church was called in and told to sign a promise that the announcement would not be read from the pulpit. As far as I know, only a few signed. Afterward over seven hundred pastors were arrested in one fell swoop. At the time I was an "illegal" assistant preacher in the town of Crossen, an administrative center on the Oder. All the pastors in Crossen were arrested too, though of course we had made provisions for this.

We had some courageous women who in fact were always braver than the men. They were ready to deliver mimeographed letters. I was the only one not arrested because I hadn't been put down on the list of pastors by the official (German Christian) church leadership. I was an assistant preacher of the Confessing Church, and hence an "illegal."

I lived at the superintendent's house, and on a rather sleepless night I prepared my Sunday sermon. The next morning the telephone rang, shortly before services began. "There's one more vicar. Just have him come to the town hall." That was me.

I started out. The way to the town hall led past the church. In front of the church a large crowd of people and police had gathered. The entrances to the church were locked. Somehow or other, though, we got into the church without any violence. Perhaps the police took off. Suddenly I stood alone there in front of the large community. At that point I didn't read out the statement from the Confessing Church, because I told myself: Well, the parishioners will get it later. I simply gave a short description of its contents and explained why the pastors had been arrested. I asked the parishioners to remain calm and to pray. I would now go to the town hall.

And I went there with an entourage such as I never had in my life before or since. The parishioners sang chorales in the marketplace. The mayor still belonged somewhat to the old school: He didn't lift his arm and say, "Heil Hitler!" but took my hand, which was quite unusual for a public official. He said: "Mr. Kanitz, you won't sign it either. Then go up to your colleagues." I said: "What do you mean up? In prison, I should think." "The prison is overcrowded, there are so many pastors there already. We had to use the upper part of the town hall." There we had a relatively comfortable prison. The arrest lasted a week, until the critical reverberations from abroad got too loud.

Once again back to that "Heroes Memorial Day" in 1935: I had scarcely arrived in our prison, on Sunday morning close to twelve o'clock, when I heard the measured beat of a drum. The military had arrived. Many of us had no inkling that Hitler had selected "Heroes Memorial Day," 1935, to resurrect the German army by introducing universal military service. This moment was now being celebrated with a great parade on the beautiful marketplace of Crossen. And we had "seats of honor" up in our prison. I'll never forget that. I broke out into tears, and I know why I was crying. I knew this meant war.

In a way I had sensed it as far back as January 30, 1933. But unfortunately not everybody had read *Mein Kampf,* which states precisely what Hitler wanted to do: annihilate the Jews and wage war.

Shortly after the confrontations over the announcement from the pulpit in March 1933, I was expelled from the Crossen church circle because I had "sinned" against the First Commandment. Speaking to my confirmation class, I had explained the commandment to "fear, love, and trust God above all things" by arguing against the national anthem, "Deutschland über alles." Admittedly the song says that Germany is to be exalted over everything "in the *world,*" but, I said, we should fear, love, and trust *God* above all things. That was treason. You weren't allowed to say that. Naturally one of the confirmands told his parents, whereupon I wasn't sent to a concentration camp, but simply thrown out of the church.

I learned about the expulsion when I just happened to be in Stralsund at my fiancée's house. I didn't return to Crossen, of course, but to Berlin. There I was asked by a man from the Fraternal Council, who at the time was responsible for the "young brothers": "Don't you want to go to Zingst? Bonhoeffer's there with his seminary." At the time I didn't know that Bonhoeffer had been to England. When he got back, he was appointed director of this newly founded seminary by the Confessing Church.

There we discussed two things that will at first strike you as unrelated. First we learned the meaning of what can be called "brotherhood" or "Christian community." In England Bonhoeffer had learned to live in a sort of monastic community (with meditation, intercessory prayer, confession, the Eucharist). In other words he learned not just to play games in his head, but to take everything one reads in the gospels and discuss it with others and to translate it into a personal life of faith, above all into a fraternal communal life. There was, for example, a strict rule that you weren't allowed to say anything about any person who wasn't there.

Secondly, none of this took place in seclusion but in a continuous lively exchange with the world. Bonhoeffer came to Berlin practically every week. He belonged to various groups and committees, and he often came back terribly shaken. What got to him was not so much what the German Christians were saying, but what the government was doing, and the dreadful things going on within the Confessing Church.

Many people had fallen away from the Confessing Church, which was gradually crumbling to pieces. There *were* some brave people, but by that time the Confessing Church was fundamentally a very sad crowd, not only because of the Lutherans, who were inclined to compromise with the Nazi state, but also because of ourselves. Bonhoeffer naturally included these events in his public evening prayers.

At Finkenwalde, we took Dietrich's interpretation of the Sermon on the Mount as our point of departure in addressing quite concretely the question of resistance and conscientious objection. In 1935/36 we were positive that for us as Christians it was impossible to serve in Hitler's army. When it came "to the crunch" — since I was born in 1910 I was drafted on May 15, 1939 — my initial hope that the Confessing Church would unanimously call for resisting the draft had long since taken wing.

Then in 1938, after the Anschluss, the Confessing Church of Prussia did something horrible. They took an oath of allegiance to the Führer, as a sort of birthday present to him, supposedly because the commissioner for churches had demanded it. It was the Confessing Church's way of expressing its loyalty. Almost all the pastors, who of course had already proclaimed at their ordination their obedience to the state, took the oath of allegiance to the Führer. (To be sure, the Confessing Church attached an explanation, claiming that God's revealed will, or the ordination vow, was the sole standard to be followed.) This was terrible. And afterward Hitler put out the word that he had never demanded the oath of allegiance.

After that the Confessing Church once again took a brave step. In the fall of 1938, when war was threatening because of the crisis in the Sudetenland, the church came out with a liturgy for peace. Actually the proposal for a prayer service that they circulated had nothing in it except this statement: "We pray in acknowledgment of our responsibility for peace; and we pray also for the others, for all men and women, whose land is threatened by war." The next day the headline in the SS paper *Schwarzes Korps* screamed, "This is Treason!" All the members of the Confessing Church in the Provisional Church Leadership (VKL) were arrested. Later when war with Poland was threatening, there was hardly anyone left who could have managed to disseminate that sort of proclamation. The Confessing Church lacked both the internal and external resources to do it.

Of course I could have followed the example of one Protestant Christian from Stettin, Hermann Stöhr. He said no to military service and was executed. Perhaps all of us really should have taken this step. But it wasn't easy, especially when one had a wife and children, which by 1939 I did. Then too I don't want to hide the fact that up until 1939 we always had one foot in prison. Time and time again the Gestapo came to my house and threatened me. The fear this evoked led to your thinking: Once you've got a uniform on, you'll be free of all this. You also get more money as a soldier. Of course, all these arguments were very poor ones.

Inge Kanitz: The day you were called up was the first day that I thought: Now you're safe from the Gestapo. In some ways that was completely schizophrenic.

JK: I'd like to say something else about the state of mind of the Confessing Church back then. When people learned that I had been drafted, I got a letter from a member of the Brandenburg Fraternal Council, one of the bravest people in the Confessing Church there. "Dear Brother Kanitz, we hope that in the coming months you will be a good warrior for Jesus Christ and an excellent soldier in the German army." He had no misgivings about that "and": "a good warrior for Jesus Christ *and* an excellent soldier in the German army."

Unfortunately I can no longer recall exactly how I reacted to that. I hope I didn't swallow the whole thing without blinking. Hindsight is always better than foresight. A German Christian might have put it, "We hope that you will become a good warrior for Jesus Christ, that is, an excellent soldier in the German army." Dietrich Bonhoeffer would likely have phrased it this way: "I hope that despite everything you may be a good warrior for Christ." As Providence would have it, Bonhoeffer himself did not have to put his pacifist convictions into practice. Otherwise he would have been killed early on. He certainly would never have taken a weapon in hand. Of course he went into counterintelligence, so he could carry on the resistance from that vantage point.

The last time I saw him was in the summer of 1943, just before his arrest. We had become good friends; he married us and was our son's godfather. I had already had many highly personal conversations with him in Finkenwalde, although he never breathed a word to anybody about his participation in the resistance, since that had to remain secret. But he was completely forthright when he saw me in the uniform of a German officer with the Iron Cross on my chest. He asked me matter-of-factly how I had gotten it. I could only answer, "I don't know myself." I most certainly did not become a "good soldier." I had only one wish, to "get through." I also had the good fortune not to be with the combat troops. Nevertheless later on I was wounded and taken prisoner. I don't want to deny my failure, in that I was after all in the army and doing my share. I had an improbable stroke of luck, or whatever it should be called, and being spared motivated me to get involved in my later work for peace.

Q: You said that at the seminary in Finkenwalde people argued that a Christian couldn't become a soldier. A few years after this when the theologians were called up, was there anyone who refused military service and was shot for it? Later on in the war were there men from the Confessing Church who deserted?

JK: The only decision we could come up with was first of all to try to get assigned to a noncombat unit, as a stretcher-bearer or a chaplain. I tried that myself, but Goebbels had issued an order prohibiting anyone born after 1906 from becoming an army chaplain. And my attempt to join the ambulance corps also got rejected. Others succeeded. Gollwitzer, for example, became a stretcher-bearer. Many people managed to avoid being promoted in the ranks.

Q: Can you once again say something about Dietrich Bonhoeffer's role in the Confessing Church? How did he himself see and justify his position? Did he maintain that the church was not allowed to call for tyrannicide, that only the individual Christian could make that decision?

JK: I wouldn't put it that way. I don't know that Bonhoeffer would have put it so theoretically: "The church may not call for tyrannicide." To the question, "Would *you* carry out the act?" he is supposed to have replied, "Yes, but I would first leave the church." In my opinion this doesn't mean that he was declaring the church incapable of resistance, but that he didn't want to burden others with guilt, because it's still a sin to murder somebody. He knew that too.

Just read the chapter in Bonhoeffer's *Ethics* on "Taking Responsibility." Bonhoeffer says there that Christians who get involved in politics – and every Christian should – can't keep their slates clean. They can only consider carefully what is the best for the good of others. There can be a borderline case where the best thing for the people's welfare is that a dictator be killed. And Bonhoeffer would have been ready to do that. It was also clear to him that in such a case he would need forgiveness. Bonhoeffer thought about leaving the church, because he didn't want to burden his church. But he knew what that church was like: It put up no real resistance.

At a youth conference recently somebody asked me: Did the Confessing Church cooperate with other resistance groups? The only answer I could give was: The Confessing Church was not a resistance group at all. Sure, there were individual personal ties with resistance fighters, but the Confessing Church as such always thought of itself only as a resistance group within the church.

Q: What was everyday life in the church like, not on the level of the leadership but in the parishes?

IK: I was not allowed to study, because back then it was still the custom that the boys got the money for their studies. So I left the Burckhardthaus Seminary to be trained as a parish helper. I had Martin Niemöller as my teacher in a lecture series on 1 and 2 Corinthians. To be honest, he bored me to tears. You always knew what was coming. We simply read something else or took some sort of notes.

Working together with Niemöller only became interesting for us when things in the church began to get "tense." Niemöller asked us whether we would help him mimeograph letters for the Confessing Church in the basement of the parsonage. Naturally we had conversations down there that would never take place in the Burckhardthaus Seminary. And so we six or seven volunteers got information that you wouldn't find in the newspapers. This motivated us to join in the work there.

Once we had mimeographed the letters, we would jump on our bikes late in the evening. I often rode as far as the Potsdamer Platz to put letters in the night mailboxes. This was because the police often stood around "suspicious" mailboxes and confiscated letters so that news that didn't suit the State wouldn't become public or make its way into the pastors' houses. We young people naturally had a lot of fun putting one over on the police.

Back then I made fifty DM a month. Of course by the fifteenth that was already used up. Through the mediation of Martin Niemöller the Dahlem parish gave me the opportunity of making some extra money by giving religious instruction to baptized Jewish children in private homes.

Then I went to the Jacobi parish in Stralsund. At the time, back in 1934, I didn't find it bad, but today in retrospect it certainly was: I was responsible for three jobs at the same time, but the church only paid for one. I was parish nurse (I had been trained as a nurse in Bethel). I was organist and choir director (I had studied choral direction in Charlottenburgh), and I was a parish helper. At five minutes to eight in the morning my pastor would send his maid and inform me: "Miss Voltmer, I don't feel well; please take over the confirmation class.

I know you can do it." In exchange for this I would be invited to
lunch. . . . I was actually on the job from seven in the morning till ten
at night: First I had to visit the sick, give injections, and put patients
into bed. Then I had to make house calls and write out music for the
choir. Afternoons and evenings I had to attend to the youth group or
the choir or women's assistance group. It was a strain, but it also gave
me great joy.

Q: What sort of work did the Confessing Church do in the Stralsund
parish?

IK: I always tried to get pupils who were either completely "neu-
tral" or who would pull together with me. I had one little ten-year-old
boy with the voice of an angel but whose family encouraged him to
steal. His father was an unemployed longshoreman with several children. The Nazis assigned him to spy on my friend Hilde and myself
because they were irritated by the success of our work with children.
One afternoon the bell rang. I thought the man at the door was some
kind of salesman, so I said: "Pardon me, I really don't have any time;
can you come later?" The man's only answer was "Heil Hitler!" and
turned back his lapel: Gestapo. So I had to make time for him.

He searched my house, and when it was over he told me: "I'm the
father of one of your choir boys. Please forgive me — I'm speaking for
myself now — but I was under orders. I was out of a job, and you go
where the bread is."

Then when I went visiting anyone, he would stand on a nearby
street corner. Afterward he would go into the house and ask the person what I had said. He was also under orders to find out whether I
brought up any non-church-related topics in the hours I spent with
the youth group. But there's no way you can do a whole hour's worth
of Bible work with a crowd of young people. Sometimes you have to
sing a folksong too, not just hymns.

I would hear about church and political events from Bonhoeffer
and my husband-to-be, and I passed the word on to a trusted circle of
older teenagers. The working young adults had the so-called red cards,
the membership cards of the Confessing Church. They also collected
money in the parish for the Confessing Church. When I went away,
there was a problem: I wasn't allowed to leave the Confessing Church
material in my official residence. This material, a briefcase with the
red cards and information sheets that got through to us, wandered
from week to week now to one young person in the parish, now to
another.

Q: Was the red card signed only by full-time co-workers of the
church or by "laypeople" (parishioners)?

IK: Laypeople, first and foremost! They made their contribution.
Our youth treasury very quickly became a red card treasury. This

money was sent along to the Confessing Church. They used it to pay the salaries of people who got no salary from the official church.

Q: What effects did the surveillance have on you?

IK: You have to weigh every word you say, because it could be put in your dossier and used against you. This kind of situation is a heavy mental burden. In September and October 1935 I kept getting the shivers. I knew the Gestapo was collecting points against me, which all together might spell prison and the end of all my plans for the future. I was hoping to get married in six months.

One evening when we came home, we found a note under the door of our apartment. I suppose it came from the father of the little choir boy. It said: "We advise you to get out of town by tomorrow night. Otherwise . . . enough said." He wanted to give us a timely warning, and we took it. I told my friend Hilde: "Let's pack our bags now, and not wait till tomorrow night." The next morning we got on the train. There were no SS men to be seen in the station, so we traveled on to Finkenwalde. Nobody checked up on us.

We were both very excited after this experience, and so I found it surprising and disappointing the way Dietrich Bonhoeffer acknowledged our arrival in Finkenwalde as if it were nothing special: "Well, here you are," was all he said. But then he included the Stralsund parish in the evening prayer and thanked God for protecting us. He later told us that we had to presume that a Christian would get persecuted. We had a little lesson awaiting us. How right he was!

JK: I was in a village south of Berlin as an assistant preacher. It was shortly before confirmation time. One evening I was sitting at my desk, while outside the Hitler youth group was singing a song I knew: "The days of the cross have passed, / the swastika will now arise, / And, thank God, we'll be free at last, / to lift our Fatherland to the skies." I knew that the young people singing that were the same ones who would be confirmed in fourteen days. So I wrote a personal letter – or mimeographed it, at any rate, because I had around twenty parents of my confirmands. I copied out the whole song, and then I said: "I have nothing against the Hitler-Jugend (back then you *had* to say that) when they sing folk songs. But in fourteen days these children want to profess their faith in the cross by being confirmed. What do you parents say to that?"

The Gestapo arrived a few days later: "You have distributed flyers. Where is your typewriter?" They confiscated my typewriter. I tried to explain to them that a personal letter, which I had put in people's mailboxes, was not a flyer. But the Gestapo ransacked everything. Our second child, who had just been born, lay in the cradle in my room. One of the officials, with a friendly glance at the baby, said: "You have an impossible profession. All that stuff is over and done with. I'll give you a bit of advice. Come over to us." Suddenly all my anxiety disappeared, and I had to laugh out loud. The idea that as a pastor I could become an agent of the secret police struck me as so absurd that I was able to have a liberating laugh. But then the official got very insolent and said: "We have other possibilities too." "I know," I told him.

IK: In the hallway he said: "If word gets out about our visit, Mrs. Kanitz, and we hear of it, that'll be the surest way for you and your husband to get to Dachau. Our visit is nobody's business. Heil Hitler."

JK: There was no reaction from the parents of the confirmands. Nor did we expect any.

Q: How were things later on at the confirmation?

JK: There too none of the parents said a word. And the children couldn't quite understand what it was all about. Naturally I never got my typewriter back.

Q: What is it like, living with fear, for example, when you're threatened with being sent to Dachau, if you continue what you're doing?

JK: You mean, were we actually very frightened?

IK: No!

JK: We were much too busy with our work for that. We scarcely had time to be anxious. Or we were together with friends.

Q: What conclusions do you draw from your experiences with the Third Reich?

JK: Very shortly after 1945 we found we had to get involved in "civilian resistance." In 1947 when I was released from prison in France, I came back to a church that had been "restored" again, that was once again just the way it had been before 1933. This was possibly the worst disappointment of my life. Because of the Confessing Church we had expected something different. Then people got acquainted with Bonhoeffer's *Letters from Prison,* where he imagines a church of brothers and sisters, which does without money and is really on the side of the poor. And it became clear: Nothing, but absolutely nothing, of that had been realized. Many surviving members of the Confessing Church tried in vain to dismantle the church bureaucracy.

Then came the 1950s, the Adenauer years, the integration of the West, and rearmament. Here in Berlin we joined forces in the so-called Unterwegskreis (On the Way Circle), mostly pastors but also parishioners. This group corresponded to the brotherhoods that grew up in the regional churches of West Germany after 1945. We tried to stick consistently to the principles of the Confessing Church, as we understood them.

In 1947 a gathering of former members of the Confessing Church was held in Darmstadt. The "Darmstadter Word," which was drawn up there, speaks for the first time of the great burden of guilt that the church had incurred in the matter, for instance, of peace, of nationalism, of social justice. It contained one of the most clear-cut rejections of Adenauer's Christian Democratic Union position. I took part in efforts to meet this position head on, but the attempt failed. Then came the antinuclear movement in the 1950s, which also affected us quite personally (I had meanwhile become a pastor in Zehlendorf). My cooperation in this movement led to various sorts of defamation. I was called "the red pastor."

IK: I remember a woman who was furious over the intercessory prayers my husband offered. One day as he was going into church, dressed in his robes, the woman asked: "Do you also pray for Khrushchev, by chance?" My husband turned around and said, "And don't you, by chance?"

JK: I also got involved with the Vietnam War and the student revolts of 1968. The student revolt hit especially close to home when I was pastor of a church right next to the Church College in Zehlendorf. At the time the students there were the "reddest" of all the "red" students, and sometimes they went a bit too far even for my taste. And the professors were positively the most "professorial." So the conflict between students and professors became especially hot. I stood in between, as a pastor who was also there for the students. We had in our parish a group for publicity work, which represented all parties and every political nuance. Unfortunately in the long run it couldn't last. After I intervened on behalf of Rudi Dutschke and others, the Christian Democrats cut me off. I left the parish and became a hospital chaplain. But I continued to be active in the peace movement and to work for the developing countries. My wife has primarily been engaged in work for children living in Vietnam. That's a brief summary of the causes we're presently committed to.

16

A Vision of Enneagram Study as Living Community in Individualistic Times

MARGARET FRINGS KEYES

❖

A writer's task, to order and present information, is formidable. We write to teach others what we have learned, but we also write to teach ourselves. Useful information develops through many people sharing and building on each other's insights. Those of us who presume to write of the spiritual journey deal with an amazing number of self-reflective loops. We attempt to awaken a force inside another, a force we only partly understand, a force that we also are trying to awaken and sustain in ourselves.

One insight, common to many cultures, many religious traditions, is that the force is communal and unitary. "The God within," "the mystical body of Christ," "the Archetype of the SELF," and the "unity of essence" are terms that hint at, but do not explain, our drive to a sense of shared consciousness. Another hunch, widely held, is that individual choice matters; yet our small power egos stand in the way of realizing our deeper unity. So we try to identify our individual developmental tasks in "waking up."

The Enneagram fascinates many of us, because it is a pattern of many patterns. It promises a complex, but understandable, way to differentiate our individual choices within the patterns of nine personality types.

When we move the Enneagram into the field of psychotherapy, it may seem we have left community in favor of a hierarchical model of a healer and an individual with defects to be healed. However, the chief difference between spiritual direction and psychotherapy is in the clinician's focus on the rigidity of the personality pattern. Both spiritual director and therapist work to dissolve egocentricity *and* bring the person back to community.

The clinician understands the severe fears, anger, depression, and despair that cause an individual to defend against waking from the

Enneagram trance state. Earlier in life that state protected the individual against real dangers. The therapist's task is to soften the defenses, by helping the individual to realize that the defenses no longer match the present dangers. The individual has better tools to use and will grow in risking deeper relationships with others. The way out of individual isolation is in realizing and creating the bonds of community.

The clinical approach to diagnosis (saying "what's so") and treatment (deciding a plan to change a portion of it) always includes a provisional hypothesis that is progressively modified in terms of new data and response to treatment. However, working with the Enneagram brings the clinician into peculiar territory and out of the psychotherapy field. Many Enneagram adepts are "true believers" and regard the Enneagram as a finished product that only needs to be learned. For some it seems to be an ideology, a belief system of revealed truths. Just as with any theory or model of human behavior, however, its labels also can become stereotypes. The Enneagram is misused when it becomes a rigid definition.

The Enneagram clusters of traits have many inner logical connections, but some widely taught relationships are still hypotheses. For example, the personality movement in stress to the next line Enneagram state is a hypothesis that needs to be tested. For many people, the stress state appears to be one farther along the line. Psychological terms such as "introjects," alternative "subpersonalities," or available "states of mind" might be better descriptions, together with an operational description of when we choose them. Psychologists can develop our deeper understanding of the Enneagram.

Again, use of the word "subtype" does not do justice to describe the libido (energy) force that the personality channels into either survival, partnership, or communal concerns. It profoundly influences use of other traits within the personality type. This most interesting idea has links to an old question philosophers, mathematicians, and theologians have studied, the relationship between ideas symbolized by the ONE, the TWO, and the MANY. Input from the philosophers in our community today can enrich our understanding.

We teach what we know and bring special gifts to our community, not only from our professional concerns, but also from the point of view and style of our Enneagram types. Richard Rohr, priest and preacher, an Enneagram ONE, is a man of the Word. When we hear him in person, his voice enters our ears and stays in our mind. His voice, in audio-cassettes, has been immensely influential in linking feeling to thought about the Enneagram. Were it not for Andreas Ebert, an Enneagram TWO, who pushed for publication, quite possibly we would not yet have his books.

Helen Palmer, a gifted psychic and counterphobic SIX, has created videotapes using panels of the nine personality types. They are compelling teaching tools for those whose primary sense modality is vision. But they go beyond this. We not only see and intuit from the nonverbal body language; we hear the voices and follow the line of thought of each type, brought out by Palmer's skillful questions.

Claudio Naranjo, musician, psychiatrist, Gestalt therapist, multicultural scholar, and an Enneagram FIVE, brings a rare depth and breadth of insight to the Enneagram. His promised opus, of which the book *Enneatypes* is only a small part, is widely anticipated by those fascinated by complex, multileveled patterns.

Patrick O'Leary, an Enneagram THREE, and Maria Beesing, an EIGHT, courageously pioneered for a wider, popular knowledge of Enneagram thought. They recognized similarities to Christian forms of spirituality. Tom Condon, a counterphobic SIX, uses neurolinguistic programming and hypnosis to help heal Enneagram distortions.

C. G. Jung, an Enneagram NINE, did not write about the Enneagram. However, he spoke of the shadow archetype, the dark rejected aspects of one's personality that must be consciously included for integration. He also developed a personality classification system based on dichotomies of extraversion and introversion, one's judging functions of thinking and feeling, and one's perception functions of orientation either to sensory data or to intuitive patterns. The dominant functions used for his classification, as in Gestalt, are *foreground*. The unseen *background*, the unknown, unlived fourth, or "inferior" function is the primary focus of treatment.

This weakest function is associated with the shadow side of the personality (the avoided transformation element). It is this reality that the person relates to and develops in the second half of life. Jung called the individual's work the process of individuation. It can also be looked at as a process of waking from the trance state of one's Enneagram personality.

I, as a Jungian psychotherapist and counterphobic Enneagram FIVE, see the Enneagram as a typology that includes Jung's insights. It differentiates the shadow archetype within its descriptions. It is compatible, not only with spiritual direction, but also with many theoretical models of therapy. I use these models and psychodrama to connect the inner world of the person to outer world concerns.

Psychological models are usually models of the founder's point of view. They shed light on aspects of reality but are not complete in themselves. We bring our own preoccupations, but we build on each other's thought. We need to share our insights in community to discover and serve truth.

17

The New Fransciscans

DIETRICH KOLLER

1.

— don't wear gala brown cowls
or that picturesque cincture.
Their blue jeans aren't designer-prewashed,
but naturally threadbare.

2.

— don't live in convents
with shiny waxed corridors,
gold-and-marble chapels,
and stuffy refectories.
They are lodged like refugees
in dumps on the edge of town,
demilitarized Quonset huts,
or perfectly normal tenements.

3.

— don't brew any beer
to slake the thirst of tourists,
but are trodden, like grapes,
by social depression.

4.

— don't live on the privilege of beggary,
or luxurious handouts.
They build themselves garrets
of leftover lumber.

5.

— don't preach lofty morality
from towering pulpits.
They prompt people to sin boldly,
and always for the love of love.

6.

— say no holy masses,
but celebrate the Lamb
in front of the gates
of nuclear weapons plants.

7.

— don't preach to the birds and the fishes,
but comfort them by fighting
for laws to protect
all endangered species.

8.

— don't write any books,
neither technical nor pious.
They read the book of souls
and tell you who you are.

9.

— and don't send you back
to the ugly old rat-trap.
They teach you instead how to blow the place up
with a well-directed No.

10.

— haven't the faintest idea of their personal stigmata,
because they're too busy
taking care of the stigmatized
on the fringes of society.

11.

— dance like dervishes
in the Vatican gardens.
They can almost convert the half-infidel pope,
as they almost converted the half-believing sultan.

12.

— all have their Sister Clare within them
and love her in the mirror of moonlight,
kiss her, reverent and fearless,
in the mirror of the well.

13.

— don't die from cancer,
but from the church,
they pass away naked,
sleeping on the naked ground,
in the arms of the poor mother earth.
And their tender *abba* spreads over them
the dark, star-sown blanket of heaven.

14.

— dissolve like salt,
and we rediscover
the flavor of life.

15.

All this may be so,
then again it may not.
The new Franciscans can also look
exactly like the old ones —
if only they manage to be pure in their essence,
not crudely identified with anything ancient
or anything modern.

18

Lucaya, the Weeper

The Story of an Indian Saint

LUCIA KOLLER

O Lucaya, rich in tears. You patron saint of all the suffering and dying Indian women to this day.

Ever since your continent was conquered, we can see you in a thousand painful forms. But with a poet's eye Reinhold Schneider has glimpsed an image of you and framed you in wonderful sketches against the background of the days of the conquistadors.

Lucaya, I want to speak with you, to reach you with my inmost heart, because you have reached *me,* and thanks to the poet's words you stand vividly before me. I want to talk with you, as with a saint, because, like the poet, I assume that you "were and are a spokeswoman for your people" and for us, the white conquerors. "A light goes forth from you" that has reached us today — down through all the darkness of five hundred years. This means that when the white conquistadors wronged the Indians, they were hating and raping their own souls.

But the soul of your master and murderer, you say, never died. Did you keep it alive for him? Did his soul dwell and survive in you, at least for as long as you lived and suffered? Should I learn from you not to despise the murderer, to shelter his lost soul in my heart? To suffer from and with that soul? This seems to me an art too new and too hard to master.

Are you stepping forth from the darkness of your nameless story, Lucaya? Lucaya isn't even your real name, but one the poet gave you. It's the name of the islands that lie to the north of Haiti and Cuba, the home of the Lucayos, who brought you over here.

You stand "in the slave market in Puerto Plata among the frightened people, who are still sick and exhausted from the sea voyage." Even though they have been transported by the Lucayos under a royal

---

After scenes from Reinhold Schneider's book, *Las Casas's Audience with Charles V.*

letter of protection and divided up among the Spanish knights to be instructed in the Christian faith, after the head count they are treated like cattle. One hears the crying and screaming, as parents are torn away from their children, husbands from their wives. Each buyer wants strong workers for the sugar plantations and presses and for the mines. You slender, delicate people cling to one another like tangled bushes or trees. You won't even manage to stand it as long as the natives of Haiti did.

You stand near an old man; you probably strike the buyers as too fragile. You probably took care of the man out of pity. Your own family members may have already been sold off or dragged away to another ship or accidentally left behind. But why did the slave-traders even bother to take the old and the weak along with them?

For you and your people the islands were the world, and this world was beautiful, with almost no dangers or terrors. It was bounded by another world, where the souls of the dead made their dwelling. Into that world, which was like the familiar world of life and yet different but not very far from it, your whole nation longed to go. "What more beautiful thing could lie in store for us than to meet with the dead?" you ask us moderns. How pure your conscience must be that you rejoice so heartily at the prospect of reunion with the dead, while we perhaps might have to fear them, because all sorts of hidden guilt would be revealed, and we couldn't dare look those near and dear to us in the eye. Among African Christians I have found a similar faith in the nearness of their ancestors. For them the resurrected Christ fits seamlessly into their world of life and death. Conversely I take the resurrected Christ as the starting point in my efforts to populate my heaven, where you have your place.

With this confident faith of yours I can understand how you, Lucaya, although you were only a bonus reserved for your buyer, immediately understood that your buyer was your master and that you had to follow him. You might even risk your life for him that very day, and let your fellow Indians perish for his sake. You native women often surrender your own people to death to save the Spaniards. You didn't understand that there could be a difference between your master and what was right. And yet no one knows what you suffered. Lucaya, you never expressed in words the unspeakable disappointment you felt at being sent not among the souls of your ancestors but among the devils in hell. You didn't even dare to ask about the keeping of the promise. You thought of the white masters as mighty beings, in whose hands you had been placed. I find this submissiveness and willingness to suffer incomprehensible and irritating.

Were you ever happy in this life? I imagine that you were, when for example your awful master left you alone with the sea and the rock on which you waited for the right wave to fling yourself down. I can dimly sense the feeling of temporary freedom the water lent you as you swam about, child of the islands. I can also hear your cries of pleasure blending in with the song of the sea. Even as a slave you went *your* way, not the way of your master.

One day he surprised you on the path to the field where the women worked. You were carrying iron mattocks in your hand, the kind the white masters brought with them as presents on their raids along the coastline of the continent. You wanted to take the mattocks to the women, because all they had to dig up the earth were their fire-hardened staffs, shamefully forced to do the grinding work of preparing the field for planting manioc. When your master stood before you, you held out the mattocks to him as his property. The image of you kneeling before him prevented his shame from turning into anger, and with your peculiar cry of joy you flew like a shadow to join the other women. With your many tricks you put your opportunities as a "mistress" to use for your people and had an intimate communion with them. You drew your ill-mannered master to *your* way, and whenever he went after you, it was to his own humiliation.

Do you remember one night on the coast? The day before, a ship had docked, sent by your master to the Pearl Coast. Under the watchful eye of the overseer the Indians sat near the sailing ship and worked at shucking the pearl oysters. They threw them into the fire to crack them open; but the pearls were blackened by the flames, and the workers often burned their hands. I see you approaching the circle around the fire and squatting down among the sweating, tormented Indians. The foremen didn't dare say anything to you. But you took steel needles out of a cloth and smilingly showed the Indians and the overseer the gleaming, undamaged pearl; then you distributed the needles among the workers. I understand that there was something in you that could never belong to your master and that he had to respect.

But how did you make yourself understood to the Spanish knights and robbers? You strange-speaking bird, how wretched must the Spanish language have seemed to you, in comparison to the wealth of Indian expressions for natural events. In her book about the Aymara Indians, *Gott im Müll* (God in the Garbage), Dorothee Sölle reports: "Groups of grown-ups sit together motionless and silent for long stretches of time, watching Ilimani, the holy mountain. They observe how the landscape changes with the shifting light. There are many subtle nuances in their language that are used to describe the phenomena of nature. An Aymara grammar lists no fewer than forty-six words for the various ways that a tree grows, extends its branches and produces budding leaves. An Aymara child no longer learns all these words, but even today he or she is taught to see and distinguish more individual details than the outsider sees." You took pains to learn Spanish, but your master much preferred to have you draw him into your language. Then he sensed a basically incomprehensible life that moves along and blooms in a way entirely different from ours, without wanting anything. Later your master admitted that his hearing became a little keener. He learned to understand gestures and glances and to feel what the words meant. Only then did he sense in you an impenetrable grief, which was drenched in profound disappointment, though that was not its source.

Once he found you kneeling near the door in the church (built of reeds with a straw roof) used by the Indians under his command. It was located between the huts of the natives, which were nothing but stalls. "It was very late," writes Reinhold Schneider. "Work was over, and the Indians had gathered with their wives and children in the chapel. Up front, where a crude, colorful picture of the Virgin was displayed, stood a mestizo boy. In a mix of Spanish, Latin, and Indian he prayed aloud the Our Father and the Salve Regina. The boy had served for a while in the house of a Spaniard who was supposed to replace the priest, but he scarcely understood the words that he uttered in a monotonous babble. The Indians kneeled and accompanied the prayer with a murmur that sounded like a muffled echo. But no third party knows what a prayer is in the presence of God."

Lucaya, you must have resembled the picture of a saint, because nothing that came from outside could have reached your inner self. You held your thin hands before your breast, your head sunk down. Both prayers – the only ones that the boy knew and hence kept repeating in a kind of chant – rose clearly and quietly from your lips. We moderns torment ourselves with meditation, wondering how to choose and formulate the right prayers. I see you with all your pain resting peacefully in God. Then again you are as busy as can be with helping people and telling stories from the gospel: how Christ came down to earth for all people, to help everyone who bears earth's suffering in his name; how he came to unite the souls of people and to build his kingdom with them, even in this world.

Naturally you bound up such stories with the notions of your people, whom you wouldn't give up. You especially liked to shift the sacred tales to the nighttime and moonlight. And you reckoned the time spent by the Son of God on earth not in days but in nights. It gave you an indescribable joy to describe how the Christ child was born at night, under the protection of the moon. "In the opinion of the Indians the moon had once marched across the sky with the sun, until the sun injured it with its shining, and the moon chose the night for itself." And so, you said, your listeners had much more reason to celebrate the new moon, because the moon had shone on the beginning of the Lord's holy way. And in your recounting of how Jesus calmed the storm he conjures up a powerful descendent of the mighty and beneficent god Luquo, on whom you conferred the honor of being one of the appointed helpers of God the Father.

But, Lucaya, the burden of suffering, which was etched into your face, was probably the most striking feature of your life as a slave. And you didn't seek to avoid it. As time went on even your increasingly unscrupulous master became aware of this. When an overseer punished an Indian, as they often did, he would hear your sobbing and find you behind a tree, the tears pouring from infinite depths down your cheeks. The sight of you admittedly angered him, and his violent words made you fall silent; but he nevertheless learned to recognize the traces of the tears from an ever deeper suffering on your face: "If a child had died on the breast of its exhausted mother, or a bearer had collapsed, he could read he signs of such events from your face before the overseer reported it." Listen to the words of this callous white man: "Thus the rift in my life grew ever deeper. There was something in me that contradicted everything that I did and gained, and I could not bear this contradiction, which the quiet girl fostered in me, out of my heart."

When the last and most terrible torture came, you couldn't take it. At your master's side you prepared to help capture slaves on the coast of Yucatan, because the slaves he had bought in Puerto Plata had died off. You landed and lured the people onto the ship with bells, scissors, and little mirrors. Once there were enough people on board, your master hoisted sail, the prisoners were thrown into the hold, and off you went. At night you lay on deck alongside your master. Beneath you, in the stifling heat the prisoners groaned. Only when the cries and groans swelled into a monotonous chant, would a sailor go down to terrorize or threaten the prisoners into silence. Lucaya, your barely perceptible crying is said to have disturbed your master's sleep even more than the piercing cries of the prisoners. He watched as you flitted to the hatch with a beaker full of water, handed it down, and, bent over the iron bars, whispered to the prisoners. The moonlight shone on your face when you came back in, and your expression was like a transparent veil of unspeakable pain. And you, white man, did it never occur to you that it was the face of your guilt?

The next morning your ship caught up with a canoe, in which two Indian men and two women were sitting. They had a little cornbread, water, and fruit; and they were rowing with all their might. They had probably run away, and they pushed their vessel on in desperation. But just as the bored sailors enjoyed shooting dolphins and sharks, they amused themselves by overturning the canoe and fishing the drowning Indians out of the water with ropes thrown over the side.

Then there was a scream. You lay on the deck, Lucaya, sobbing to break your heart. Lucaya, your heart had been saturated with pain and had no room left for any of the late, wretched, hardened love or care that your white master might have been able to offer you.

You were seized by a dreadful, nonstop crying fit. Although it was so quiet that nobody else in the house could hear it, it drove your master out as soon as he came home. He brought you a wooden crucifix; you took it into your folded hands, and your face lit up with bliss that was just as incomprehensible as your suffering. It was as if your mortally wounded soul was soothing itself. The crying dried up, slowly, but they could tell that the end wasn't far off. Only once, when the dimming glance of your eyes sank into the eyes of your earthly master, with the all-penetrating power that only dying looks have, did you betray how deep your pain was. You sadly asked whether he didn't feel that he was in still greater need of compassion than the Indians were, and that they had felt just as much grief for him as for their brothers.

Your master had a narrow little grave dug near the chapel. He wouldn't have dared admit to himself that he was mourning for a Lucayo girl. But once he passed by the grave, which had been adorned by somebody else's hand. He found Indian women and children there. They tried to flee, but he thought of you and bade them stay. . . .

—

Lucaya, because of you I understand the paintings and embroideries of the "weepers" on the pottery and clothing of the Diaguitas, the Indians from northern Chile whom I have come to know a little. I would like to honor them and the Mapuche women from southern Chile, friends of Sister Caroline in Santiago de Chile, with my reflections on this story of suffering.

19

Paul in Athens

Or the Efforts of Many Christians to Hold a Dialogue with the Pagans

MARION KÜSTENMACHER

❖

Now while Paul was waiting for them [Silas and Timothy] at Athens, his spirit was provoked within him as he saw that the city was full of idols. (Acts 17:16)

Here Luke is describing a situation that couldn't be more up-to-date: Paul, who wants to proclaim the gospel of Jesus Christ, who has dedicated his entire life to his faith in Christ, has arrived in Athens. And Athens is one of the greatest metropolises of his age, the spiritual and cultural center of the ancient world, a kettle bubbling with exotic colors — but there's something wrong. It's a rich, flourishing city full of businessmen, philosophers, artists, foreigners, globetrotters — and *idols*. Countless sculptures of gods, goddesses, heroes, and demigods stand in the temples and public squares. What stirs the pride of the Athenians is a horrible outrage to Paul, the pious Jew, who has the prohibition against graven images from Exodus 20:4 ringing in his ears. Just imagine that, *a city full of idols*. Let's call the city Munich or San Francisco or New York or Berlin. Everywhere we look it's swarming with cults and techniques and therapies, do-it-yourself or with a guru, everything from horoscopes to Tai Chi, from Rolfing to rebirthing, from hakomi to shiatsu massage, tantra to tarot cards, bioenergetics, you name it.

It's enough to make one dizzy. Or do we feel pious compassion for the unbelievers getting taken in by this fraud, who flock to these courses and spend all kinds of money? Do we feel helpless shock because we simple Christian parishioners can't do anything about such superstition? Anxiety because more and more people are falling away

---

Originally delivered as a reading of Acts 17:16–34 at a conference for Baptist pastors.

from the faith and seeking their salvation in esoteric substitutes? Insecurity over the nagging question of why God allows all these terrible aberrations to begin with, when the pure gospel wants to come to all men and women with our Lord Jesus Christ? Perhaps we also feel something like, "Thank God, this sort of thing isn't going on in my parish." Perhaps we also have a massive need to throw bulwarks up around us because it's dangerous to get involved in any way with esotericism.

We often have the same experience that Paul, a typical provincial, had when his anger flared up, when his spirit, as Luther says, flew into a rage, upon seeing the sights of cosmopolitan Athens. The view of the reality he finds himself confronting is more than sobering. Paul, the most zealous champion of a brand new religion, faces an immense gamut of offers from competing religions that takes his breath away. Doesn't the same thing happen to today's Christians? At some point we have come to believe in Jesus Christ; we have set out full of joy and enthusiasm. We have dedicated our life to him. God's call has become our vocation, sometimes even our profession. And now we stand there *mano a mano* in the supermarket of religions where the people serve themselves as needed, but seldom turn to the dusty shelves of the Christian churches.

Nowadays people who are wondering about the meaning of life and looking for help with their problems no longer necessarily expect a solid answer from their pastor and their church. From the Christian standpoint we first of all have to acknowledge a paradoxical situation: Never was there more interest in religion than there is now, and never was so little of it directed at the traditional custodians of Christianity. Today's academic theology is not unfairly disdained by Evangelicals as impotent and shrugged off by our contemporaries as unreal. The theological "guild" is, with few exceptions, no longer capable of talking about God in a way that people can understand and that leads them to faith. It seems that people prefer to go anywhere else to raise the issue of the deep-down meaning of life and to satisfy their religious needs. The religious experience they're seeking is something they're not getting here. Everyone chooses from the smorgasbord of religions whatever strikes him or her as helpful. In the marketplace of ideologies and worldviews the churches seem to be stuck with unsalable merchandise — assuming they even take the trouble, like Paul, of actually venturing out into the market.

As an editor for a German publishing house I know this from my own field: All the Christian publishers are losing their readership just as the major churches are losing their members. The erosion of the churchly environment is instantly reflected here. So the publishers are grappling with the same problem that the pastors are. Many Christian presses are secularizing their offerings, just to keep their heads above water. On the other hand the esoteric bestsellers are piling up in the bookstores. One of every ten books sold in Germany today deals with the questions of life and meaning from an esoteric perspective.

Isn't that enough to make you cry? I just wish that when we have our own confrontation with esotericism, which is our dialogue with the pagans, we can, like Paul, first of all be aware of our own feelings. Paul was seized by *outrage*, a clear, well-defined feeling, and it served as his starting point. He doesn't console himself with a pious verse from the Psalms. He doesn't write some sort of self-righteous letter to the editor about these godless, apocalyptic times. He doesn't stick his head in the sand; he doesn't deny or repress anything. He looks out and senses what's going on inside him. That's the first thing you have endure. To be begin with, the Jew in him is indignant. Already a zealot for God's cause when he was named Saul, he sees his holy God offended. The idols violate the *Jewish law* prohibiting graven images; and Paul's anger wells up from his need to have this law respected. Paul, who has been driven by his powerful experiences of God to traverse the whole Roman empire as an apostle, now stands amid the religious fairground of Athens, having some very concrete human experiences — experiences of himself. What he sees profoundly wounds his religious sensibilities. I think this is the first important point for us when we meet the new pagans in our midst: We shouldn't immediately tell ourselves, "What they're doing is dangerous, not allowed, against the Bible and church tradition." We have to say, "What I'm seeing here wounds *my* religious sensibilities, unleashes resistance in *me*, strikes *me* as dangerous, threatens *my* image of God."

We are all specialists in denying feelings, especially the negative "non-Christian" ones. But we must be allowed to have *our* feelings, strong feelings. Otherwise they have us. We mustn't be pious figurines; we should experience ourselves as flesh-and-blood human beings. We don't need to suppress anything, neither aggression, disappointment, or rage. This is the first step, the transforming element, on the path of inner healing: really to look at our own wounds, which lie beneath, and find expression in, our feelings. We have to do this in every encounter, including the encounter with esotericism. The way we go about dealing with esotericism, and with our own spirituality, shows how we deal with *Christ in us*. Here Paul takes the step from looking away, from denying the facts, to sincere, painful anger. We have to let this experience touch us physically. It is painful and profoundly human: "The Son of man must suffer many things" is how Jesus announces his path as Christ in Mark 8:31; and Mark adds: "And he said this plainly." In Athens Paul let these feelings pour over him, and we can learn this openness from him.

So he argued in the synagogue with the Jews and the devout persons.

Oh, yes, with so much unbelief all around, it feels good that there's always the synagogue, where the pious Jews sit who already know *one* God and praise him in their services, and where as a cultivated Jew one is among one's own kind, where everything is familiar, the liturgy and the texts, the questions and the answers, where you come and feel at home, where you're understood. Are you familiar with that? Your parish as a place of refuge, where the world is still in order? Where you know who you are? Where you have something to say, where your words carry some weight? Paul has had a massive, painful experience that has not exactly strengthened his sense of self. Looking on your own anger, or some such negative feeling, drains your energy, makes you weak and insecure. All of us know these moments in our spiritual life, when our inner wounds are laid bare, as they were with Paul. What more obvious solution for him than to seek warmth and security among the Jews, his "own kind," in the synagogue and regain his self-assurance? A bit of infantile regression, the psychologists would say. Sure, but at the same time it's the right step to take at this point. Paul heads for the place where he had his first religious experiences: back to the childhood source of his experiences of God, back to the synagogue, where the word of God is read out and the blessing given, the parish, tradition, the church's nourishing soil, where we have our roots, the spiritual family we belong to. We all need this. It's legitimate and healthy, as long as we don't use it as a narcotic and remain stuck there, unwilling ever to leave the "synagogue."

Here is how I translate this principle for my work: Why should I bother, as our publishing house puts its program together, to do the high-wire act of having a dialogue with esotericism? After all we could always turn out beautiful, irreproachable texts full of biblical citations and Christian poetry. That way I would get no grief from pious booksellers or irate reviewers. Among the surviving Protestant publishing houses in Germany, alongside the scholarly theological ones, practically the only presses still operating are those that serve the "Jewish Christians": the church's insiders, the covered wagons drawn in a circle — the pious, charismatic, evangelical camp. A press like Claudius, with authors such as Richard Rohr, who also speak to the new pagans and "gentile Christians," has to face a constant barrage from devout conservatives. Or do we take the position of many pastors: Why should we confront the frequently syncretistic ideas of the esoteric types? Why shouldn't we exclusively care for our two hundred "regular customers," our faithful brothers or sisters in the faith? That takes enough time and energy as it is. . . .

If we do that, then we chose to remain in the "synagogue" and settle

down there. This is a spiritual temptation, like the one Peter had at
the Transfiguration. He wanted to build three huts on the mountain
and remain there: "It is good for us to be here," he says. Richard Rohr
is forever telling us that it's good for our spiritual life if we can make
a conservative start. But that's no reason to put off launching out on
our own spiritual journey. Anyone who, thanks to his or her spiritual
history, has personal access to the rich Christian tradition, already has
a precious treasure that many others don't. But faith is not a permanent
status that one just gets to and sets oneself up in, as if in a hut or a
"synagogue." It's a process, a story, into which God draws us and that
gets us going, so that Christ finds room within us.

> *[And he argued] in the marketplace every day with those that chanced
> to be there. Some also of the Epicurean and Stoic philosophers met
> him. And some said, "What would this babbler say?"*

Thus Paul can't stay in the synagogue. He stands in the middle of the
marketplace, every day. Belief in Jesus Christ leads us into the midst
of the world, not away from it. Spiritually speaking, Paul's presence
in the marketplace is, I believe, an unprecedentedly important statement by our text, because we so often pass over this difficult point:
It means leaving behind the security of my faith-experiences that I
could previously have. Letting go of the safe models. God is a God of
the Exodus, a God who leads us, as God did the people of Israel, into
a country of new, broader encounters with God.

American Christians borrow an image from the westerns: We can't
stay hunkered down behind a circle of covered wagons. God needs us
to be settlers seeking out a new country. Unfortunately this nervous
mentality is spreading in conservative Protestant communities. Many
of us don't want to join Paul in taking the step out of security, because
we're afraid and perhaps we already know what's headed our way:
difficulties.

Paul dared to move out, and he *immediately* ran into all sorts of difficulties. He disputes with representatives of different philosophies,
the Stoics and Epicureans. Paul in alien territory, himself alienated,
deeply vexed, does what all theologians and many Christians do in the
same situation: he argues. We're all familiar with these exhausting disputes, debates, and TV discussions: They all itemize their arguments,
try to convince or convert the other, consider the other unteachable
and pigheaded, and end by saying: "What would this babbler say?"
"Babbler" is literally a "grain-picker," those who want to show off their
laboriously scraped-together ideas. We would call them hairsplitters.
That changes nothing: Paul is a trained theologian, but in dealing with
the worldly, philosophically cultivated Athenians he runs aground in
exactly the same way we do when we argue with esoteric types (and

there are some very sharp people among them) about reincarnation and similar topics. Or when we meet people who are fed up with the church and have pulled out of it and we try to clobber them with debating points and clever arguments or to dazzle them with dogmatic niceties and theological pirouettes proving that the only place to find God is the church.

Esoteric types often (and rightly) criticize us Christians because *they* have been wounded in their religious sensibility by the church; they felt completely misunderstood and so they finally left. This is how Abraham Heschel, the great Jewish philosopher of religion, describes what we need in the encounter with people who think and believe differently from us: "The symbol of God is man. Every one. God made us in his image and likeness. Hence every person must be treated with reverence, as befits the representative of the king of kings. Veneration for God is shown in our reverence for humanity. The fear of insulting or injuring another has to be as deeply anchored in us as the fear of God. To be arrogant to a person is the same as blaspheming God."

So the point is not to argue over who's right, whether all religions have equal rights, or whether Christianity occupies first place, etc. Instead we Christians have to demonstrate a change in *attitude*, expressing reverence for God in every person. Jesus expressed this by washing the feet of the disciples. Each of us can find his or her own Christ-gesture to express this reverence. In Paul, as he disputes in the marketplace, the "Pharisee" has once again broken through, and this also continually happens to us. We aren't ready to accept the other for what he or she is, the image of God. We operate on the level of *negotiation*, we propose a deal: *If* you change, if you think, feel, and believe as I do, you'll get the gospel from me. Then you're saved. This is the classic attitude of the Pharisee in us. This attitude sets conditions. It makes us the righteous and the other person the sinner. With this wrongheaded attitude we don't stand like Christ alongside the other person but over against that person.

> *Others said, "He seems to be a preacher of foreign divinities" — because he preached Jesus and the resurrection. And they took hold of him and brought him to the Areopagus, saying, "May we know what this new teaching is which you present? For you bring some strange things to our ears; we wish to know therefore what these things mean." Now all the Athenians and the foreigners who lived there spent their time in nothing except telling or hearing something new.*

In the Greek original this passage is at once comic and tragic, because the Athenians think Paul wants to preach to them about *strange gods,* a new pair of gods, *Jesus* and *Anastasis.* They take *Anastasis,* the feminine noun meaning "resurrection," to be the name of a female deity. The mutual *misunderstanding* couldn't be greater. The disputations have gotten nowhere, and Paul's attempt to preach ends miserably. Thus the Athenians absolutely can't understand and accept the gospel; the domain of their religious experience is totally different and can't be opened up with this sort of preaching. Nobody understands anything, and not one of the pagans gets converted.

Actually now he could pack up and go — if there hadn't been a few people who thought that they perhaps could after all *learn* something from this foreign expert in a new eastern religion. So they keep Paul with them. They're interested in everything new. There's something exotic about him and his new teaching that promises them new experiences. And here comes the next turning point of our story, as Paul himself notices. The Athenians, our modern esoteric types, far from the church, are deeply interested in having experiences: experiencing themselves, experiencing God. Behind today's phenomenon of the new religiosity, with its countless variations, we find, first of all, a grand religious quest by many men and women who are asking serious questions and have to be taken seriously. The modern pagans who surround us as they did Paul in the marketplace of Athens bear within themselves the same longing for God as we do. We all know Augustine's saying, "Our heart is restless till it rest in Thee." Ernesto Cardenal puts it this way: "Deep inside everyone the same flame glows, the same thirst burns. God is hidden in the innermost core of all creatures and calls us."

So Paul, standing in the middle of the Areopagus...

Hence the Athenians expect to hear something new from Paul. They're ready to listen to him, and they take him to the Areopagus. The Areopagus was the oldest law court in Athens; its jurisdiction in Roman times (when Paul was there) extended only to religion and education. What is the meaning of Paul's presence here? The Athenians bring Paul to a place that is *alien* to him. He doesn't choose the spot; they bring him where they want to hear him and can understand him, in the middle of the Areopagus. In this context the Areopagus means: the place of *decision*. Where do I belong, spiritually speaking: on the side of the self-righteous or on the side of Christ? But Christ always stands in the middle of the pagans. Later in the Letter to the Ephesians Paul managed to formulate this: The pagans are coheirs of Christ and belong to his Body, along with the Jews. Paul has to betake himself into their midst; he can't speak to them from a remote churchly observation post. This changes a great deal. In Paul's case the whole initial angry stance is transformed. What he then delivers is not some sort of prophetic juridical discourse, no harsh thundering, no accusation against the pagans, no polished theological settling of accounts, all those familiar features of his work. On the Areopagus Paul finds a new *standpoint* in dialogue with the pagans, from which he can launch his great speech. Paul has allowed a process of inner *healing* to work on him. He has learned to look more closely at things. He's now learning to see with the heart. Attentiveness of the heart (David Steindl-Rast) leads him to the reverence for other people that Abraham Heschel spoke of. Notice the new tone:

> *Men of Athens, I perceive that in every way you are very religious. For as I passed along and observed the objects of your worship I also found an altar with this inscription, "To an unknown God." What therefore you worship as unknown, this I proclaim to you.*

In his address Paul attends to the dignity of his listeners (some of these were women, as the end of the text reveals). He respects their religious feelings. (The Greek word for "religious" also applies to superstition.) In the first instance Paul names everything, without making value judgments. This is the Christ-attitude that all spiritual masters, all mystics, and all mature Christians develop. It is the look at what really is, but it is a loving look, which leaves the others room and makes the process of growth possible.

Anyone who, like Christ, really goes among the (new) pagans, or who, like Paul, really *tests everything and holds fast what is good,* will find the right point of contact, as surely as Paul did. Paul found the altar to the unknown god. In the ancient world such altars were built as a means of protecting oneself from the wrath of gods whose name nobody knew. So once again the motif of wrath emerges, but this time as a threatening judgment of a strange god, whom we fear, from whom we must protect ourselves. Isn't it exciting that Paul first had to meet this unknown aspect of his God before he could tell the Athenians about this God? He had already learned from his Damascus experience that our own religiosity can lead us astray – and has to accept correction from God. Paul let himself be confronted "freely and openly" by this aspect of God that he had never known before; and for this reason he can now grasp and stir the religious feelings of the Athenians to their profoundest core. He sees their striving to reach God, and he does not condemn it. He sees their fear of God, and he doesn't condemn that either.

> *The God who made the world and everything in it, being Lord of heaven and earth, does not live in shrines made by man, nor is he served by human hands, as though he needed anything, since he himself gives to all men life and breath and everything.*

Paul preaches God, the Creator of the entire cosmos, no God of Judgment, no punishing, avenging God, who persecutes or condemns the sinner and pagans, as we so much enjoy doing. The whole cosmos lives and vibrates through the power of God. It bears God's signature. All of creation is a blessing: Atoms, molecules, organisms, plants, animals, people, all come forth from a single tremendous, loving source, the creative Word of God, the blessing that flows out from God. A God of blessing! The exegete Claus Westermann has pointed out that in the Bible God turns to humans primarily in two ways: through saving and through blessing. This God of blessing is the one whom Paul first preaches to the pagans. This is to be our point of departure when we speak of God as the Lord of heaven and earth (Gen. 1:9: "And God saw that it was good"). The universe is a solid foundation and bears us up.

Without this experience, which Paul passes on here, religion will strike us as nothing more than false security, as pressure to perform, as a bunker protecting us from the outside. Here Paul lets himself fall into the arms of God the Creator. At this point of his own spiritual process he finally puts his trust in contemplative experience: God snatches up everyone. Whoever wants to preach the gospel to others must first be able to let go and fall into the endless universe of God's love. Take, for example, astrology, that widespread religious sport, which many Christians are so quick to condemn up and down and to dismiss as superstition. I don't want to champion astrology here, but I see *behind* it the profound, often unconscious, but genuine wish that vast numbers of people have to discover a connection between themselves and the world. We do speak about this in church when we call the universe God's good creation. But have we *experienced* it? Have we let ourselves *fall into* it? Has this blessing flowed over our skin? Do we breathe in and out this joy over the creation? Is it written on our faces? Do we share it with *all* people?

> *And he made from one every nation of men to live on all the face of the earth, having determined allotted periods and the boundaries of their habitation, that they should seek God, in the hope that they might feel after him and find him. Yet he is not far from each of us, for "In him we live and move and have our being"; as even some of your poets have said, "For we are indeed his offspring." Being then God's offspring, we ought not to think that the Deity is like gold, or silver, or stone, a representation by the art and imagination of man.*

Paul is really sharing here. He holds back nothing for himself. What he's sharing is the gift of grace: God comes to all people. God is not far off. *We* live in God. *We* are God's offspring. What has happened here? Paul has reached the *WE*. Here he has become a brother, here he surrenders himself, as Jesus did, to those who listen to him. If he hadn't gone through all the other stages of his spiritual journey, this would have been merely a slick rhetorical flourish or a rather repellent attempt to get chummy. That's why it's crucial for us to take all the steps. We always want to skip over some of them. We want to convert others, to call them to turn their lives around, without having let go of ourselves. We want to build the Christian community without becoming part of the Body of Christ ourselves. We even want to be pastors and advisors without having really looked at our own wounds and injuries. That way we may have *religious* experiences, but we can't have experiences of *God*. We can have religious symbols, golden images and thoughts that we then set up as the Athenians did. The point, however, is not to *have* a symbol but to *be* a symbol. We see God's symbols, "God's offspring," not because of what we *have*, but because of what we (potentially) *are*. That's what Paul is saying here. The Athenians have forgotten that, like all men and women, we represent God's image. This is their ignorance, beneath which lurks their anxiety.

> *The times of ignorance God overlooked, but now he commands all men everywhere to repent, because he has fixed a day on which he will judge the world in righteousness by a man whom he has appointed, and of this he has given assurance to all men by raising him from the dead.*

Actually the text says, "what God has certified for everyone." In his religious life Paul has taken the many steps from feeling wounded to the false faith that wants to protect itself and always be right, that is constantly arguing, until he reaches a state of inner healing. But not until making this traverse can he say here: The experience that has brought me here is true, the journey is true, the process is true. And because God has resurrected a man from the dead, all men and women can have this faith experience, they can take this trip into their own forgotten condition of being the image and likeness of God – just as I have.

When Martin Luther launched the Reformation, he did so with a wholly personal question that was tormenting him: *How can I "get" a gracious God?* He got his answer in Romans, from Paul, the Apostle to the Gentiles. I believe that Paul can also help us today. But *the central question* that necessarily torments us today would have to be phrased: *How do I "get" an experiential God?*

This is the question troubling the esoteric types and the new pagans and all the people alienated from the church who now stand in front of our locked church doors. It's the question that we finally must face ourselves. And to do this we mustn't simply look at Paul's theological statements in his letters. We also have to look at the movement that brought him there. We have to consider the experiences that he exposed himself to by, among other things, his apostolate to the pagans. When people alienated from the church or followers of other religions criticize Christianity as rigid and narrow and repressive and dead, when they say that in the church we have only negative expe-

riences with people, but no experiences with God, then it's our turn
to ask ourselves a very personal question: *How do I "get" an experiential God?* We *know* that Jesus is the Christ, we *know* that the Bible
is God's Word. But have we also *experienced* that? Are we not, on the
contrary, anxiously striving to avoid our *own* experiences of God —
and those are radical ones, as the Bible everywhere reminds us — and
referring instead to the experiences of others, passed on by tradition?

Nowadays among us Protestants the traditional and official church
props itself up on biblical revelation and its tradition. The church
has always showed itself mistrustful toward visionary and mystical
experiences. Do we really still sense in ourselves that deep burning
longing to be God-seekers, as Paul was, a man whose whole life we
have to define as a *journey* to Christ? Paul never met the earthly Jesus,
but he did meet the resurrected Christ, and he had to struggle long and
hard to be acknowledged as an apostle. He is the star witness of the
fact that the Christian religion too can make possible, can bear, and
can integrate direct, not handed-down, personally acquired religious
experiences. This drives Paul to the pagans, because there is a direct
path to Christ for the pagans, independent of the law. A pagan, he
realized, didn't first have to become a Jew (circumcision according to
the Law of Moses) to become a Christian.

To the Jewish Christians of his day this was an incredible affront,
and it led to arguments in the primitive church and to the first Apostolic Council. If we consistently apply it to our present-day situation,
Paul's position is every bit as explosive and scandalous to some church-
going Christians: Today's unbelievers or esoteric types don't first have
to pass through the funnel of conforming to our whole ecclesiastical
tradition and culture, our "Law," in order to become Christians. I am
no more infringing on tradition as we have it or on the order of the
community than did Paul, who was proud that he himself fulfilled the
Law. In just this way I am at home in my church. But if we want to
go further and, like the Jewish Christians, demand "circumcision" of
the modern pagans, insisting that they reject or defame their previous
religious experiences, if we present them with the church's morality and doctrine of sin without first making it possible for them to
experience the great blessing of God the Creator and the gospel of
Jesus Christ and to share all this with them, then we fall far beneath
the standard set by the resolutions of the Apostolic Council, which
are undergirded by wisdom and love and the Holy Spirit (Acts 15),
instead of infusing them with new life for our age.

> *Now when they heard of the resurrection of the dead, some mocked;*
> *but others said, "We will hear you again about this." So Paul went out*
> *from among them. But some men joined him and believed, among*

them Dionysius the Areopagite and a woman named Damaris and others with them.

Not everyone who hears the gospel immediately opens up his or her heart to it. Some listeners may mock it, others may initially dismiss it: it makes practically no difference. The important thing is how Paul manages to deal with this. He condemns no one, he doesn't evangelize himself to death, he doesn't despair, he doesn't succumb to preacher burnout. His trust in God has grown enough that he can "go out from among them." He can let go. He knows: These people have not been abandoned by God; I can and must leave them in God's hands. And so he must endure what we must endure: that *we* see only a few people opening themselves to Christ, that *we* will always see only a part of God's great work, that God takes deep breaths, which continue beyond our last gasp and which can reconcile the world — whether *we* see it or not. To this point we should hold fast, with Paul. In my encounter with Richard Rohr I have experienced how abundantly God responds to such trust, and for that I am very happy to say thanks to him here.

20

Rock and Wellspring

Personal Notes on My First Meeting with Richard Rohr

WERNER KÜSTENMACHER

On March 1, 1977, when I looked out the airplane window and saw the United States of America for the first time in my life, I wept.

No other country has so attracted and preoccupied me. I was born in 1953, so I grew up in the strong cultural pull from America in the postwar period. My brother listened to the Armed Forces Network and wore an Elvis hairdo. My sister had a very American "petticoat," and I swapped German Mickey Mouse comic books for American Superman and Mighty Mouse comics with a little black American kid. In our family the word "USA" was always charged with a special magic. Around the turn of the century my grandfather had worked for a few years in a German bookstore in San Francisco, where he had also met his wife. So it was understandable that I was excited and overjoyed when at age twenty-three I had finally managed to land there myself.

The first impressions are burned into my memory as if on a photographic plate: the faintly seedy charms of Kennedy Airport in Queens; the nightly skyline of Manhattan, which my Indian taxi driver was extremely proud of; the first night in a YMCA hotel, with police sirens howling twenty stories below us.

The goal of our little group of theology students and a woman social worker was New Jerusalem, the community founded by Richard Rohr in Cincinnati. How fitting — for me — that the New Jerusalem lay in the United States.

My first taste of New Jerusalem consisted of my being separated from my travel companions and being put up all by myself in one of the communal houses. Bull's-eye, right from the start. The eight "tenants" had held up dinner especially for me and welcomed me like an old acquaintance. For the first time during the trip I had the feeling that they were not just friendly to me but really interested in me.

The next morning there was breakfast, with a built-in prayer session. People prayed aloud – I was used to that from German prayer circles – but...simultaneously. Sometimes the pious confusion showed signs of turning into glossolalia. All this accompanied by pink cornflakes and Vitamin D milk.

The next day someone from the house took me to the community "center," where we Germans were to meet Father Richard together. At the time he was thirty-four, in other words five years younger than I am now. But I can recall that the title "father" made immediate sense to me. He greeted me, just as the people in the house had, like an old acquaintance. And without wasting time on small talk he got right down to the subject of theology. "Our theology is incarnational," he said, adding that if you want to live the incarnation of God, that will take you to martyrdom and the cross. He thought of this orientation of his community as a counterprogram to fundamentalism, the prevailing theology in American churches. "Fundamentalists don't take religion seriously; they save the saved and convince the convinced." Americans, he said, were stuffed with sermons. The thing that really caused a sensation was the complete community of goods in New Jerusalem, the common life, and above all the lifestyle shaped by faith.

"Sharing" was the most striking word for me in New Jerusalem. That meant that in the evening everybody told the others what he or she had experienced during the day. But everything else was shared too: salaries, cars, the house. The demands that Richard made of the community were very stiff. But he never identified with "his" community, and he recognized the dangers of a personality cult. At the same time he never dodged the expectations we had of him. One experience made this especially clear to me.

I have long debated whether I should write about this, because it was a very intimate episode in the life of the community. But this experience left a unique imprint on my faith. Whenever doubts gnaw away at the foundation of my faith, my thoughts return to those days in Cincinnati. It has been fifteen years since that time.

A young woman from our house got hysterical fits in the evening. Screaming and crying she lay in bed. She screamed all sorts of religious things. In the rounds of conversation before, she had described herself as "very emotional," and had she been in Germany she might have landed in a psychiatric clinic. These attacks grieved all of us. Somebody was always watching over her in her room, while the rest of us prayed for her down in the kitchen. Finally she fell asleep and spent a completely peaceful night.

But the next morning the attacks resumed. I sat upstairs on the attic floor. One story below me the sick woman was shrieking like an air-raid siren. I sensed an enormous, peculiar energy in the house.

My heart beat as if it would burst. The mood I felt then still remains to conjure up the situation even today. There was a hectic to-and-fro in the house, and a heated conversation on the phone. Then I heard Richard Rohr come in. What happened after that I could only listen to, as if it were a radio play. I heard repeated screams, some of which seemed to come from a completely different person, then a loud thud and a rather eerie silence.

When Richard came out of the room, I must have looked at him with a very troubled expression. He took me aside and explained to me exactly what had happened. It wasn't an exorcism, but a "deliverance." In all communities that take faith seriously, he said, the opposing forces are obviously mobilized. Just as in the healing narratives in the New Testament they had asked the spirit in the sick woman to give its name (which it did). This was followed by a private confession. Finally the sick woman had taken the Eucharist. Now she was asleep, and Richard thought she would feel much better afterward. She might not even remember most of what happened. And that's exactly how it was.

Such experiences, Richard said, strengthened his own faith, because he knew that evil will always be defeated in such cases: "Jesus is the victor." At that moment I was convinced that this is true. The peculiar energy in the house had disappeared; I was completely calm. The thousand doubts that I had about the whole episode, all the "purely psychological" explanations, the skepticism whether anyone could really be cured in this way — all that had just now vanished. "Jesus is the victor" was a phrase I had often heard in the CVJM [the German YMCA] and had never particularly liked. But now I saw the whole world, my whole life concentrated in this saying.

Ever since then that Saturday afternoon in Cincinnati lies in my memory like a foundling at the front door. It doesn't fit. It doesn't fit in with what I experienced before and since, and with what I learned in theology. It doesn't fit into the evangelical models that otherwise defend every biblical miracle story with tooth and claw against modern attempts at explanation. It certainly doesn't fit in with official academic theology. And it doesn't even fit in with the other Father Richard, the one I met, heard on cassettes, and read in his books. Yet that Eucharist at the sickbed is for me the secret to the mystery of Richard Rohr.

That Saturday afternoon in Cincinnati strikes me as a visit to a gigantic subterranean wellspring that supplies a great city with water. You can put the water from the faucet to all kinds of wonderful uses without ever seeing its source. Even someone who knows the wellspring can, needless to say, go on drinking tap water. But now and then doubts arise whether the water isn't being chlorinated at some point or whether the rust from the pipes can't be tasted. For me Richard Rohr is the messenger from the wellspring. He has contact with the great primeval rock of our faith. I don't envy him that because I have a sense of how painful this contact is.

He is a typical American, embodying the wonderful features of this country: the freedom to look and think. Without blinders he looks around, picking up ideas on all sides. Here like many Americans he is, in the good sense, careless. This is the reason why the United States is a leader in the many areas of research.

At the same time Richard Rohr is a very untypical American. This begins with the fact that he is a Catholic, and Catholics are a minority in the United States. He can complain bitterly about the lack of tradition in the major America churches and about the dogged narrow-mindedness of the "Jesus and me" theology that refuses to learn anything from history. He has the rock-solid physical trust in the power of the sacraments that is generally lacking in most American Protestants, who are directed by reason and emotions. This, by the way, is probably one of the causes of the spiritual cleft between North and South America.

The strengths of Richard Rohr, the typical/atypical American, come together most beautifully in his talks about the Enneagram. Christian faith has always gained strength by reflecting on alien models of thought with a broad-minded heart and taking them up in prayer. It is rooted in a brave spirituality that need not fear evil spirits. "But test everything; hold fast what is good" (1 Thess. 5:21). This principle, unfortunately, is often misused. Both Evangelicals and charismatics, traditionalists and progressives – they all build walls around their thought and declare certain regions taboo. I've experienced this so often in my life that sometimes I think that's how it has to be.

But no, Richard Rohr has shown me that it *doesn't* have to be that way. You must test everything. And hold fast what is good. For this I am thankful to him from the bottom of my heart, and happy to be able to put it down for him here in black and white.

– 21 –

AIDS — The Wounds
That Can Blossom

FRANK LORENZ

❖

At the Border

I am with S. at the train station. This is the last stop before the border. The concourse is full of life. Many people arriving, some leaving. A few are alone, with heavy trunks, others with friends or parents accompanying them. S. is carrying his own backpack. Suddenly we notice that S. has to leave earlier than we thought. We go out to the platform, and after a while we are practically alone. S. looks around: "Already?" We embrace, continue to clasp hands for a long time until S. lets go and gets on the train. I wave to him until I can barely see him. I stay behind, while S. goes across the frontier.

S. was one of the first patients under my care at the Basel Lighthouse. He was twenty-five and had been an IV drug user for some time. He had gotten the AIDS virus by sharing needles. We were the same age when he entered the Lighthouse. He was very silent, wrapped up in himself, while I was always bustling around.

The Lighthouse is a home for AIDS patients in need of care. We, the care-providing team, are responsible for supporting the patients and helping them to do what they can't (any more). In the process the patients themselves decide what they don't want (any more). Thus in the Lighthouse we have encounters and contacts, mostly on a daily basis. These are often remarkable, and sometimes intense.

For me S. was the more intense kind. After he died, I met his father, and we talked. That is, he asked questions, only in a veiled fashion, because he wasn't used to talking about himself and his thoughts and feelings. In conversation with S.'s father I discovered that I had a lot to learn: I had to arrange and formulate my ideas so that this man could understand me and get a handle on what I was saying. He questioned me as the nurse of his son and as a theologian. I noticed that what I

126

had previously learned about (and with) theology and the church was now being directly questioned and challenged.

A Kind of Paradigm

With this counseling session and with others that would take place later something in my life, and hence in my theological work, came into sharp focus: AIDS. In other words, I have "my people" in mind, when I read or hear something or make some comment of my own. I find myself asking: Could you tell them that? As you might imagine, this gets me to pitch overboard some apparently quite important things. On some issues I become belligerent and lose my temper, for example, when I hear sickness being called "God's punishment" meted out to a group of people for some sin of commission or omission. But on the other hand I have discovered new, immediate, unexpected access roads to theology, a new language, and a surge of vitality through and with "my people."

AIDS has become a kind of "paradigm" for my theological work. I have developed three criteria, crucial questions that I continually pose to myself and to any new theological notions I meet with. (1) How do you relate to the "marginal groups," with the "outsiders," with those who are alien to you, or "totally other"? (2) How do you deal with the body and sexuality? (3) What do death and dying mean to you?

These three themes characterize some of the darkest regions in the thinking and propaganda of both the official church and traditional society. If we spell them out down through the epochs of history – which is a history of the winners and rulers – we see the consequences of the deliberate wedding of social morality and the Christian message.

The Others

Every center has its "marginal groups." The so-called outsiders – in the case of AIDS, this unfortunately means above all IV drug users and gay men – have for the most part been hushed up, and sometimes shot down. If the church did anything for them, it was usually some sort of "charity," given out with the attitude of the *beati possidentes,* the people who know what's good and bad, what's normal and abnormal. These benefactors generously handed out a few of their possessions, wealth, knowledge, and salvation, without really sharing. Leonardo Boff calls this "assistentialism." In every case it masks anxiety: fear of the "others," of the so-called drug addicts, because they are living out the hidden longing of our time, a life of the nonconformism that is forbidden to us. They allow themselves our domesticated ecstasies. There

is the fear that there might be still more between heaven and earth
than the supposed consensus admits, that there might be a "more"
that we all yearn for, that might burst into reality and break down
the everyday routine, something that exists, even though it positively
ought not to.

Body and Sexuality

Fear of gay men and women — homophobia — is closely tied in with fear
of one's own unlived sexuality. Anyone who refuses to deal openly and
honestly with his or her own body and sexuality will never be able to
accept homosexuality, whether male or female. Our social consensus
continually lends its support to this by assigning fixed roles for men
and women. The upshot of this is that we all have a long journey
ahead of us before we can live in our bodies without struggle and
stress, before sexuality, minus the usual clichés and cultic language,
can become part of our humanity.

By functionalizing sexuality, the church did one more thing:
"Procreation" became the sole purpose of the dark (but now safely
channeled) "power of the instincts." Pleasure and love become un-
necessary words, and the once profoundly physical language of the
Bible's message, even the "body of Christ," was turned into a hollow,
ethereal verbal flourish.

The Last Taboo

Ultimately death and dying characterize what no one denies is the
final taboo in this third of my contemporary thematic complexes.
"Death and dying" unmask the spirit of our age, which is a spirit of
compartmentalization. We build walls separating private and professional life, the normal and the abnormal, the healthy and the sick.
In the neatly separated quadrants of life we create institutions and
structures that continually harden. We have gotten used to eliminat-
ing what irritates or interrupts us, what restricts the "routine flow of
seemingly unlimited life" (J.C., a student).

Separation causes pain, anger, and depression. It is widely recognized that depression, in its various manifestations, is the disease of
our time. But it is concealed and pathologized. People suffering from
it are put into institutions — they simply shouldn't be the way they are.
There psychotropic drugs insure order and peace. The "remedy" for
pain, rage, and depression is generally called "avoidance." And since
death is the final separation, at a time like this it must become *the*
problem, the most taboo territory of all.

AIDS — "Other Islands of Your Longing"

"AIDS is the last appeal for human kindness" (D. Sölle). AIDS makes the deepest wounds in society and the church visible and palpable. Men and women with AIDS personify these wounds. But these wounds can begin to "blossom," to borrow the language of Franciscan mysticism. They can become the place where we Christians, where the church(es) experience healing as the "body of Christ." AIDS can help us to discover another acronym, in German, Andere (other) Inseln (Islands) Deiner (of your) Sehnsucht (longing) (M. P. Meystre).

At first glance this may seem a crazy idea: What has hitherto been considered the quintessential destroyer of life can heal. This is neither cynicism nor calculated optimism. It is not meant to be false, cheap consolation; nor should a deadly illness ever be instrumentalized or exalted. But I have gotten to know a fair number of people who have found their identity, the way to themselves, through this disease.

AIDS confronts Christians with the task of overcoming fear and prejudice and meeting those whom the church's doctrine and practice have for millennia turned into untouchables. Going part of the distance with people who have AIDS, sharing moments of life — sometimes the last ones — means once again taking the path of the Galilean. It means rediscovering his scandalousness and vitality; it means restoring content to the message of unconditional love that has often become unbelievable and bringing that message precisely to the marginalized and powerless. Toward these people theology has a compensatory function: to confess guilt, to alleviate pain, and to take care that it and the church never again provide the spiritual superstructure for exclusion and oppression.

AIDS is also a "sickness" in the body of Christ. Accompanying people with AIDS on their way means that — to a certain extent — the boundaries between HIV-positive and HIV-negative, between the sick and healthy, become unimportant. Through the solidarity of the "physical," through the coalition of the "sexual," loving, injured, tender, hoping, and brave people, the "body of Christ" is joined together. A "road community" full of grief and joy will evolve, because it's a matter of life and liveliness, and of death and dying. Everything will find a place in it.

For Christians and their churches AIDS is a *status confessionis.* We are challenged to take sides and to confess what we believe. We are challenged to live in truth, to call the games, constructs, lies, and abuses of our time by name. We have to learn to persevere on the crosses of our society: hostility to the body, intolerance, exclusion, and hatred of the "others," the "foreigners," maniacal worship of power and progress, protecting property and assets and the compartmentalized mind-set. Through AIDS the church can once again become the "body Church" (K. Marti).

At night during last Lent and Eastertide I kept watch at the bedside of C., a young woman. She was tormented by terrible dreams and couldn't bear being alone any more, because she had crossed the boundary between her inner and outer reality in both sleeping and waking. Together we worked out the fantasy that an angel was sitting or lying next to her on the bed. This led to her noticing that when she turned over she had to be careful not to lie on his wings and break off a feather. During this time I rediscovered something that I thought had been locked deep down in the trunk of my childhood: the idea of the "guardian angel." Attending people with AIDS, even on their deathbed, gave me the possibility of fitting back together some of the fragments of the shattered images from my childhood.

So, in conclusion, the question remains: Are we ready to let ourselves be changed by and with people who have AIDS? Are we ready to let this message burrow deeply within us, ready for its personal and institutional consequences?

I myself have to spell that out every day with "my people." For example, U., whenever he's awake, continually shouts, "Somebody come!" That's his way of saying everything, whether it's too hot or cold for him, whether he's thirsty or in pain. His brain and central nervous system are diseased, the left side of his body is paralyzed, and so he struggles all the more with the right side. And with "his" line. It expresses anger and rage at what is taking his life, at the disease that he will die of. "Somebody come..." to take it all away, the pain and suffering and death, as I translate it. I have often wondered why U. uses just this line and not one of all the other possible lines — shorter ones, for example, like "Help!" To this day I don't know why. But I do know that this line is the main reason why I feel so close to him, and it teaches me the most: teaches longing for life, rebellion against whatever stands in the way of life, and then too: vulnerability, fear of what will happen, fear of loss, especially of losing people. "Somebody come!" This is John the Baptist and John the Disciple in one, future expectation and present reality.

Yesterday when I left the Lighthouse after my shift, U. was still alive.

22

A Whisper of Love

GERALD MAY

⚬

These words came to me as if whispered by God. They make me think of Richard Rohr and his courageous heart and ministry. The piece was first published in the Newsletter of the Shalem Institute, Mount St. Alban, Washington, DC 20016, and is used with permission.
–

I know what is inside your heart.
I see your courageous impotent love, and your fear,
   and the tears you would cry if you could.
And I do so love you.

I feel how you hate your own selfishness.
When you see my poor ones on the street,
   I melt as you detest your defenses against them.
I feel your deep heart-secret:
   you wish you would not run away
   but could embrace those poor ones, kiss them,
   love them completely, caress their souls.
And I so love you.
I know how you feel, deep, so deep,
   when you bar your doors and secure your house
   and invest your money and try to enjoy your possessions.
   I know your dis-ease, your unrest,
And I love you
   and I drink from your discomfort and find it good.
No, it is not guilt, nor shame;
   I know the taste of them, and spit them out.
It is your impotent love, your stifled love, your helpless love,
   your yearning love that feeds me,
Yet I starve, I thirst. With you.

You are so rarely aware of me,
   how I embrace you as you read the morning paper,

My arms cradle you, my breath is on your hair
  as you listen to the news.
I know your unspoken feelings, for I am closer to your heart than
  you are now or ever will be.
I feel your love, screaming out against injustice,
  bleeding, wounded from the pain of others,
  love become revulsion when the agony is too much,
The starving children, the hungry homeless, the tortured innocent,
  and all the broken, broken hearts.
You cannot bear it, so I must
  almost alone.
I drink up what I can from your love
  in little sips, but I starve, I thirst, and ache for you.

And I love you and cry for you when you cannot,
And I love you and cry in you when you must turn away
  and go about your business.
And when you can cry, I kiss your blessed tears
  and drink from them.
You feel my pain, you see my beauty,
You ache for my goodness.
And that is me, loving you and birthing in you,
Again and again, coming to you
  In utter surrender.
Oh how I wish you could know
  How completely I am surrendered to you,
For if you knew that, even just a little,
You could not help but surrender to me.
  Your love would awaken
And we would become a mountain spring and a sparkling ember
And we would grow, into river and flame,
  into ocean and lightning
Cleansing, searing, burning, renewing the earth.
Your love would grow wings of power and wisdom
And together in unbearable passion we would fly and die
  and fly again;
Our courage would encompass the heavens.
Knowing nothing but our love we would look
  straight into the heart
  of every broken being, every creature,
  every plant and mountain
And live in them, and caress their wounds,
  and bring them nourishment,
  and die for them and with them.

We would be relentless, my love.
We will be forever.

My dreams, my dreams: I do not even think of letting them go.
Your fear says you can do so little,
    you can only bear so much,
    you simply have to cope.
And I do so love you.
Open to me, my love. Just now, in this moment
    and the next
Surrender to me,
And let your surrender be so complete, so utterly perfect
    that the only thing left that is yours is your searing love.
No plans left, no strategies remaining,
No comprehending of anything,
No defenses, no coping, no adjustment, no compromise.
Only love, love delicate, love fierce,
    love angry, love complaining, love overjoyed,
    love mistaken, love triumphant, love broken, love aching,
    love driving you crazy.
Relinquish everything to make room for my madness in love;
I will show you the way when you can no longer bear not
    knowing it.
I will fill the emptiness of your heart with spaciousness of love.
I will clear your mind so you may nurse from wisdom's breast.
I will fill the incompleteness of your body with light and power.
Bear the exquisite pain with me — I will bear you.
Share the sheer joy of life with me — I will burst with happiness.
Bear the loss of what you thought was me,
    To let me be free in spaciousness.
Bear with me when I seem like nothing to you
    Nothing to hold on to
    Nothing to know
Only trust and fidelity, hope and abiding, reaching, open.
I do love you so.
Love me, love me; I ache for you, my love.
You need not know how.
You need not know how.
Know only that you love.

23

To Our Four Children

A Letter from Dresden, Three Years after the "Change"

RITA AND PETER MEIS

> *When your children ask you in time to come, "What is the meaning of the decrees and statutes and ordinances that the Lord our God has commanded you?" then you shall say to your children, "We were Pharaoh's slaves in Egypt, but the Lord brought us out of Egypt with a mighty hand... to bring us in, to give us the land that he promised on oath to our ancestors." (Deut. 6:20-21, 23)*

To our four children:

Whether you actually will ask us this sort of question remains to be seen. But if you were to ask us about it tomorrow, our answer would have to be: No.

No, it wasn't Egypt. The first half of our life wasn't marked by slavery and bondage. Neither rods nor fleshpots would serve as valid evidence of the life that lies behind us. Perhaps then you'll look silently at us and wonder whether satisfied slaves haven't always been the worst enemies of freedom.

You're right to sense that we have a hard time with the new freedom. We didn't break into spontaneous applause when we got it. Will you ever believe that inside limitations we had real experiences and found our way to maturity through them?

What remains for you a passing episode has left a permanent stamp on our life: forty years of real, live, dictatorial socialism. But they were also forty years during which we lived, loved, and suffered. Your parents belong to the generation that — unlike your grandparents' and yours — is made up of the children of socialism. Well, then, what is this time worth to us? What is left over from it, and what has to be rejected?

It's a good thing that your eyes betray these questions. We have to talk about them. Tell stories. We mustn't duck the reckoning we owe ourselves. But above all, we have to secure the traces of our past. This means resisting the arrogant West German tendency to make us believe that everything we did was just an emergency solution, not worth holding on to, and hence deserving to be tossed onto the garbage dump of history.

No, it wasn't Egypt. Rather it was something like the "Babylonian Exile." As I search for a valid interpretation (one can't create meaning without it), it occurs to me how frequently and urgently we preached about the letter from Jeremiah to his banished people: "Seek the welfare of the city... and pray to the Lord on its behalf, for in its welfare you will find your welfare" (Jer. 29:7). We tried to face this mission — not, to be sure, with any more bravery than most, but with some perseverance.

Of course, "exile" can be used to describe a situation that one can only endure, that one must refuse to consent to (at least within oneself), and that one can only long (at least secretly) to be released from. And in that case this paradigm doesn't apply to us. We never dreamed, the way your grandparents did, of winning back national unity (although of course we did suffer bitterly from some unfulfilled longings).

The place we are coming from, therefore, is probably best described with the image of the "wandering people of God." They are on their way through stages (desolate ones too) of history because God needs them to be at this one or the other. The people don't find comfort, rest, or a real home, but in each case they set up their protective tents. Our people were in various places in Saxony, almost always very close to their Slavic neighbors.

If you ask about the most important experiences we had on this path with others and with the church, if you ask where we are at home, there seem to be at least three things worth holding on to, in the face of all the unfortunate developments.

1. The forced distance from the state and its power did us good. We have an uncanny, stunned feeling to see the current efforts by our church toward a "restoration." The church won't admit the fact that we live in a nation that is secularized (and that has perhaps even, in Bonhoeffer's terms, "come of age"). At any rate the diabolical interest that the state security ("Stasi") system took in many of us shows that back then despite the required distance we did, as far as possible, bravely and even publicly give political witness. We're not crying about this experience. It really makes us sad to see how incapable we are of offering clearly defined resistance to the current pressure for church and state to reach an accommodation. Perhaps Jesus declares those that mourn blessed (and not the resigned ones), because grief always creates a bit of distance, indeed a kind of homelessness. On

the other hand, the abandoning of distance is matched by the all too voluntary abandonment of blessedness.

2. We were more credible and probably more useful to Christ because our lifestyle fit in with the simple people we were near to. By contrast the continual enticement of the old Adam (the driving force of the new system) is one of the worst experiences that our hearts now have to fight with every day. Having to learn the "wisdom theology" of the market economy ("thou shalt crave," "thou shalt distrust," etc.) implies not just the unhappy relinquishment of simplicity; it also makes us more lonely.

Perhaps Jesus calls the poor (in their undiscovered innocence) blessed for another reason too: because he wants at least to keep alive our powerless longing for simplicity.

3. It was a good school that God put us through, to make us pay a price for being Christians. To be sure, nowadays some of the recognition we get feels quite pleasant, and we don't long for the return of the reprisals (which those who were least persecuted most often took to be persecution). But when Jesus' followers no longer irritate, provoke, or disturb others, it seems to me that something's wrong with their following. When Christians are no longer a problem for the world, maybe they become a problem for Christ.

Perhaps Jesus calls those persecuted for justice' sake blessed because nowadays accommodation also means consenting to injustice.

But please don't think we were heroes. We came up short in terribly many areas: Along with our church we were silent in the face of the fraudulent elections that went on year after year, and in the face of the Wall, but above all we never faced the economic questions. We underestimated the economic weakness and corruption of the socialist state and learned to accept the division of Germany as a consequence of the war and as a positive factor, improving European stability. Were we to blame for that? Perhaps.

We brought you up thinking that your children – our grandchildren – would have to live in this circumscribed socialist world. Were we to blame for that? Did we unconsciously tie you down?

So what's left is not a reverie of bygone years, but a bone-deep irritation. Socialism never really earned a halo. But what perplexes us now is the fact that the overcoming of inhuman conditions always seems to promote spiritual misery. Will it really be our destiny "to seek the Garden of Eden only to wind up in a wasteland, which we afterward try to convince ourselves is despite everything a bit of Paradise" (G. Kunert)?

You have to give us time to reorient ourselves. In any case we haven't arrived yet. The overhasty satisfaction of some of the East Germans who have "come home" is surely just a superficial sense of comfort. And should it turn out some day that the strength of your parents can do no more than adjust to the status quo, in other words that we have to pass on the will for change into your hands, you should realize that it takes a certain distance to do this.

And so (to borrow an image from the New Testament) as the current march into the "holy city" proceeds – an entrance that has its triumphal features, despite the economic troubles – you mustn't forget the countermovement of the suffering Christ. Jesus "suffered outside the city gate...Let us then go to him outside the camp and bear the abuse he endured. For here we have no lasting city" (Heb. 13:12–14).

In the GDR distance was decreed, because that way Christians could be "launched" better. Back then we thought our exclusive mission was to carry the gospel, as best we could, into the cities and villages and to let Christ take shape there. Sometimes this would be done merely through our existence, sometimes through purposeful actions and plain political talk. This "going into" has been so deeply imprinted in us that we find the thought of "going out" (earlier we'd have called it a fatal flight from the world) hard to accept as something essential. And yet we sense that being a Christian in today's social configuration has more to do with distance and letting go than we are ready in our hearts to do.

You notice how these lines are fragmentary and not fully developed. Perhaps too you can see the alienated groping of our generation, which comes from a different world from yours and must find its way anew. But if you too should read these lines in the spirit of people who have been made insecure, then they may nonetheless fulfill the function of the friend described in an Eastern Jewish folktale:

> A wanderer once got lost deep in the forest. After a while a second man got lost and ran into the first one. Without knowing what had happened to him, he asked the first man the way out of the forest. "That I don't know," he replied. "I can only show you the paths that go deeper into the thicket, and then let us look for the way together."

This is the path we hope to find with you.

24

Men's God, Women's God

Questions about the Christian Image of God and Humanity

CHRISTA MULACK

❖

Sunday after Sunday all around the world men and women in Christian communities pray, without the slightest hesitation: "Our Father, who art in Heaven, hallowed be thy name..." Without the slightest hesitation they call him "God the Father." Naturally we don't ask about the Goddess, our Mother, because that would be primitive, pagan, un-Christian.

The "God of our fathers" turns out to be a man's God. The word of God is exclusively the word of men. Men have chosen what experiences are worthy of being handed on in the Holy Scripture. Men determine where experience of oneself ends and experience of God begins. Male experiences of God are holy. Female experiences of God are pagan.

But, to begin with, let's stay with God, the heavenly Father. I have some questions for him: Father in heaven, you are described to us in the New Testament as caring, loving, forgiving, compassionate, and faithful. Then why don't you see to it that fathers on earth also become like you: caring, loving, forgiving, compassionate, and faithful? Why are we much more familiar with such behavior from our mothers? Why are the fathers of our time not ready to nurture their children, to look after them with love? Why do they watch as fathers on earth abuse and rape their children and wives? Why are weapons more important to them than food and education for their children? Why do we have a Father in heaven and a fatherless society on earth? Many of us don't know our fathers. Many fathers fell in the war. Others deny being fathers. Up till now killing has been more important to earthly fathers than fatherhood.

We know our mothers. They have always cared for us, even under the most trying conditions, which men have created for them.

Why are the fathers missing on earth, and not the mothers, while in heaven the Mother is missing, not the Father?

God, if you are really our heavenly Father, why do you set such store on being the only one revered? Why is only your name hallowed and the name of our mother passed over in silence? In your creation a father is only a father by means of a mother. Without mothers there are no fathers. Supposedly the opposite *can* happen, as we know from Mary. Why does it apparently mean so little to you that we humans also venerate our Mother in heaven and hallow her name? Without a heavenly Mother people will learn neither to honor their mother earth nor their earthly mother. But didn't you teach them that they were to honor their father *and* their mother? On earth as it is in heaven. Both realms belong steadfastly together. Jesus taught us that. These connections are becoming increasingly clear to us women. When people don't learn to honor their Mother in heaven and to hallow her name, they're all the more prepared to exploit Mother Earth, to rape and destroy and silence her. Then earthly mothers become powerless accomplices of male interests. But when only the heavenly Father is revered, people are all the more prepared to kill, die, and sacrifice their own children for the honor of the Fatherland.

The fathers of this world — and, following their lead, all the rest of us — have forgotten there can no more be a fatherland without mother earth than a father without a mother. On earth as it is in heaven.

What sense does it make to go on venerating our heavenly Father while our Mother Earth is going under from the harm inflicted on her by earthly fathers? What sense does it make for women to go on being ready to give all honor to the divine Masculine Principle, and so as to seal their own powerlessness, preventing the breakthrough of feminine forces?

In the name of a male God women have learned to disregard, if not to despise, themselves and their own sex. Without the slightest hesitation they also assumed that divinity has nothing to do with femininity. In the name of a male God women have learned to confer divine forces on men, to lend them divine power. They likewise never hesitated to assume that divinity had to do only with masculinity.

The myths and theological structures thought up by male theologians were always designed to make the female sex get the worst of it, to exclude women from the domain of the holy, the divine, and hence the domain of power as well. Meanwhile many women are now insisting that what the Bible says about the beginning of the human race must at long last come true: man *and* woman are the image of God. Thus the truly divine can be described only in masculine *and* feminine symbols, or else it must petrify into an idol. In the symbol of the goddess they resurrect the hitherto missing feminine half, and thereby link up with the early Christian traditions, which spoke of a Lady Sophia alongside the Lord God. In the Holy Spirit, who in truth is a *Spiritess* (i.e., the Hebrew word for spirit, *Ruach,* is feminine), these traditions sanctified the feminine aspect of the deity. Jesus refers quite unequivocally to this double aspect of the divine when he warns the scribes (in Mark 3:28–29): "Truly I tell you, people will be forgiven for their sins and whatever blasphemies they utter; but whoever blasphemes against the Holy Spirit[ess] can never have forgiveness, but is guilty of an eternal sin." This is surely one of the most serious sayings of Jesus handed down by tradition. But if this divine *Ruach* can be blasphemed against independently of God the Father, why can't she be venerated independently from him as well? We can sense traces of her everywhere, once we have learned to perceive them. In the form of a dove she came down from heaven to Jesus as he had himself baptized in the waters of the Jordan. She called him her beloved son. And theologians also know that Jesus thought of himself as a son and ambassador of Wisdom, for whose message he was ultimately crucified. Behind the voice of the Logos at the beginning of the Gospel according to John is actually concealed Lady Wisdom, as theologians have discovered. If we put her back in again, the hymn reads as follows:

In the beginning was Wisdom;
she was the primeval deity.
All things are made through her,
nothing came into existence without her.
In her was life,
and life was the light of men and women.
And the light shines in the darkness,
and the darkness did not grasp this.
She was the true light that enlightens everyone
who comes into this world.
She was in the world, and the world is made through her,
but the world knew her not.
She came into her own, and they did not welcome her.
But to as many that welcomed her she gave the power
to become children of wisdom, believing in her name.
And Wisdom was made flesh and dwelt among us,
and we saw her splendor,
a splendor of the only-begotten son,
full of grace and truth.
And from her fullness we have all received, grace for grace.

Why aren't we allowed to know that these words were once intended for the veneration of a goddess, as theologians have shown?

Why do men need to make the authenticity of Christian doctrine dependent upon the exclusion of female divinity — which Jesus thought so important? But then too why do many women despise their own sex so much that to this day they deny the connection between divinity and femininity?

Our false image of God is tied up with our false image of ourselves. We have learned that rationality and aggressiveness constitute masculinity. Sensibility and feeling, by contrast, are feminine. Women are still being forbidden to have their own thoughts, as men are forbidden their feelings. And in this way only male religious insights and perceptions have been turned into unchallengeable "revelations of God," while the religious experiences and needs of women found no expression in theology, and to this day may not be integrated into our Christian understanding of the faith.

So long as the church doesn't attend to this problem with more passion, so long as it doesn't espouse theological *glasnost* and admit the truth that its theological statements are closely linked to psychological and anthropological perspectives and circumstances, it will do justice to nobody — neither to Jesus' call for conversion, nor to the God of the New Testament, who makes all things new. The church can become a place of salvation only when it breaks off with all dead ideas and misogynistic teaching, when it provides us instead with healing symbols and accepts responsibility for the consequences of its acts. But when the church refuses to be the site of a new way of behaving, it can at most remain a place for dreaming. While we are still kept waiting for the new behavior, there is no holding up the dreams of the new human person:

At some point, when men overcome their fear of their own feelings, they will stop assigning the realm of feelings to women.

At some point, when women overcome their fear of their own thinking, they will stop mechanically repeating what they've been taught and publish their own ideas instead.

At some point, when men let go of the fear of being ridiculous, they will stop making women ridiculous.

At some point, when women are no longer afraid of coming off as incompetent and dumb, they will stop trusting male theologians more than their own religious feelings.

At some point when men no longer need to fight for power, it will be enough for them to rule themselves instead of women too.

At some point, when women have seen through to the cause of their feelings of powerlessness, they will insist on acting autonomously instead of renouncing the job of getting their own needs met.

At some point, when men accept their own vulnerability, they will no longer need to hurt women, children, and other men.

At some point, when women stop orienting themselves to the vulnerability of men, they will take their own injuries seriously, instead of swallowing them in the name of peace.

At some point, when men stop killing off the tender, sensitive sides of themselves, they will also end the destruction of the environment.

At some point, when women no longer think of themselves as the advocates and administrators of male sensitivity, they will order men to stop their world-destroying operations.

At some point, when the church has become the place where liberated women and men can meet,

- they will meet one another with curiosity instead of with dogmatic formulae;

- they will talk about the differences in their faith and celebrate what they hold in common;

- they will not only discover in what life situations they need a Goddess Mother and a God the Father, but also when it is time to leave both behind and experience new dimensions of the divine.

25

The Wilderness Temptations and the American Journey

Resistance and Contemplation in a Quincentennial Perspective

CHED MYERS

Over the past three decades many North American Christians concerned with justice and peace have sought to realize the balance Thomas Merton advocated between "resistance and contemplation" (see Douglass 1972). Richard Rohr has been deeply involved in that search. Merton wrote often of the relationship between contemplation and the desert, and it was perhaps in part because of this that Rohr moved to the American Southwest in 1987. It is in this spirit of "desert resistance and contemplation" that I offer the following reflections to Richard.

—

> I will tell you something about stories [he said]
> They aren't just entertainment. Don't be fooled.
> They are all we have, you see,
> all we have to fight off illness and death.
> You don't have anything if you don't have stories.
> Their evil is mighty,
> but it can't stand up to our stories.
> So they try to destroy the stories,
> let the stories be confused or forgotten.
> They would like that, they would be happy
> Because we would be defenseless then.

Leslie Marmon Silko, *Ceremony*

More than anyone else Thomas Merton reanimated the modern quest in Western Christianity for a spirituality that, in the spirit of the desert fathers, would engage the demons of our time in a struggle for history. Reflecting upon the paradox of the desert in modern life, Merton once wrote (1956, 17ff.) that the desert fathers believed that the wilderness was special in the eyes of God precisely because it was undomesticated by human society. For the contemplative it was a place to go just to be. Yet because the desert was also "the country of madness" and "the refuge of the devil," anyone "who wanders into the desert to be himself must take care that he does not go mad and become the servant of the one who dwells there in a sterile paradise of emptiness and rage."

In the mid-twentieth century, however, Merton lamented, the desert had become transformed by human technology, particularly in the Southwest. Here the desert was "the birthplace of a new and terrible creation, the testing-ground of the power by whom man seeks to un-create what God has blessed." It was also host to "fantastic, protected cities of withdrawal and experimentation and vice . . . sordid smiles of the devil upon the face or the wilderness." So, Merton concluded:

> When man and his money and machines move out into the desert, and dwell there, not fighting the devil as Christ did, but believing in his promises of power and wealth . . . then the desert itself moves everywhere. . . . The desert is the home of despair. And despair, now, is everywhere.

The contemplative had to face this despair, wage war upon it with hope: "that war is our wilderness."

In response to Merton's challenge, we who work in the Southwest often collaborate with the Nevada Desert Experience, a Franciscan-inspired campaign of prayer and resistance. There we must confront the unholy trinity that perhaps best characterizes the demonic in our society:

- the grim opulence of Las Vegas, parable of North American instrumental, objectifying materialism;

- the dark violence of the government's nuclear weapons test site an hour north of town, symbol of U.S. militarism and its destruction of the land;

- the cry for justice of the Shoshone people upon whose land both sites dwell in violation of treaty, representing the tragic legacy of forced dispossession of native peoples by the dominant culture.

This confrontation took on even greater poignancy during the 1992 Quincentenary of Columbus's arrival in the Americas, a *kairos* moment that has raised deep and abiding questions for people of faith concerning the profoundly ambiguous European project of "civilization" in the "New World."

Remembering the Story: *Mimesis* or *Mimosis*?

Native American writer Leslie Silko's warning, placed on the lips of an elder in the opening lines of her acclaimed book *Ceremony,* ushers us directly into the heart of the matter. The continuing debate about how to interpret the European conquest of the Americas and its legacy has to do with myth and history, memory and amnesia, responsibility and denial — that is, about *which stories* will be used to construe our national experience. Will the highly mystified narratives of Progress and Manifest Destiny prevail for yet another generation? Or will we begin to listen and learn from the long-silenced voices of the many marginalized peoples of this place?

"Stories are all we have to fight off illness and death." This is the wisdom of native American cultures struggling to survive the centuries-long holocaust of European domination. Yet it holds true for *all* peoples, not least those of us who continue to look to the biblical narratives to combat the viruses of greed and violence that infect the U.S. body politic. But if the stories of the first Americans have been suppressed and in some cases "forgotten," our scriptural traditions have been "confused." Too often the Bible has been expropriated into the service of the historical narrative of oppression. This confusion has rendered Christians, too, "defenseless" against the powerful myths of empire.

The biblical Story of liberation has often been mishandled by people of faith — *dis-membered,* so to speak, by abuse and misrepresentation. In fact, this was a problem even within the Story itself, which is why the renewal traditions in the Hebrew Scriptures emphasized the discipline of *re-membering.* Thus the Deuteronomic refrain: *"Remember* the long way that the Lord your God has led you" (Deut. 8:2).

This focus upon *re-membering* is what Eric Auerbach called *mimesis:* the invitation to "re-produce" the liberation Story in our own lives. In other words, the Bible is not just another text for us to interpret; it also *interprets* us. Conversely, the Deuteronomist warns that when people of faith do not practice *mimesis* they simply become like "the nations around them" (Deut. 8:19f.). This is *mimosis,* defined by Webster as a condition whereby people simulate the pathologies that surround them.

A good example of a modern tradition of *mimesis* is the Christian church's liturgical journey through Lent. We *re-member* the Story by retracing Jesus' footsteps to the Passion, and practice countercultural disciplines in order to mitigate the effects of *mimosis.* Customarily we inaugurate this Lenten journey by reflecting upon the story of Jesus' temptation in the wilderness (found in Luke 4:1–13 and Matthew 4:1–

11, expansions of Mark 1:12f.) — to modern sensibilities a strange if familiar drama.

Liberal scholarship understands Jesus' struggle with the Devil in terms of the apocalyptic combat myth (angels vs. the principalities) that shapes so much of the New Testament worldview. Conservatives argue that it is a blunt reminder of the reality of evil. Psychological/ spiritual interpretations see it as a dramatization of Jesus' internal struggle over his character and vocation. And radicals (e.g., Clarence Jordan) read it as a parable concerning the seductions of economic, political, and religious power that must be resisted by all true disciples.

Each of these interpretive traditions preserves part of the truth of this story. Yet the story's most remarkable characteristic is precisely its narration of the primal struggle between *mimesis* and *mimosis!* What follows is a kind of "Quincentenary reading" of this text, reflecting on our North American struggle with story and history, *particularly* for those of us who are Christian inheritors of the dominant culture.

"Led by the Spirit into the Wilderness for Forty Days": Jesus on a Vision Quest

In preparation for his mission, Jesus follows a mysterious yet com- pelling calling to radical wilderness solitude. He fasts. He is alone. His mettle is tested.

Let us imagine for a moment Jesus' desert retreat as a kind of "vi- sion quest," a tradition found among native peoples the world over. (My purpose is not to argue for cross-cultural correspondence, but by analogy to situate the biblical story in American soil and the rich spiritual traditions indigenous to it.) The vision quest is a ritual pas- sage, somewhere between what Joseph Campbell (1988) calls the "initiation ceremony" and the "hero-journey." Largely lost to modern urban cultures, it survives still among most land-based tribal peoples. Among Aboriginal Australians it is referred to as "going walkabout," what elder Guboo Ted Thomas describes as the "renewal of the Dream- ing" (1987, 90ff). The California Yuki practice a kind of mix between ghost dancing and the sweat lodge. Pueblo people follow the ancient traditions of the kiva society. And the Sioux name it *hanblechia,* vision-seeking.

Christopher Vecsey attempts to characterize the journey: shamans "with the help of guardian spirits travel to the land of the dead in order to restore the lost or stolen or diseased souls . . . out of love for their community" (1991, 120f.). Thus the popular account of a Lakota shaman, *Lame Deer, Seeker of Visions,* opens: "I sat there in the vision pit . . . all by myself, left on the hill-top for four days and nights with- out food or water. . . . If *Wakan Tanka,* the Great Spirit, would give me the vision and the power, I would become a medicine man and perform many ceremonies" (Lame Deer and Erdoes 1972, 11f.). The vision quest is both a very real *exterior* adventure beyond the margins of society and an *interior* passage of cleansing. Yet the journey to the "spirit world" is also a sojourn through mythic time to encounter the identity and destiny of one's self and one's people, to *re-member* the story with which to combat "illness and death."

This is surely descriptive of Jesus' venture deep into the wilderness. Following the third gospel's version of the story, we cannot but notice at the outset the use of "forty days" (Luke 4:2). That this was meant to invoke Israel's forty-year wanderings in the wilderness after Egypt has often been pointed out. But what exactly is the connection?

Jesus is somehow *interiorizing* the experience of his people, but I suspect not in the sense that modern religious existentialists (liberal or conservative) understand it. What if Jesus is doing more than dealing with "personal demons" in order to "individuate"? What if he is *retracing the footsteps of Israel through story-time,* in order to discover where his people went wrong? Jesus believes that his people have lost their bearings, having given in to *mimosis.* He must therefore go back over this ground, and this time practice *mimesis.* Israel's footsteps tread right through his own soul.

This vision quest is a *radical journey:* Jesus must move beyond a diagnosis of pathological *symptoms* to the *root-causes* of the historical crisis of his people. He understands that to forge a different future one must seek *reparation* of the past — especially the repressed and denied past, the traumas that remain deeply embedded in the collective psyche of the present. As Freud put it, "What is unconscious is bound to be repeated." Or: "Those who ignore history are doomed to repeat it." It is the same insight.

But where to begin such an overwhelming task? Sociologist of religion Robert Bellah reminds us that a nation's "myth of origins is a strategic point of departure because ... where a people conceives itself to have started reveals much about its most basic self-conceptions" (1975, 3). For Israel, the myth of origins was placed in the Exodus wilderness. So it is there Jesus, "in the spirit world," must return.

Israel's distinctive identity commenced when they were sprung by Yahweh from Pharaoh's imperial straightjacket: "I will bring *My people* out of Egypt" (Exod. 3:10). Similarly, Jesus' distinctive identity has just been confirmed at baptism: "You are *My child,* the Beloved" (Luke 3:22). Now Jesus, like his ancestors, must struggle in the wilderness to discover what this vocation means.

The temptations are a fundamental test of this identity. "If you are the child of God..." taunts the Devil in refrain (Luke 4:3, 9). This is the question Jesus must answer: Who am I/we, and what story defines me/us? Are my people still interpreted by Yahweh's liberation narrative, or by the story of captivity under Pharaoh's imperial system?

Satan's vocation is to lure us into those other narratives that compete with the biblical one for our allegiance. And the stories of Herod and Caesar, the National Security Council, and the six o'clock news are seductive indeed, for they sing of prosperity, power, and prestige. Jesus can resist them only by staying rooted in the Story. Thus his counterrefrain is "It is written..." (Luke 4:4, 8, 12).

"Give Us Our Bread Day by Day!"

Jesus now stands, in this mythic moment of vision quest, at the point of Israel's origins: alone in the wilderness, surrounded by nothing but the barren rock of the Judean desert, hungering, and understandably anxious about bread (Luke 4:3).

To be in Exodus means to face the harsh realities of life outside the imperial system. This is the first test of character, and in the Story Israel did not find it tolerable:

> The whole Israelite community grumbled against Moses and Aaron.... "Would that we had died at the Lord's hand in the land of Egypt, as we sat by our fleshpots and ate our fill of bread! But you have led us into this desert to die of famine!" (Exod. 16:2-3)

In the Story, however, the God who leads from slavery also offers sustenance: Israel receives the gift of *manna*. But Yahweh's "alternative economy" had a very specific character. The arrangement was that every family would gather just enough bread for their needs. Moreover, the *manna* was given day by day; it could not accumulate (except of course for the Sabbath). No one was to live in surplus, no one in deficit (Exod. 16:12-20).

There was a lesson in all of this, about the connection between the concentration of wealth and enslavement. And this lesson was to be passed on: "Keep an omerful of *manna* for your descendants, that they may see what food I gave you to eat in the desert" (Exod. 16:32). But it was forgotten, and in the settled life of Israel in Canaan the orthodoxy of the nations prevailed: "surplus extraction" and "capital accumulation" inexorably took the place of equitable distribution.

Economic stratification thus became a central complaint of the prophets later in the Story: "The spoil of the poor is in your houses; what do you mean by crushing my people, by grinding the face of the poor?" (Isa. 3:14f.). The imperatives of commercial profit had eclipsed the principles of justice: "We will make the *ephah* small and the *shekel* great, and practice deceit with false balances, buying the poor for silver and the needy for a pair of sandals, and selling sweepings of the wheat" (Amos 8:5f.). And fidelity to international markets had replaced allegiance to God's economy of reciprocity and grace: "I will go after my lovers; they give me my bread and my water, my wool and my flax, my oil and my drink" (Hos. 2:5).

Satan's challenge to turn stones into bread invokes that primal wilderness anxiety about sustenance, ridicules the divine economy as foolishness. Why not exploit the land for profit? After all: *surplus equals security.* Can Jesus renew the Story by making a different choice at this archetypal crossroad?

He does, by recalling the lesson of the *manna:* "Not by bread alone." This does not imply a repudiation of economics in favor of the "higher spiritual life," as is the usual interpretation of religious privatists. No, Jesus is countering with the first of his three citations from Deuteronomy, the book of *re-membering.* Here he cites Moses' warning to the people as they stood at the borders of Canaan, with its promises of prosperity, not to forget the principles of the divine economy (Deut. 8:3 = Luke 4:4). He is resuming the journey on "the road not taken," where the true measure of social wealth is not affluence, but "enough for everyone."

This principle will be *re-membered* again by Jesus at other crucial points in journey. It has been noted that the three temptations in Luke correspond, in reverse order, to the first three petitions of the Lord's prayer (see Luke 11:1–4). (I will refer to this simply as "the Prayer," since it is definitive of what disciples should ask for, just as Exodus is definitive of "the Story.") Moreover, Jesus *reenacts* during his ministry these same three themes, turning them into object lessons.

Jesus' Deuteronomic defense here is echoed in "Give us our bread day by day," the central petition of the Prayer (Luke 11:3). And it is *reenacted* in his feeding of the poor *in the wilderness* (Luke 9:10–17). There, while his disciples' cannot see past market constraints (9:12f.), he demonstrates the *manna* economics of sharing and justice: "And all ate and were satisfied" (9:17).

"May Your Sovereignty Be Realized!"

The second temptation both escalates the conflict and retraces the next stage in the journey of Israel. Satan parades "all the kingdoms of the world" before Jesus, and offers to grant him vassal-jurisdiction over them (Luke 4:5–7).

The narrative here is very matter of fact in its analysis of state power. First, the notion that a pantheon of principalities could be viewed "in a moment" suggests that all forms of political hegemony are essentially the same: seen one, seen 'em all. Second, there is no question but that they are all administered under the authority of the

Prince of Death himself: he can "deliver them to whom he wishes" Indeed! Third, the power is the glory — and therein lies the seduction. Would that the churches could maintain such a clear perspective on politics!

Israel faced this crossroads in the Story, a moment poignantly narrated in 1 Samuel 8. The community of Israel again gathers in complaint, this time demanding "a king to govern us" (8:5). The concentration of wealth *necessitates* the centralization of power. The elder Samuel, representing the old republican federation of the Judges (Judg. 21:25), inherited from the wilderness, warns of the dire consequences of such a political project. It will mean the construction of a military machine and compulsory conscription (8:11–13), state expropriation through eminent domain and oppressive taxation (8:14–18).

But Israel was losing its vision of "holiness" — that is, its distinct identity. "No! We are determined to have a king over us so that we also may be like other nations" (8:19). Sure enough the house of David would soon establish oppressive hegemony throughout Palestine, making Israel indistinguishable from the other powers. *Mimosis:* A people liberated from Pharaoh were on their way to becoming like him.

This drift, too, was contested in the Story, as Jacques Ellul points out in his book *Anarchy and Christianity.* The Hebrew court historians, defying the conventions of antiquity, systematically reproached rather than eulogized the "great" kings of Israel. In addition, "for every king there was a prophet... often a severe critic of royal acts." Ellul concludes that the Hebrew Scriptures "ascribed no value to the state, to political authority, or to the organization of that authority" (1991, 55).

At this crossroads, too, Jesus again takes his stand. Once more invoking Deuteronomy, he plainly identifies the issue as one of "service" and the sole sovereignty of Yahweh (Deut. 6:13 = Luke 4:8). This time the exhortation is taken from the heart of Moses' sermon on *mimesis,* the *Shema:* "Hear O Israel" (Deut. 6:4ff.). If a people's true identity follows from its "relations of production," so too from its system of governance.

This is *re-membered* too in the second petition of the Prayer: "May *Your* sovereignty be realized." To pray this was to delegitimize every alternative jurisdiction; otherwise would we not simply have been instructed to ask God's protection over the king-of-the-moment? And again later Jesus *reenacts* the principle, by subverting the conventional expectations of political leadership in his own messianic practice, all the way to the cross (see Luke 19:38; 23:1–3). It seems the first-century authorities understood perfectly the implications of

Yahweh's exclusive sovereignty; it is *we* who have gotten the Story "confused."

"Your Name Remain Holy!"

What an extraordinary preface to the third and final test of characters: "And then the Devil transported Jesus to Jerusalem, and set him on the pinnacle of the Temple" (Luke 4:9). Satan with Jesus in tow. Satan with access to the holiest place. Satan quoting Scripture. It ought to give us pause about every religious claim to represent God.

Satan knows that behind every political economy is a theology, so he turns the tables and thumps his Bible. But he chooses his text carefully: Psalm 91. A powerful statement of God's protection of those who "abide," it is all too easily misunderstood, like so much of Scripture. When read through the hermeneutics of power and privilege the psalm becomes a tune of entitlement, a hymn to invulnerability, and finally an ode to empire. We know how "A Mighty Fortress Is Our God" (Ps. 91:2) can become a song of the Reich — and thus truly what Phyllis Trible (1984) would call a "text of terror." And indeed it did, in imperial Israel, and every Christian empire since.

What Jesus confronts in this last temptation is the ultimate form of idolatry: identifying God's name with our historical projects. This is the theology of entitlement: God is on our side. We will prevail "though a thousand fall at your side" (91:7, a favorite verse of military chaplains), because "our cause is right, our cause is just." Divinely appointed, historically favored, we stride the globe, treading upon evil empires and trampling two-bit dictators in disfavor (91:13). And utterly convinced of our own innocence.

In the Story the currents of economic and political domination culminated in the construction of the centralized Temple-State under the Davidic dynasty. Originally envisioned as a storehouse for redistribution of the community's surplus, the "house of God" became the reification of imperial Israel's power and privilege. Instead of a place where sacrifices were offered on behalf of the people, it became a place where the people were offered in sacrifice to the state. So again the prophets railed:

> Do not trust in these deceptive words: "This is the Temple of the Lord...." Has this house, which is called by my name, become a den of robbers?... Therefore I will do to the house that is called by my name, in which you trust... just what I did to Shiloh. (Jer. 7:4, 11, 14)

Jesus is about to *re-member* these very words.

Waving Psalm 91:11f. in front of Jesus' nose, the Devil urges him to "take the fall" for empire, assuring him that he will be "borne aloft" by the theology of entitlement. And what a vantage point Satan offers, on the rooftop of the great Second Temple of Herod, above the gleaming capital city of Jerusalem, the center of Israel's universe! It is of course a symbolic perch, the highest place in the "dwelling place of the Most High" (Ps. 91:9). In other words, we are now at the heart of the historical project in question.

One final time Jesus clings to the Deuteronomist: "You shall not test the Lord, as you did at Massah" (Luke 4:12 = Deut. 6:16). The argument comes full circle, for at Massah ("place of temptation") wilderness Israel again despaired of sustenance and pined for Egypt (see Exod. 17:7). Jesus has again chosen the "road less traveled": the radical Yahwist principle of nonidentity, the hedge against every legitimization of domination. It is the leading petition of the Prayer; everything depends upon the holiness, the "otherness," of God's name. The "I am who I am" is no empire's patron, but the animator of the only true historical project: human liberation (Exod. 3:14). And to dramatically emphasize the point, Jesus culminates his public ministry by enacting Jeremiah's ultimatum to the Temple system, invoking the authority of the One who cannot be domesticated (Luke 19:45-20:8).

Having failed to seduce Jesus, the Devil departs, seeking a more "opportune time" (Luke 4:13). The word here, remarkably, is *kairos* — Luke's pointed reminder that the moment of choice for the New Order always has the potential to be an antimoment of capitulation to the Old Order.

"Lead Us Not into Temptation...": Europeans in the American Wilderness

That *kairos* confronts us today in the Quincentenary moment — and the Lenten journey — challenging us to *re-member* and *reenact* the vision quest, to examine the choices of our ancestors and lay bare the roots of *our* national pathologies.

Indeed, the three archetypal crossroads that faced Israel and Jesus also pertain to the story of the Europeans' America. There is not space here to relate our own complex national journey — that is better done by "revisionist" historians such as W. A. Williams (1980) and Howard Zinn (1980), who have adequately demonstrated the tragic ways in which we in the United States have been seduced into empire by our leaders. But perhaps a few generalizations can capture the essential contours of these fateful turning points.

It is true that the origin myths of European immigrants, from Columbus to Cotton Mather, appealed to the biblical stories (see Myers 1991). The religious refugees, economic adventurers, and soldiers of fortune fleeing Old World oppression most often understood themselves to be on Exodus in the New World wilderness. The question is, did these myths symbolize a social practice of *mimesis* or *mimosis*?

The settled subsistence or pastoral nomadic peoples the Europeans encountered in North America had not, for the most part, proceeded down the paths of economic exploitation, political centralization, or empire – for whatever reasons. One need not romanticize pre-Columbian cultures as "noble savages" to acknowledge that with few exceptions their economies operated within the limits of the land's hospitality, their politics remained local, and their alliances limited in power. As Kirkpatrick Sale (1985) put it, these were essentially *bioregional* cultures. Ironically, the largest regional political matrix extant at the time of contact – the Iroquois Confederacy – was characterized by equal representation and pluralism and inspired several key ideas of the colonial drafters of the Constitution.

The European "Exodus" had a different agenda, however. As Puritan preacher Samuel Danforth put it, they were on an "errand into the wilderness." This mission was not about subsistence but prosperity: it aimed to tame, "civilize," and exploit the Promised Land and its peoples. From the beginning ideologies of entitlement and ethnic superiority contaminated the self-understanding of this self-elected "Chosen People." For the European, history could only be about "Progress."

Thus the story of our ancestors in the Americas has been characterized by driving indigenous communities off their lands and destroying or expropriating the natural resources upon which these cultures depended. Reflecting upon immigrants as *uprooted* peoples, Maori sovereignty activist Donna Awatera draws the bitter historical conclusion: dispossessed from their own land, Europeans could *only* dispossess others. So they set about recreating the Old World in the New – its commercialized relations of market-exchange and wage-labor, its technological materialism of surplus-value. "The love of possession is a disease with them," said Sitting Bull of the European neurosis.

From the colonial silver mines of Potosi and fur trade of the old Northwest to the modern clear-cut logging of the Pacific Northwest and strip mining in the Southwest, freedom for the European American has been fundamentally associated with the right to exploit the land for profit. Our people have indeed turned wilderness stones into bread – and mountains into coal pits, forests into board-feet, rivers into interstate power grids, deserts into weapons test-sites, and ultimately, human life into just another commodity. It is hardly too simplistic to say that up to the present the result of this historical project has been to universalize alienation from the land. Economic exploitation became economic domination became economic determinism, reaching now to every corner of the globe. This is the story of "Progress," the first temptation.

"The Power and the Glory..."
America as Empire

W. A. Williams (1980, 36–54) reminds us that there was a real debate among eighteenth-century colonial revolutionaries about the political destiny of the new nation. Virginian John Taylor, for example, envisioned a loose federation of republics and criticized centralized federalism: "The executive power of the United States is infected . . . with a degree of accumulation and permanence of power, sufficient to excite evil moral qualities."

It was however the expansionist designs of Jefferson and Madison that prevailed, a spirit reflected in verse penned by two of the latter's friends:

> Shall we ask what empires yet must arise . . . / when British sons shall spread / Dominion to the north and south and west / From th' Atlantic thru Pacific shores.

Once like Israel a "pilgrim people," European Americans too were becoming like the kings they had supposedly left behind.

The nineteenth century saw the completion of the "domestication" of the entire continent and its native peoples, from the Louisiana Purchase to the Mexican and Indian wars to the closing of the frontiers. This spawned a new project: the consolidation and concentration of U.S. wealth and power. After the Civil War there was increasing urbanization and industrialization, the rise of robber barons and corporate capitalism. This was the era of Manifest Destiny, federal domination "from sea to shining sea" — the second temptation.

But it was at the turn of this century, with the annexation of Hawaii, Puerto Rico, and the Philippines, that the U.S. made its most decisive and fateful choices to become an imperial people. And with this came acquiescence to the third temptation: placing God at the service of our historical designs. The spirit of imperial piety is perhaps best exemplified in President McKinley's infamous comments to a Methodist Church delegation in 1899, justifying U.S. colonization of the Philippines:

> I went down on my knees and prayed to Almighty God for light and guidance. . . . And one night it came to me this way: . . . that we could not give [the Philippines] back to Spain, for that would be cowardly and dishonorable; that we could not turn them over to France and Germany, our commercial rivals in the Orient, for that would be bad business and discreditable; that we could not leave them to themselves, for they

were unfit for self-government.... There was nothing left for us to do but take them all and to educate the Filipinos and uplift and civilize and Christianize them.... Then I went to bed and slept soundly and the next morning sent for the chief engineers of the War Dept.

Such sentiments have characterized U.S. foreign policy throughout the twentieth century, persisting to the present in Bush and Schwarzkopf's invocations of God during Operation Desert Storm.

We who are members of the dominant culture, inheritors of this profoundly flawed legacy, must face the truth. The Devil tempted our ancestors in the wilderness, and they followed him, just like the old Story. We have become like the idols we worshiped: economically and politically dominated and dominating, children of empire.

But there is hope. Jesus retraced the footsteps of his people and showed it is possible to resist the primal temptations to which they succumbed. He summons his disciples to the same struggle with the Prince of Powers: "You who have stood by me in my temptations I commend to the reign of God, as I have been commended" (Luke 22:28). Thus the conclusion of the Prayer: "Lead us not into temptation, but deliver us from evil."

"Today This Scripture Is Fulfilled": Re-vising the Story

There is a peculiarly Lukan epilogue to the temptation narrative, which also functions as a prologue to his gospel Story proper and which is germane to the hope for renewal in our time. The same Spirit that drove Jesus into the wilderness now leads him toward an equally formidable challenge: he must prophesy to his own people (Luke 4:14–16).

Here is another mythic moment. Back in his hometown church, the former altar boy walks to the front, opens the Bible and thumbs to Isaiah, takes a deep breath, and reads:

The Spirit of the Lord...has anointed me to bring good news to the poor...to proclaim liberation to the captives and recovery of sight to the blind, to let the oppressed go free, to proclaim the year of the Lord's favor. (Luke 4:18f. = Isa. 61:1f.)

Jesus closes the book gently, fixes his gaze upon the congregation, "The Story begins again, here, now" (4:21).

With this, Jesus' vision quest to retrace the journey of Israel arrives again at the present and leads to the future. Isaiah's vision of the healing of Israel is *"re-vised"* – that is, "seen again." The old Story is reanimated: a people enslaved are again offered the journey of liberation, given another chance to embrace the just economics and the nonoppressive politics of the undomesticated God. But Jesus' synagogue audience does not have "eyes to see" this *re-vision* of their history (Luke 4:24–30). The Old Order is too familiar, the myths of entitlement too strong. The same must be said of our own people, our own time, our own story.

What might it mean to rediscover an Exodus identity in this Quincentenary *kairos?* Jim Corbett — southwestern rancher, Sanctuary conspirator, Quaker — in his brilliant book *Goatwalking* argues that the wilderness wanderings of Abraham, Moses, and Jesus bespeak of the vision of a *cimarron* community:

> A *cimarron* — sometimes anglicized to "maroon" — is a domesticated animal or slave that goes free. The antonym of *cimarron* is *reducido* ("reduced"), used by the Spanish conquistadores . . . to characterize and classify tamed Native Americans (1991, 4).

He reminds us that this is an American tradition: during the first centuries of the Conquest escaped Indian and African slaves "marooned" themselves on remote islands or highlands, setting up liberated communities outside the domain of colonization.

Corbett is *re-membering* the true character of Exodus journeying: *as the reversal of the grand march of Progress!* Wilderness "errantry," he contends, is a defection from the dominating, objectifying practices of settled "civilization," characterized by the exploitation of nature for the purpose of accumulating wealth. "To live peacefully as members of wildland communities, human beings who have been domesticated to live by possession must become untamed," must break our "cultural compulsion to remake and consume" the world. And he reminds us that any attempt to "go feral" today must reckon with the spiritual demands of a vision quest: "Whoever leaves the world to wander alone in the wildlands should be prepared to meet a devil or two, when busyness ceases to drown out the dreamside."

We return, then, to Merton's insight: Today, "everywhere is desert." We cannot escape the Metropolis; it is within and around us. Choosing Exodus over Progress for people of faith in North America will mean summoning the courage to face our *mimosis* of the dominant cultural pathologies. By *re-membering* our national experience we can understand the temptations that historically have "led us into *mimesis.*" Then the Spirit may empower us to resist the Devil's seductions — which are now thinly disguised in the transnational grandiosity of the post–Gulf War "New World Order."

The good news is that if we repent — that is, *change directions* — we can *re-vision* our story, the ideals and hopes of our people. But if the next five hundred years are to be different, we must listen to the silenced stories of all those whom the imperial narrative has marginalized, the voices of *every* culture and race and class. We need to learn from the first peoples of this place, whose ancient wisdom may yet help us. And we must rediscover and dance again to that national music that has competed dissonantly with the anthems of empire – tunes such as "liberty and justice for all," "I have a dream," and "Give me your poor huddled masses."

This will be the longest Exodus; the Quincentenary is only the first year of the rest of our lives. It will be a journey of resistance and contemplation into the heart of our own collective darkness. Surrounded as we are in capitalist culture by stories that are mere entertainment, people of faith must practice *mimesis*. Then, like the Indian elder, we too can confess: "Their evil is mighty, but it can't stand up to our Story."

References

Auerbach, Eric. *Mimesis.* Princeton: Princeton University Press, 1968.

Bellah, Robert. *The Broken Covenant: American Civil Religion in Time of Trial.* New York: Seabury, 1975.

Campbell, Joseph, and Bill Moyers. *The Power of Myth.* New York: Doubleday, 1988.

Corbett, Jim. *Goatwalking: A Guide to Wildland Living, A Quest for the Peaceable Kingdom.* New York: Viking, 1991.

Douglass, James W. *Resistance and Contemplation.* New York: Doubleday, 1972.

Ellul, Jacques. *Anarchy and Christianity.* Trans. G. Bromiley. Grand Rapids: Eerdmans, 1991.

Lame Deer, John Fire, and Richard Erdoes. *Lame Deer, Seeker of Visions: The Life of a Sioux Medicine Man.* New York: Simon and Schuster, 1972.

Merton, Thomas. *Thoughts in Solitude.* New York: Farrar, Straus and Cudahy, 1957.

Myers, Ched. "We're All in the Same Boat: A Reflection on Gospel Journeys and the Quincentennial." *Sojourners* 20, no. 8 (October 1991): 30ff.

Sale, Kirkpatrick. *Dwellers in the Land: The Bioregional Vision.* San Francisco: Sierra Club, 1985.

Silko, Leslie Marmon. *Ceremony.* Penguin, 1977.

Thomas, Guboo Ted. "The Land Is Sacred: Renewing the Dreaming in Modern Australia." In G. Trompf, ed. *The Gospel Is Not Western: Black Theologies from the Southwest Pacific.* New York: Orbis, 1987, 90ff.

Trible, Phyllis. *Texts of Terror: Literary-Feminist Readings of Biblical Narratives.* Philadelphia: Fortress, 1984.

Vecsey, Christopher. *Imagine Ourselves Richly: Mythic Narratives of North American Indians.* San Francisco: Harper & Row, 1991.

Williams, W. A. *Empire as a Way of Life.* New York: Oxford University Press, 1980.

Zinn, Howard. *A People's History of the United States.* New York: Harper & Row, 1980.

26

The New Jerusalem Community, Cincinnati, Ohio

FOUR DISCIPLES

SIMPLY PUT, Richard has been our father.

Not in an emotionally warm, physical sense –
although we each may have some strong emotions regarding
    him,
and his presence here has been very much "felt" for years after
    he's been gone (for better or worse) –
but Richard has been a father to us,
a strength, a wisdom beyond his years
that makes you sit up and take notice even when
you swore to yourself that you really didn't need a father at all.
He led us, guided us, taught us, through some of the most
    important years of our lives.
The community here may or may not last some years;
but we who knew him are forever changed.
What he engendered in us, individually and collectively,
will always affect us.

What follows are a few reflections by three brothers and sisters
who lived through, witnessed, many of the fifteen years that Richard
was with us. Ed and John write as those who were closest. Anne writes
in the intimacy of the Spirit, which so many of us share, each in
our own way, having encountered Richard. As St. John wrote, a full
accounting of everything that he did and said among us would fill, at
least, several books. Richard has been a singular blessing to us, for
which we will always thank our loving God.

BILL LONNEMAN

TO BETTER UNDERSTAND the truth of what happened between us, I will write of you in "relational" terms. Aren't you, after all, the one who enticed the community with the image of the Trinity, urging us to break through its obtuse theology to experience the relationship beyond?

It is odd to me how you are known throughout the world as the founder of New Jerusalem. Just a word, certainly, but one that feels so sterile, planned, or manufactured. Does "founder" express the profound excitement of our own Big Bang, our birthing, in which God chose you to play cocreator? Perhaps now, in the 1990s, we're embarrassed to admit we were (and still are) searching for the Father; but then, in the 1970s, it was what our hearts yearned for.

Could any of us possibly have confused you, smooth-faced, naive boy-wonder with the Creator, Father God? Oh, yes, but more often than not we were grateful and grace-filled to be led by you to the Father, Abba, daddy, the-one-who-delights-in-us, the one whom we thought only had a right hand to sit by. "Behold the manner of love the Father has bestowed on us, that we should be called children of God, for such we are."

You seemed your truest self here as brother and teacher. Realistically, only a few of the young men were drawn close to you as friend, brother, and disciple. All of us, though, knew you as teacher, rabboni, opener of the Word. The well-read among us recognized and delighted in your ability to extrude the gems of wisdom from brilliant philosophers, psychologists, and theologians and remake them in the light of the gospel. Most importantly, none of us were left unscathed by your revelation of Scripture where the two-edged sword pierced our minds, hearts, and souls. Our reality was turned inside-out, and since then I personally have only been able to trust and believe in that which is incarnational, paradoxical, or paschal.

Many have said that your moving to Albuquerque has allowed New Jerusalem truly to become church/community. Like the dumbfounded disciples who were left staring up into space on Ascension, we also stood astounded, agape (but not dumbstruck), looking westward as you left. Loss, grief, joy, anger, and acceptance washed over us in this new baptism by death. Perhaps only then could the sky break open as over the River Jordan with the Spirit of God coming down on us, naming us again his Beloved, People-of-Mine. And as the Holiest of Spirits re-creates us each day, so too does your spirit still shape us. You are our community's holy ghost with an edge. You are the one who haunts us still in the late evening hours, in the corners of our consciences, in uncalled upon moments; urging us, beckoning us to build and live in this kingdom that is and is not yet.

I have been created to dance for God on a stage that (I fear for my soul) is much too small. I dance hard and fast and often furiously but always with a grateful heart for you father/brother/holy haunter.

ANNE MARTINA

꙳

IN THE ALMOST TWENTY YEARS that I have known Richard, many things have come to pass and many blessings received because of my relationship with him. There have been many tapes, videos, books — many words, maybe too many. I have heard Richard speak hundreds of times, accompanied him across the country on traveling teams, been arrested with him for civil disobedience in Washington, D.C., and participated with him in other protests and rallies. But the other side of the activism was experienced without many words, in the quiet of the hills of west central Kentucky. This contemplative experience would prove to be of great significance along Richard's journey as well as the journey of three of his disciples/sons. In 1985, Richard left New Jerusalem to spend a month praying and being with "God alone" in Thomas Merton's hermitage at the Trappist Monastery of Gethsemani-Bardstown, Kentucky. Fred, John, and I ("the Boys") have become brothers because, I think, we have allowed ourselves to be "sons" and allowed/taught Richard to become "father." The power of the father/son relationship has been for all of us, life-changing and allowed us, in the end, to be fathers. Also life-changing was the experience of Gethsemani as the three of us were privileged to join Richard for the last days of his retreat. The following are journal entries:

May 11, 1985

If indeed there are lines of energy,
I have been sucked in.
If there are really angel-visitors,
I have been graced.
If there is a simple response for what has happened to me
A simple response for a simple man,
To explain how I find myself to be in God
Please explain what has happened to me and who is responsible.

To say that confusion abounds would be an understatement. But I can point to one holy night where I was branded with a sizzling iron, enslaved by a merciful freedom. I was uprooted, overturned, and left dazed by my enslaver. Who is responsible? Along the journey's path there are occurrences, oases that I am not able to name but wherein my soul finds freedom and knows grace. Elements of the "spiritual" break through the self-created self and caress you/me into a knowledge of something wonderful, perhaps God. It happened this night.

It must be difficult to sort out my confusion. Deep well, pathway, images, and hazy remembrances of wine-filled nights overflow and flood my days. My mind cannot stray from the well. It feeds and refreshes me. Graced, gifted, blessed, no matter the words, I know that the brothers have experienced "mercy within mercy within mercy."

To prepare for the weekend at Gethsemani, I picked up a few of Merton's books and read about his entry into the monastery and his need for a hermitage. Richard had been there for almost thirty days and I wondered if he had changed and become different on a spiritual level and therefore different with me since I have no spiritual level. I am sure that God spoke to him and instructed him to disassociate himself from me. Fred and John are going and I am somewhat concerned that I will be a third wheel and not understand what I will see or experience.

May 12, 1985

Saturday morning finally arrives and Fred and I went shopping for provisions. (Three cans of soup, four apples, a box of granola bars, and two gallons of wine.) We pick John up, and knowing that we will not eat "real" food for at least twenty-four hours, we stop at Burger King for two double whoppers with cheese, fries, and pop. Fred, of course, orders a "Whaler" and coffee. It's "holy" food.

The ride down was pleasant enough. We have always sung together, the three of us, for years. Harmonies weaving throughout. We talk about the dynamic of our relationship with Richard and with each other. Richard has had to practice what he preaches about God's unconditional love. It surely must be difficult for him to continue loving the three of us. We are not exactly the perfect sons (except for Fred — he's a THREE). We traveled well out of our way. Actually we got lost and arrived an hour late. Richard was on the road (literally) looking at his watch, tapping his foot in disgust. "You're late!" He got in the car and we discovered we would not have to sneak around as we were prepared to do. We were expected and welcomed by the abbot. On the road, Richard had found "the perfect symbol" for his days at the monastery. That's just great. It was a hubcap with spokes gathered at the center. All things lead to the center. We comment that there is nothing there once you arrive and the three of us feel that Richard has lost his mind.

We are escorted to the guesthouse and meet Brother Bruno, a lovely old man I had met once before. He loves Richard's tapes and he knelt on the floor the last time we were there for a blessing. His gentleness and humility were profound and typified the monastery. We were led through the guesthouse and near the church sacristy met

Brother Justin, a young monk with a shaved head and lengthy red beard. Dressed in jeans and T-shirt, he is gracious, simple, and forgiving of our tardiness. He paints icons for the chapel and is obviously very talented. He shows us some of his paintings but is humble and praises the work of others who, he says, "Do much better work than I." He suggests that we see his room. Richard declines the invitation for us, thinking that we might disturb someone. We protest and Richard finally asks that we see the room. We are led to a small cubicle that reminds me of my college dorm. Then it's outside to barns, bees, lakes, and hills. We begin the trail that will lead us to the garden where two statues dominate: the apostles (the brothers) sleeping side by side by side, unable to stay awake with Jesus. Further on the trail we found the statue of Jesus, hands raised to his face. We are all moved by the sights. We climb another knob and joke that one of us is not in top shape to be running the hills.

Returning to the monastery, we leave Justin for the first of many times. We know he is crying as he leaves, and our hearts ache. As he walks away he turns and asks "Please, call me Dale." Dale is his pre-Trappist name. I believe he begins to see the relationship we all share and is pained that he hasn't found the same intimacy and "brotherhood" in the monastery. We begin our walk to Merton's hermitage, excited about finally seeing it, when a deer crosses the trail directly in front of us. The house is how I expected it and remembered from the few pictures I'd seen: isolated, rustic, fishing-camp style. We wondered if Dale could come back with us that evening. After evening prayer, Richard makes our request. Dale agrees and will sneak back after prayers. We hear he's excited. We walk a bit and look for fossils with John. He is such a boy and, of all of us, has the most childlike innocence. The love we have for one another is genuine. I am sure Richard had no idea of the eternal bond created when he introduced us years ago. Dale is already at the house when we return. We crack open the first of the two gallons of wine. We drink and talk about Merton, the monastery, community. We question Dale about the monks seemingly being at arm's length from each other. "God alone" or "God, alone" — either emphasis leaves me feeling empty. It must be the wise man who can understand Merton's "When I am alone, I am no longer lonely" (*Sign of Jonas*). As the night goes on Richard selects from some of Merton's first copies and reads to us. It was perfect!

> Sweet brother, if I do not sleep,
> my eyes are flowers for your tomb...

I reach for Fred to make sure he is okay and to let him know that I too am thinking of his brother who had died several years ago. We go on to talk about Merton's death and the premonitions he had:

... Everything that touches you will burn you ...

The night continues. Lights go out, a fire is lit and soon Richard must convince Dale to begin the long walk back to the monastery. Somehow I think the walk will be longer tonight. We all go to the front porch to say goodbye. We try to sing for Dale but it sounds terrible. We try again and improve. We begin singing a 1960s song, "Find the Cost of Freedom," and Dale begins to sing with us. "Mother earth will swallow you, lay your body down." I am blown away. He is one of us, just a boy really, in a monk's suit. He said it himself. He is a "marked man." We hug him goodbye and he refuses, almost, to let go. We walk down the moonlit trail, crying. We stand silent, not knowing what to say. Something happened. Who is responsible?

We continue to talk and enjoy the wine. We are not too drunk to know that we are blessed brothers who have been given more than we deserve. Sometime in the early morning we gather in Merton's little chapel. Richard prays "with a grateful heart" for the days in this space. We pray for Dale, with him I think. Around 2:30 A.M. John sleeps on the mattress by the fire, Richard disappears to his room. We forget to say "goodnight." We figure that he needs time to himself this last night. Fred and I talk a bit then fall asleep. The brothers, side by side by side, unable to stay awake while the fire blazes in the darkness. I wake a number of times, sleeping bag in disarray, my bare back frozen on the cement floor. At 5:00 A.M. I feel a tick crawling on me, my fourth for the night and I escort him outside. Fred and I awake at six, knowing we had experienced something profound yet unable to explain it. All we are able to do is look into each other's eyes and question what had happened. Luckily we experienced the same thing – the experience of being "in God." We put on a pot of coffee, for times like these, and embrace. Life is good. Who is responsible? After the coffee and some sawdust-like granola bars we head down the trail looking for deer. Finding none, we return past a clearing we've named "Merton's Driving Range." Richard wakes and we decide to head for Carl's hermitage on top of one of the knobs – forty-five minutes up, thirty minutes down. We make it back to the monastery just in time for liturgy. We are invited by the abbot to join the monks in the sanctuary. After Mass we are told that Dale is unable to say goodbye. He will write and explain.

I hope someone can explain. To write in words the experience of knowing God, knowing my brothers, my father as living in God is beyond comprehension and certainly beyond explaining in this journal. There are lines of energy, charged somehow with grace. We got in the way.

Suppose a man were once in his life,
to vanish into God for the space of a minute.
                                                    —Thomas Merton

May 13, 1985

After writing last night, I had a wonderful time of silence outside on
the front porch. I can see the silhouette of the tree that symbolizes
You in me, me in You. I was able to pray for John and Richard now
in New Mexico. Everything has become more beautiful, and there is
very little that I find to criticize. An odd thing happened when I went
to bed. I felt all my loves merging together into one love. Strange, eh?

May 14, 1985

I attempted to stay alone with you tonight but fell asleep at the Center.
I feel at peace with everyone for some reason. I asked to know you
in a deep way, and I believe it is happening. These evenings are great
and I appreciate Steph's giving them to me. She seems to understand
that something holy has happened to me. You must surely be a simple
God and a God of the simple. It cannot possibly be as difficult as I
make things out to be. Moving to Albuquerque remains the center
of my thoughts lately. I feel that I could see you in the desert. My
time is limitless, and your love is everlasting. I am quite content to
know you little by little. Still no word from John yet. He's so bad at
calling.

May 19, 1985

I just left Fred. It was good to talk with him about Gethsemani. It far
surpassed what I would call a religious experience. It became a unifier
of God in me, me in God. I'm so grateful that I have not experienced
this alone but have found understanding and similar "conversions" in
my brothers.

May 21, 1985

John called regarding property in New Mexico. Richard will stay on
in Albuquerque and hopefully talk to the bishop. John cried while we
talked. Something deep is happening in him. Bless him and Richard
both.

                                                    ED COLINA

FROM TIME TO TIME we have encounters with people that will leave a mark on us for life. Father Richard has been that person for countless numbers of people. I count myself among some of the lucky to have walked with him in his discoveries into Love. From the very earliest days with him I began to see a journey, a dream that wanted to take root. I didn't know if he was revealing some truth to me, or bringing out some deep part of myself that had never seen the light. It was this kind of nurturing that made it easy to risk your heart. And risk is the key word in his early teachings. But risk was not without its reward. I was becoming a son to Father Richard, and a new life began to open up before me.

In the days that followed and as the community grew I watched like a wide-eyed child at the marvels the Lord worked through Father Richard. Too countless are the number of lives touched by his goodness. There were the little moments too, moments when his own childlike nature would come forth and marvel at that which adults barely see. He knew of his power as father figure and of his littleness. He would say, "Words will not save anyone," and we would laugh at the number of tapes he has made. But his were not just words. I have seen his faith in action – from caring for an infant in the middle of the night to speaking the gospel before the powers of injustice.

I have with many others been taught the joy of the "freedom of the sons and daughters of God" by this man, that freedom to live as the little ones of God.

I have also seen the hidden Father as only a son can. It is that which will forever bond me to him.

May we take action for those who have no voice and come to know the joy of Christ.

JOHN HERDTNER

27

Richard Rohr and the Enneagram

HELEN PALMER

❖

The context in which I met Richard is as interesting as the man himself. He came to an Enneagram class that I was teaching in Santa Fe. It was many years ago, at the time when growth material was first going mainstream. Our participants were the same sangha of therapists, artists, academics, and locals that have welcomed all the inner-life traditions to America and given them a home. Richard was the only priest in evidence, and he fit in remarkably well.

The Enneagram has since come to world attention, but I still feel that I speak to the spiritually committed minority of different social groups. From my point of view, everyone who walks in the door is interested in the inner life and follows some form of meditation practice. I like living in a systematic delusion. From my perspective every policeman, teenager, housewife, and politician is a seeker. While I know that isn't true, it makes me feel secure to generalize from my small sector of the world.

Years later I heard that Richard had published a book on the system. He had been teaching in a sector that I knew nothing about. From his perspective, most people look Catholic; from my perspective few of them are, but he and his coauthor seemed to have taken a broad-minded approach to the material because my students were enthusiastic. Eventually it was translated from German to English and one of them brought it to me.

It was a good description of Enneagram territory without a fence in sight. No red ink, no cautionary warnings, no guards surrounding a reader's mind. The book is written for Christians without discounting other routes. It could have been otherwise. Maps like these have been a subject of discussion and warfare for generations. They focus our anxiety about the inner journey. It makes us nervous when an experience on our route is also claimed by others, because when you enter new country, your map is all you own.

Each tradition has a path to the spiritual territory. They coincide at certain teachings, where they share a common view. The Enneagram is one such crossroad, joining personality with the inner life. It attracts people from every imaginable sector and is currently moving through international channels, business, and the Catholic Church. I follow the oral tradition, which relies on speakers to represent the nine Enneagram types. The Asian panels are my favorite. A real United Nations scene. Hong Kong business people, Anglo expatriates, Buddhist housewives, a Chinese nun. The sound technician at these events winds up wreathed in smiles because the panelists speak English with different accents. The tech bangs his earphones in the sound box at the back of the hall. He doesn't know which channel to amplify because the voices and bodies don't match. He's got a Pakistani who sounds like a Scotsman, a Filipino with a Texas drawl.

I credit the Rohr book with precipitating a lot of this good will. It somehow fits my memory of him, the only religious in my training group. How remarkable, how ordinary all of these people seem to be with each other. They are not necessarily liberals, they are not stretching their minds. They are sitting there being themselves, telling their stories to each other, as if we did this every day. I like to look out at an audience with people dressed in religious habits and a good percentage in business suits – people attracted to a crossroad teaching who are otherwise separated by race, religion, and class.

In the last five years I've been traveling. In every class there are several who are there because of Rohr. They think it's a good thing to watch their thoughts and feelings. They think it's part of their Christian path. So again, I'm living in an encapsulated delusion. Now I think that every Catholic is a seeker. I think it was a stroke of genius, although probably unintentional, that the Enneagram came out in Germany coauthored by a Lutheran minister and a Catholic priest. It seemed to me, in my systematic delusion, that every little town in Germany has two church spires, one Lutheran and one Catholic, sometimes on the same block. I like it when people come to class from those little towns to study the material that I learned in a different setting.

Last month I talked to Richard on the phone, the first conversation that we've had in years. We're planning to teach at a psychological conference in Washington, D.C., and I'm thinking that it's going to be okay. His talk is about sin and conversion, and I'm leading practices to develop inner perception. I think it's going to be great. We'll show up and look like we've been there all along.

– 28 –

Prayer and Protest

ANDREAS RICHTER-BÖHNE

❖

In the Spring of 1977 together with some friends of mine I visited the New Jerusalem Community in Cincinnati, where I got to know Richard Rohr. Living in the community for a week was enough to deepen in me a longing for a believable lifestyle in the church and in society. I remember the conversations we had about Dietrich Bonhoeffer. We talked about his attempt to put "Prayer and Action of the Just," in other words contemplation and struggle, spirituality and action, to the proof in his own life and in the life testimony of the church. "Our being Christians today will consist of only two things: in the prayer and action of the just among men and women." And so in Germany during the Nazi period he stood all by himself, which has made him all the more fascinating ever since. He has become a sort of church father and saint for those who are fighting for a radical lifestyle in the imitation of Christ. His words and deeds are a continual source of strength.

And then we also talked about Bonhoeffer's vision of "common life." This is another longing that has impelled me since those days in Cincinnati: longing for life in a community of brothers and sisters, who are truly committed to one another, both with their poverty and their gifts, with their wounded souls and their desire to become whole; the longing for life in a community where God's service touches the depths of one's personal life; the longing for life in a community that, by being with one another and for one another, perceives and endures the inner strife of each person and of the world at large, while taking liberating steps toward conversion.

In the early 1980s when NATO was rearming with Pershing II and Cruise missiles, I spontaneously found myself joining the Christian initiative "Life without Armaments." I joined the regional group in Heidelberg in January 1983. We began to prepare ourselves for acts of civil disobedience and launched a campaign in front of NATO headquarters in Heidelberg. We took our inspiration from Martin Luther King, Jr., Mahatma Gandhi, and the Berrigan brothers. During these months I read, along with others, Jim Wallis's book *Call to Conversion*. This critical American voice against the planned rearmament in Europe helped us in our preparations. It created a feeling of solidarity and prevented us from making sweeping judgments about the United States and its people.

In June 1983 Richard Rohr, accompanied by Jim Wallis, visited West Germany for the first time. During the German Protestant Church Assembly they delivered lectures and led Bible study groups. A few days before this they had been arrested at a peace demonstration in the rotunda of the Capitol in Washington, D.C. They had gathered there to pray for peace and against the nuclear arms race. The grounds for their arrest was that it's against the law to pray in the Capitol.

Now they had come as guests to Germany and were visiting us in Heidelberg. There and on a weekend with them in Würzburg I "grasped" existentially for the first time in my life that my decision for political resistance was a *spiritual* decision. That is, from this point on it was no longer a moral decision, in the sense of appeals like, "Defend yourselves now, finally!" "At long last, do something to fight it!"

The "second conversion" I experienced then was one of the most moving moments in my life. I realized that the energy for my commitment came not from a "you must," i.e., from the law, but from the fact that God was unconditionally taking charge of me in my utmost depths. This released in me a feeling of tremendous solidarity with "the others." Can it be right in God's eyes that we in the West threaten the people in the East with massive overkill, while the poor are still waiting for justice?

On that June weekend in Würzburg we held a worship service together, we sang, and we prayed. I told the group about our planned civil disobedience. Earlier Jim Wallis had told us about Filipino friends of his who were exposed to severe persecution and threats against their life. One of them had recently been murdered. All this shook me and left me feeling very vulnerable.

Together with others I went back encouraged to Heidelberg. There we prepared ourselves for action. The most important development, to me, was that we began to meet regularly for prayer. Finally we planned that in October we would join with nonviolent groups to carry out a "prayer for peace-cum-blockade" at the main gate of NATO headquarters. At once I and others became aware that we couldn't pray together at this sort of place *without first having discovered with one another the power of prayer.*

Part of the campaign was a three-day fast from August 6 to 9 (in memory of the dropping of the atom bombs on Hiroshima and Nagasaki) on the sidewalk across the street from NATO headquarters. Here I discovered how prayer becomes a source of power. It took away my fear of the imponderables in the nonviolent actions. We chose as a motto for our fall action "Choose Life."

During the period leading up to this action I had learned of a letter from the bishop of my Protestant regional church in Bavaria. On September 22, 1983, he had written to all the church's co-workers and to the parish councils:

> In recent weeks and months there have been widely publicized negotiations about securing and maintaining the peace.... In discussions about the question of peace the Sermon on the Mount can help us recognize and achieve our specific contribution as Christians to the cause of peace.... With respect to prayer Jesus warns us, first of all, "Whenever you pray, do not be like the hypocrites; for they love to stand and pray in the synagogues and at the street corners, so that they may be praised by others" (Matt. 6:5). Prayer has been given to us so that in all our cares and trials, including our concern for peace, we can turn to God. Thus, we may not use prayer in order to be seen by people, to draw attention to ourselves and our goals and to increase public support for our opinions. Prayer is not a tool for demonstrators. Whoever does such things, as the Sermon on the Mount says, has already gotten his reward.

Bishop Dr. Hanselmann passed the same judgment on the fasting actions: "Fasting for peace has...a deep meaning. However in our days fasting also seems to be serving the purpose of demonstration."

This letter struck me to the core. Had I landed on the side of the hypocrites, had I already "gotten my reward," because I was fasting for peace and praying, on the street no less, draped with a placard reading "No more Hiroshimas"? Was I misusing prayer and fasting?

The bishop's letter said nothing about the possibility that the people who were planning the installation of nuclear weapons — quite often involving God in the process — had "already gotten their reward." The bishop's concern was aimed at people like me: "I am worried that some among us vehemently invoke the prophetic service of the church in order to lend emphasis to their personal opinions."

Then there was mention of the actions of civil disobedience, and the label of false prophets in sheep's clothing was applied to those who "prepare young people for so-called violations of the rules or encourage them to do so." Finally those who carry out actions of civil disobedience were reminded "that by showing disrespect for our free, democratic legal system they are sawing vigorously away at the branch on which we, far better placed than many others, are sitting."

I had had long discussions with my friends in our peace group about the spiritual and political aspects of our actions, and in a long letter dated October 9, 1983, I addressed the bishop:

Your statements betray . . . more concern with internal church developments than with the ongoing process of rearmament, and the increased
danger it brings with it. I had already gotten this impression at the Pente-
cost session of the brotherhood of pastors this year, when you said that
there were already so many atomic rockets stationed in our country
that it didn't matter if more were added. . . . And with regard to the positions taken by other church leaders, it occurs to me that anxiety over
the peace movement is greater than the fear of the prevalent security
policy.

This is the only way I can explain your one-sided interpretation
of the Sermon on the Mount. Your selection of verses alters its actual context . . . The Sermon on the Mount begins with the encouraging
words of promise in the Beatitudes, not with any warnings from Jesus.
The first thing it says is "Blessed are you!" Next the reality of the community gathered around Jesus is described as "light," "salt," and the "city
on the mountain." This means the public profession and testimony of
Christians before the world. Only after this do we hear the critical remarks on prayer or its misuse for demonstrative purposes. But, as I see it,
this criticism can just as well refer to prayer during church services and
in the privacy of one's own room. Self-righteousness and hypocrisy are
not attitudes that automatically mark the actions of Christians in public.
In the individual case it all comes down to the content and purpose of
the action.

But you have raised Jesus' statements to the level of absolute principles, from the height of which you try to define prayer. On the basis
of the context and the overall testimony of Scripture I maintain that
this is not a legitimate approach. The ideology of deterrence is one of
these forces to which we have surrendered ourselves and which we
must combat in obedience to our faith. Thus when we pray and sing at
demonstrations or other actions, we are doing this simply because our
identity as Christians is on the line there, because we have reason to
cry out, but also to praise God and to ask God for peace. We are bound
to say this to all men and women, witnessing to what Christians place
their trust in and protesting against what must not, for God's sake, come
about. We can resist only as praying individuals.

In a brief response the bishop referred to numerous statements
in recent months on issues concerning the arms race. This was also
the reason, he argued, why he had said nothing on this point to the
church's co-workers.

A propos of my objections to his interpretation of the Sermon on
the Mount, the bishop replied:

No one disputes that the reality of Jesus' community as salt, light, and
the city on the mountain relates to the public profession of Christians.
But aren't actions of civil disobedience sometimes prematurely, uncriti-
cally, and falsely equated with this gospel testimony? In that case where
is the proper distinction and correlation between Law and Gospel, be-

tween justification and sanctification? . . . I cannot "combat" the concept of military deterrence as univocally as you do "in obedience to the faith." I cannot simply dismiss the historical experiences of this century. Theologically speaking, I stand by — as I suggested — the necessary distinction between Law and Gospel and the doctrine of God's two modes of government. I reject any acknowledgment of the "status confessionis" on the question of peace. This is not a special pleading for political abstinence and merely private piety, as I have clearly pointed out in the lecture "God Sits in Command," which I gave at the synod.

On October 16, 1983, we prayed with about 250 people in front of the entrance to NATO in Heidelberg. Channel 2 of German Television carried a report about it. The police let us alone. Later I took part with others in further actions of civil disobedience: a blockade of the Bismarck barracks in Schwabisch/Gmund, in Mutlangen where Pershing II's were stationed, at the military training area in Wildflecken (1984) and in front of a poison gas storage site near Pirmasens (1988). I was twice arrested and convicted. My former girlfriend, who is now my wife, spent twenty days in prison. I tried all the available legal options, all the way up to the Regional Court of Appeal, because I couldn't understand why my activity was "reprehensible." Friends paid my fines.

By the way, I still remember very clearly my hearing before the Regional Court in Ellwangen, where in response to my motion a subpoena was issued to the American soldier whom I had supposedly "forced" to arrest me. I asked him whether he felt forced. He answered, laughing, "No, that's my job." He didn't care. As far as that goes, almost all the experiences I had with GIs and their dependents "on the other side" were positive. Back in Heidelberg we kept trying to engage them in conversation, we attended American church services in Mark Twain Village, had discussions with army families, wrote up fliers in English, and continually tried to have a dialogue. We did all this prompted by faith, and for precisely this reason they weren't our enemies. What a hollow theoretical ring many of the church's words have, appealing for reconciliation and peace in places where there is no peace! How self-centered some of the church's activity is, when it never enters into real political discussion. Seeing this in my church and its leaders kept making me feel sad, and it still does. Even when it abstains from or discreetly withdraws from questions of life and death, the church is always political. When I take a close look at the history of my church in this century, I also realize once more why the lack of civilian courage and prophetic witness has become institutionalized in Germany. "Priests" (who in Germany are also state functionaries) are simply not inclined to being prophets; perhaps they will turn radical when they're retired.

My companions and I got a completely different impression from those American bishops who dared to speak out and act bravely and clearly against their government's policy. They leveled their prophetic witness at the divinization of national security.

Since then the world has changed. The East-West conflict has eased up. But the challenges for Christians and their churches have remained the same, as have the patterns of theological and political argument — as in the Gulf War. The problems have shifted, and even intensified. With all the economic and military resources now at its disposal, the Northern Hemisphere is defending its wealth against the poor in the South. The politics of deterrence is seeking out the South as the new enemy. The cry for justice grows louder. As the destruction of the natural foundations of life proceeds apace, the battles over who will get what are becoming harsher.

I am thankful for those experiences that I had in the early 1980s and that I've tried to describe here with the use of personal documents. I understand the "conversion to life" that I had back then as a basic change in the direction of my life. Nevertheless I remain a groper, a learner. I would like to continue on the path I have taken, together with others, to whom justice, peace, and the integrity of creation have become a lifetime task. I would like to continue my journey, together with people in many countries who, as I have seen, are deeply dependent — in their neediness and longing, in their love for life and justice — on divine love. Only God can touch and heal our sorest points (and I have many). I've spoken about one of them here — and of a hope that does not leave us high and dry.

There is hardly anyone who has conveyed this to me in personal meetings, in speeches, and in books the way Richard Rohr has. Back then he encouraged me to venture into my own vulnerability. I was immediately able to believe that God's love will always be enough and to spare.

I say thanks. And I also mean thanks for the fact that God keeps alive in us the longing for the kingdom beyond the boundaries of the continents, beyond cultures and languages. This is a community that gives a foretaste of the life in "justice and peace" in the one world to which we are en route.

Note: I would like to express heartfelt thanks to the bishop of my church, Dr. Johannes Hanselmann, for permission to quote from our personal correspondence.

29

Ode for Dorothy

PAT FLATLEY SIMMONS

❖

Mother, you were a beautiful ship
Broken, on your maiden voyage,
On the rocks of patriarchy.

Faithfully, I swabbed your rotting decks,
Daily I raised your tattered sails.
Vowing I myself would be unsinkable.

Now the sea has taken you to herself.
My curses and tears go with you.
I stand on the stony beach alone.

—Mary Vineyard

It's June 6, 1989. Tuesday morning in Harrisburg and the rain is pouring outside my window. I'd forgotten what continuous rain for days looks like. It's gray out. It's looked like dusk since yesterday afternoon when my brother and I left Mom at Warren State Hospital. It's rainy and gray every day in Mom's life.

I hadn't realized that my brother last saw Mom two and one-half years ago when she moved from the hospital he manages to the one at Warren. He tells me that he had already written in his guilt file that he didn't intend to accompany me on the last two-hundred-mile drive of my sixteen-hundred-mile pilgrimage to see Mom. I had no idea it would be so painful for him too. She had loved him. Is that even harder? I struggle to remember dates and believe I last saw Mom five years ago. She's been certified manic-depressive for twenty-three years.

When we pull on the hospital grounds, it's a scene from a Du-Maurier novel. A Gothic-appearing building with tall spires. Pulling into the "castle of the damned"? My brother said earlier that maybe we'd get lucky and drive off the road. No one would ever know that it wasn't an accident!

My brother is treated deferentially by the staff as he's the superintendent of a sister facility. We arrive at 2:00 P.M. Upset stomachaches had prevented us from stopping for lunch. Mick says he's shaking. We laugh and tease to deal with our anxiety. Home to the wilderness!

Mom's in the Israel Building Infirmary. She's suffering from pneumonia and she almost died a month ago. It seems like Mom "almost died" a hundred times. The facility is nicer than most nursing homes and not at all like a mental hospital. The staff is adequate and pleasant. I recall the years of visiting her in mental hospitals where she mothered young female patients. This woman who appeared to dislike her daughters. My family story is that Mom was gentle and "nice" as a young woman and never got feisty until she was "sick." Things were bad as early as 1952. She wept uncontrollably and hid in her bed for days. I became the enemy in her mind. Did childhood demons catch up with her? Dad confirmed for me that he wasn't home much. He worked two jobs and "brought home the bacon." In the 1950s, that was the defined beginning and end of the father's job.

Mom's not in her bed in the infirmary and we are told that she's in the dayroom. She's asleep when we go in. She looks like an old hag, toothless, leaning back with her mouth open. I remember that my mother was a beautiful woman with olive skin, green eyes, and beautiful light brown hair. Her hair looks greasy and her hands are gnarled and crippled.

The nurse wakes her and she looks past me and says, "Mickey." She does something strange with her tongue when she speaks without teeth, which she refuses to wear; it's hard to understand her. She looks at me from her lifeless eyes and says, "Patty." The haglike appearance leaves and I see an aged nursing home inmate like a hundred thousand others. I cry and do nothing to control it. She stares and stares. I vowed never to cry in front of her thirty years ago! I hug her and Mick leaves us alone.

I show her my new granddaughter's picture and the sad, old features produce a toothless grin! I say it's Jessica's child and ask if she knows that Jessica had a baby. She says, "I know." I bring out another child's picture and a group photo of my four children. I say the oldest is twenty-seven, and she responds, "My God!" Was her life already over when they were babies?

Mick comes back with a nurse. She asks Mom to name her company. She looks at Mick and says, "Mickey." She stares at me deliberately for awhile and says, "Maureen." Mick laughs and says, "Mom, you're still an old fox. You know who *she is!*" She says, "Patty." Mom, will you *never* love me?

There's a delightful old woman with a broken hip at a short distance and she keeps asking us to remove her restraint tray as she "has to leave now." My brother, the pro, says to me, "Isn't she a wonderful old woman?" He keeps telling her so gently. "Now, you know that you have to ask the nurse." Mick tells me that many of the persons who work with this population are "saints," but it's obvious he feels the patients are too! My brother who doesn't know that he's one! A man sits on the couch and tells me that he smokes five packs of cigarettes a day. He holds a bag of urine. The television speaks of the student deaths in China, and he says that it's good to get rid of as many of "those" as possible. For some unfathomable reason the ignorance of his statement doesn't alter my compassion for him. Strange.

In the course of one hour, Mom asks for and I give her five glasses of water. Mick worries about dehydration, although he sees no symptoms. He tells me it's bad politics to criticize the staff because they're in power positions and can take it out on the patient when the family leaves. Instead he says, "My mother drank five glasses of water. You may want this on the medical record." Always so gentle. The nurse answers kindly that staff is careful to see that Mom gets enough necessary water. She adds that if she could, Mom would drink water all day. I think that if I lived here instead of sixteen hundred miles away, I could bring my mother glasses of water. Did she bring me water when I was little? I wonder if she loved me then.

Mick leaves again and Mom stares in my eyes and says, "How can you do this to me?" I feel the old, deep anger welling in my chest. "How can *I* do this to *you?*" I say to myself. I flash on the incidents of physical abuse and the years and years of emotional battering and meanspiritedness; of hearing over and over that I was worthless and the hell involved in building some self-esteem. The pain over never having mother to shop with or to talk to a grandmother who helped with the kids. Trying to be a parent from the time I was eight or nine, cleaning, packing lunches, caring for my infant sisters when they came later, trying to smooth waters and make her happy. To myself, I scream "Do *you* have no recollection of the hell you put *me* through? Nothing's changed! I'll always be bad in your eyes!"

Neither of us looks away and I know she sees my pain in my eyes. But something happens. I look and suddenly see the tormented, suicidal, addicted woman my mother was at midlife: pregnant with her fifth child, overwhelmed with self-contempt. Crumbling. And I am again a young adolescent recently changed from good girl and mother's helper, screaming back at her after years of her needling and my needing, slamming her door, my door, any door, yelling how much I hated her. "Mom, I needed you so desperately. I loved you so much. Why couldn't you love me?" my eyes now say. To my surprise I say, "Mom, you are a good woman. You had it very hard. You've suffered horribly. I know that now. I'm so sorry." She mumbles something at me and I brace myself and say I don't understand. She says slowly and clearly, "You are so beautiful." I had told Mick earlier in the car as we exchanged Mother stories that Mom told me shortly before my wedding at age twenty-one that it was a mistake to have beautiful women in my wedding party because people could see I was much less attractive. I told him it was years before I could look at my wedding pictures and see I was a pretty bride. Ironic that she would use the word "beautiful." I feel forgiveness and love.

So Mick and I sit longer and tell her again that she is good. We say again that we know how she's suffered and that we know she did the best she could. She stares and begins to moan a low moan — almost as if freed to speak of her woundedness. We all hold hands in communion. The tired green eyes look at me and I realize that I will probably never hear that my mother loves me. And I feel the *need* to hear it has been surrendered. I think that I may be saying goodbye to her forever. Just then Mick says, "Mom, someday, somewhere we'll all be together again and this time we'll be happy." For a spirit-filled magic moment, we believe. It's time to go. Mick leaves. She's still staring at me! How can I leave her? Love and grief well up in me and I say from my depth, "I love you, Mom." And a beautiful old woman says to me, for the first time I recall, "I love you, too."

Postscript: Dorothy May Flatley died on July 2, 1989. Rest in God's peace, Mom.

30

Moving Beyond Limits

CHRISTINA SPAHN

Several years ago I saw a puzzle that seems pertinent to the topic addressed in this article. The instructions were to connect nine dots placed as follows with four straight lines *without lifting the pen or pencil from the paper or retracing a line previously drawn:*

If you attempt this you'll find that this task is impossible if you draw lines only within the perimeter of the square formed by the dots. The solution is to move one's writing instrument *beyond* the square:

Why this puzzle seems relevant to this article is that, however superficially, it illustrates how easily and arbitrarily we can set limits that are premature or, worse, unneeded. This proclivity is restricting in daily life. It can have dire consequences when we're dealing with faith, morality, and our relationship with God and our world.

During the past several years we've learned a great deal about the developmental process through which human beings grow and mature. Lawrence Kohlberg, who describes six stages of moral development, and James Fowler, who describes a parallel six-stage journey of faith growth, have contributed greatly to the developmental awareness. This has significant implications for the individual, the church, society, and the entire human community.

Very briefly and sketchily: These developmental theories describe us as all starting at the same place. As little children, we were inclined toward concrete images and lacked the ability to deal with the abstract. Our faith was the faith of our parents. And, because we believed them, we accepted the existence of God with the same enthusiasm and trust we had for Santa Claus and the Easter Bunny. Incapable of distinguishing between religious imagery and other types of imagining, we believed what family members believed.

On the moral level, we were more motivated by rewards and punishments than we were by a love of goodness. We simply had not yet developed the capacity to be otherwise.

Later in our lives, after age eleven, most of us entered another level of growth, one from which the majority of people never emerge. This is the level of the conventional, that stage at which our faith and our sense of morality rely heavily on what we perceive as legitimate authority. A person at this stage has moved beyond that described above. In contrast to the young child whose faith is unreflective and unquestioning or, in the older person, superstitious, this person recognizes the validity of institutionally sanctioned beliefs and moral codes. Something is to be believed and laws are to be followed because authority demands it. Conformity is the primary characteristic of this stage and security is its reward. A conventional stage person identifies strongly with the religion, society, peer group, nationality, or whatever is perceived as an authority and is bothered by others who don't deliver similar allegiance. Such phrases as "My country: right or wrong," "The Bible says it, I believe it, and that settles it," "Just say NO!" indicate a conventional level of development.

A major characteristic of this stage is that faith and moral conduct are still determined from outside oneself. One has not yet grappled with the questions, doubts, and inconsistencies through which faith is not only professed but also internalized. This process, which moves one to mature faith, requires considerable courage, and many people are unwilling to exert the energy required. Entry into this process, where we feel more like we are losing faith than deepening it is a risky business. It is generally only in retrospect that we understand and appreciate what has been happening.

A second reason why so many people remain at the conventional level is that churches, governments, and family structures affirm and support this stance. Conventional people don't tend to rock the boat; postconventional people are not nearly as interested in maintaining the status quo. Some of the present tension between hierarchical power and various movements in the Catholic Church seems directly related to a desire that people live within the limits of institutional understanding, that they stay within the square.

Church leadership seems to be saying in effect: "We know what's best for you." And people the world over are responding. "There's more!"

This sense that there's more, that it's necessary to move beyond the boundaries of religious convention, is one of the characteristics of mature faith. This faith recognizes that Truth is greater than dogma, that charity is more important than law, and that personal and communal integrity demand the enfleshment of such values as justice, compassion, and respect for human dignity.

Individuals of mature faith are in process and consciously so. They can live with questions, apparent inconsistencies, and lack of certitude. Their faith is posited not primarily on the authority of another but on their own examined convictions. Like the Samaritans whom Jesus met after his encounter with the woman at the well, they believe not because of the word of another but because they have heard and experienced for themselves (John 4:42).

Persons of mature faith are not mavericks. They have done the hard work of internalizing their faith and, therefore, embody it. Franz Jaegerstaetter, the Austrian peasant who defied church and country and was beheaded for refusing to join the Nazi army, was such a person. So, too, were Archbishop Oscar Romero and thousands of other Central American men and women whose deaths have born silent witness to their belief that faith is more than religious behavior. It is significant, too, that we remember that the stance of Jesus of Nazareth was hardly conventional! The questions Jesus asked and the enthusiasm with which he was popularly received made both political and religious authorities very nervous. They wanted conformity, but Jesus was empowering people to move beyond that. He had to be killed!

All this seems important to remember because the journey to maturity is a solitary one, but one that has been modeled countless times before. To move beyond the conventional is to risk both internal and external opposition: the internal arising from self-doubt and fear of the unknown; the external resulting from the misunderstanding and hostility of individuals and institutions. Yet while this journey is solitary, it has communal implications. Change in institutions happens only when change has occurred in individuals who, however much on the fringes, somehow identify with those institutions. Because some are willing to risk walking into the unknown, the church, society, and humanity come to new levels of self-awareness and possibility.

31

The Call to Emptiness

AVIS CROWE

In my late thirties I went into the wilderness of my soul. It was a long journey into the heart of paradox, for I discovered that in the emptiness of my life was the ground of fulfillment. All of this happened at Pendle Hill, a Quaker center for study and contemplation near Philadelphia. It is as far removed from a true wilderness as one can find. An alternative adult living-learning community, it is also an arboretum with lush grounds abounding with trees, flowers, space – and people who are all on a spiritual quest.

I had already gone back to school once, the "real" kind, some years earlier. I had left New York City and the world of commercial television production, in search of . . . what? Something that would fill the void, satisfy the inchoate longing that had dogged me for years yet remained unmet in spite of career changes, lifestyle experimentation, a dozen addresses, and even more personal entanglements. A graduate degree provided temporary satisfaction. I had recognized the need for drastic change and had acted on it; I felt a sense of accomplishment and had a paper in hand that proved I was capable. Confirmation came when I landed a satisfying job as an arts administrator. I had even found love and looked forward to marriage. I gave up my job and moved halfway across the country. Then the first domino fell: The love affair ended and the rest of my life came tumbling down around me. I was nothing at all: I was unlovable, unemployed, and alone. I felt very empty. Like a wounded animal I limped back to the East Coast, crawled into the dark hole of depression and stayed there for nearly two years.

As I looked back much later, I could see that the amazing grace of the soul had been my constant companion during that period. It took the form of caring friends who insisted I get help; it led me to a Quaker meeting where I recognized the spiritual nature of my longing. It was grace that helped me find a skilled therapist who received my tears, helped me through the tangled byways of the past, and set me on a path of healing. It was grace that drew me to Koinonia Partners in Georgia, where I began to learn firsthand about community and radical

church and where the true spiritual journey began. And it was grace
that led me to Pendle Hill with its peculiar curriculum of classes that
included such titles as "Compassion and Community," "Monasticism,"
"The Plain People." It was a class called "The Wilderness Journey,"
taught by Sonnie Cronk, that was pivotal for me. More than pivotal,
it was transforming.

During the ten weeks of the class I walked with the likes of the
desert fathers, Thomas Merton, Caryll Houselander, the Little Sisters
of Jesus, and many others. In their company I experienced the interior
desert and found amazing possibilities there. The desert, I discovered,
was not a wasteland at all, but a unique terrain that is home to a wide
variety of living things. I looked inside myself and where before I had
seen nothing, I found a woman waiting to be born. I had come face
to face with paradox and felt at home there.

Midway through the course, we went on a silent weekend retreat at
a historic Quaker meeting house in rural Pennsylvania Dutch country.
We had been encouraged to think about our own emptiness in the
silence. I stared into the fire, wrote in my journal, watched out the
window as Amish horse-drawn buggies passed by in the winter chill.
Some of the words I reflected on were those of St. John of the Cross:

> A sail can catch the wind and be used to maneuver a boat only because
> it is so frail. It is the weakness of the sail that makes it sensitive to the
> wind.

It was a new concept for me, but I knew it as Truth, knew it physically, in the center of my body. For the first time I began to have
an inkling that in my loneliness, the place where I felt most empty,
was strength. But it was just an inkling. The word "empty" was laden
with negative experience and assumptions for me. To be empty was
to be hungry, needy, unloved, and unacceptable – a condition to be
remedied with food, career, husband, children. All of these eluded
me except food, which was both comfort and curse. Yet, here was
John of the Cross, and others, knocking that askew and pointing to
an extraordinary notion: that emptiness – weakness – was where the
real strength lay! That a vessel must be empty in order to be filled;
that to be a channel, one must be free of impediments; that the reed
flute must be hollow in order to receive the player's breath; that to be
empty is the way, in fact, to becoming full.

In a moment of revelation I realized that emptiness is ... *not* nothingness, which had been my greatest fear. Rather, it is the foundation
of a truly vibrant faith and action. I felt almost breathless as these
ideas first crept, then tumbled, into my consciousness, into my blood-
stream. I heard in them an invitation: a call to stand in the midst of
my own emptiness and live there for awhile, experience it fully, claim

it — even proclaim it. If I could do this, I just might come to a place of receptivity at which point transformation could truly happen.

I wrote in my journal:

> I've turned the corner. My perception has shifted: from aloneness as something to regret and grieve over, to something positive, something to be celebrated as the condition that has been given me. What I have *not* been given is as much a gift as are the things I have been given (which I am also beginning to see and acknowledge!). I feel ripe and open and available, as though the ideas and words I've been reading and struggling with are being made of flesh . . . mine.

But that was in 1982. The sharpness of insight and discovery has faded over time and in the wake of the extraordinary turns my life has taken. I had gone to Pendle Hill as a student for a year and had seen the glass of my life half-empty. During four more years on the staff it became half-full, then overflowed. In those five years I began to see things from the perspective of the downside-up kingdom, as Sonnie Cronk liked to characterize the kingdom of God. In the process of embracing my own emptiness I opened myself to possibility for the first time. Gifts beyond any earlier imaginings were given to me as a result: a life-companion, time in South Africa, ministries that opened up at Pendle Hill teaching courses in journal writing and leading retreats, work I was able to continue during our Cape Town sojourn. And now, after years of living in apartments or other people's houses, I have my first home here in New Mexico. It has been a decade of unexpected blessings, a time of filling up with life's abundance.

But as this winter approached, I could feel the cycle turning. In nature there is a cycle of seasons. The fruitfulness of spring and summer give way to autumnal shedding of leaves that reveal starkly beautiful skeletons of trees, and then to the lengthening darkness and the hard ground of winter. Fields lie fallow. Bulbs are planted and wait for spring, unseen beneath the crusty earth. This cycle repeats itself over and over, each one a time of recovery and of preparation. There is in me a similar cycle. My life has become so full that there is not much room for the working of the spirit. I have all but abandoned the regular journal writing and periodic retreats that had become essential parts of my life. I find myself moving too fast, talking too much, becoming short-tempered and resentful of people. Almost without realizing it I have allowed myself to get caught up in activity and now find myself living in the shallows, no longer anchored in the deep.

Once I had chosen "Emptiness" as the theme for the retreat I will lead at the Center in February, I realized with a start that it was *I* who was being called to emptiness. It was I who was being reminded that it is time once again to lie fallow, to sink into winter's embrace, to let the leaves fall away, the leaves of activity and personal plans,

needs, dreams as well as recurring hunger for approval. When my
husband accepted an invitation to go to England, I decided to remain
here. I think now that I was acting on an inner knowledge that I
needed to slow down and empty out. Perhaps grace is at it again! I fight
emptiness, know how hard it is to go into the wilderness. But I know,
too, that God comes with me into that place, leads me through it to
the other side where I am able to live more authentically and closer
to the roots of my faith. In emptying out I can once again become a
hollow reed, to be played by the One who has created all things.

32

Radical Grace
and Radical Christians

Confronting the Idols Closer to Home

JIM WALLIS

Richard Rohr is one of the best teachers the church has today. His passion is to link the spiritual life with social transformation. His Center for Action and Contemplation is well named, for it seeks to be a place where the interior life is brought together with the urgent cry for justice in our contemporary world.

What we most need in our time is a spirituality of transformation, and Richard Rohr is one of the clearest voices pioneering the unmarked path to such a vision. He challenges those whose psychologizing and spiritualizing become the narcissistic self-absorption so characteristic of our times. And Richard also challenges those who would plunge ahead with the battle for justice without being aware of the interior battlefields of the soul and spirit. The former can so easily become irrelevant and the latter so painfully destructive.

I am convinced that a deeper understanding of the grace of God may be our only salvation. Richard believes that the true way to be genuinely "radical" is, indeed, to trust and embrace such grace. It is not insignificant that the CAC's publication bears the title Radical Grace.

I am honored and grateful to submit a contribution to this volume on the occasion of Richard's fiftieth birthday, for he is an old and dear friend. Of all the things I considered sending, I finally decided on an article I originally wrote for Sojourners *many years ago, and one of the few I come back to again and again. It reflects upon the meaning of radical grace for "radical Christians." It is revised for this book.*

For activists to reflect upon the grace of God is a difficult, troubling, and dangerous thing. It is difficult because we often feel there is so little time. Indeed, I remember having to stay home from an important antinuclear action the weekend I wrote this piece, in order to meet my deadline. That decision itself cleared my mind and heart for the reflection. To open ourselves to the grace of God is troubling because many of our favorite habits, assumptions, and "idols" will come under rigorous scrutiny. And it is dangerous because such contemplation may lead to our conversion. But it is a conversion we desperately need and secretly long for.

This article addresses many of the questions that Richard has devoted his life to. And it points to the direction that Richard Rohr continues to call us. Thank you Richard, and happy birthday!

—

For by grace you have been saved through faith; and this not your own doing. It is the gift of God — not because of works, lest anyone should boast.

—Ephesians 2:8, 9

Grace is the logic of a loving God. There is nothing we can do to earn it, win it, or deserve it. Grace is simply a gift, not a reward. We can receive it only by faith, not through good works.

As familiar as that is to us, we have great difficulty coming to terms with the meaning and reality of grace. We seem to find innumerable ways to deny the grace that is the free gift of God's love to us. Either we abuse it and make grace self-serving, or we dismiss its reality altogether by acting to establish our own righteousness. In twisting God's purposes to suit our own or in striving to justify ourselves through our own efforts, we have, in fact, denied the grace of God. In so doing, we have denied ourselves the ability to simply rest in that grace, to be changed and used by God's love.

Perhaps the greatest denial of grace in our time lies in its abuse. Dietrich Bonhoeffer named it "cheap grace." The grace of God is cheapened and distorted when used to cover over our sin rather than to cleanse it. The language of grace is impoverished and exploited when employed to justify our disobedience and lukewarm attitude.

True grace convicts of sin, softens the heart, and prompts repentance. Cheap grace overlooks sin, hardens the heart, and breeds complacency. True grace accepts and redeems the sinner. Cheap grace accommodates to and justifies the sin.

As Bonhoeffer reminds us, grace that comes at such a heavy cost to God cannot be used cheaply. Grace is not meant to obscure the path of discipleship and obedience. On the contrary, grace opens that path to us. Cheap grace proclaims salvation without repentance. The evangelism of cheap grace has no real power to challenge either our personal status or the political status quo.

But there is another denial of grace among us. It often rears up in reaction to the cheap grace most prevalent in our churches.

The reaction to cheap grace can be so strong, the emphasis on radical discipleship and obedience so firm, that eventually there is little room left for any grace in our lives. The response to cheap grace can wrongly lead us to the loss of grace altogether. Its replacement with new forms of works righteousness is a great danger to those who call themselves "radical" Christians. This danger is my chief concern here.

Radical Christians face the tendency to seek justification in our lifestyle, our work, our protest, our causes, our movements, our actions, our prophetic identity, and our radical self-image. It becomes an easy temptation to place our security in the things we stand for and in the things we do, instead of in what God has done. It is a temptation to depend on things other than God's grace.

In our reaction against cheap grace, we are always in danger of producing radical alternatives to grace. In our desire to be obedient to the gospel and to prove our faithfulness, we could lose the freedom and the power that come from resting and fully trusting in God's grace as sufficient for our lives and for the world.

In the language of the passage from Ephesians, radical Christians have things they tend to "boast of." These are the things that can most easily become idols for us. They are not the idolatries of the established society and the comfortable church. We have identified those and confronted them so often that they have become familiar and easily recognizable. Therefore their power over us has been diminished.

But there are idols closer to home. We are less able to recognize them and can, therefore, more easily fall into their grasp. In very subtle ways, they are the idolatries that have the most power over us.

Idolatry must be identified and unmasked if it is to lose its power. Illusion is, in fact, the source of an idol's power. We place our trust in that which is not trustworthy but appears to be. We are deceived by the image of the idol that replaces that which is worthy of our trust.

Not to fully trust God's grace is to engage in illusion. It is to underestimate the power of sin and death and to overestimate our ability to overcome it. Not to rely on the work of Christ is to rely on our own work to save ourselves and the world. When we don't trust grace, we take ourselves too seriously, while not taking sin seriously enough.

What are those things in which we are tempted to place a false trust, things that threaten to become idols for us, things that can become substitutes for grace?

Our lifestyle can become an idol. To live simply is a biblical virtue, especially in a society choking on its own consumption and waste. Economic simplicity clears away the material obstacles that block dependence on God. Living with less also helps open our eyes to the suffering of the poor. It enables us to participate more easily in their struggle for justice, instead of in their oppression. The motive for living simply is that we might love both God and the poor more freely.

But it is not a simple lifestyle that justifies us. It is, rather, God's grace that enables us to live more simply. Displaying our style of life as if it were a badge of righteousness contradicts the whole spiritual foundation of economic simplicity. We live simply not out of obligation and guilt but to be less hindered in serving God and the poor. It should not be a duty, but a joy. Our lifestyle must not be used to judge others, but to invite them to share in the freedom and the grace we have found.

It was the worst tendency of the Pharisees to seek justification before God through their scrupulous lifestyle. May we never be like the Pharisee who stood beside the tax collector (read: the wealthy corporation executive) and thanked God that he wasn't such a sinner. Complex legalisms employed in the name of simple living could well rob us of the freedom and joy that are the intended fruits of such a lifestyle.

Our identification with the poor can become an idol. That the God of the Bible is on the side of the poor and the oppressed is beyond dispute. Christ's presence among the lowly and the afflicted is a doctrine drawn from the very heart of the gospels. But taking up the cause of the poor can have its own pitfalls.

There is a tendency among concerned people to romanticize the poor and their poverty. Poverty is ugly and bitter, and the poor suffer from the same sinful human condition as the rest of us. It is insensitive to represent the poor and the brutal circumstances of their lives as uniquely noble and virtuous. That may serve the fantasies of people experiencing downward mobility, but it will not serve the needs of poor people.

The suffering of the exploited is too easily exploitable. The misery of the poor advertises well to serve the personal, ideological, religious, and financial interests of others, and new forms of colonial exploitation replace old ones. The poor become the objects of public rhetoric, the targets of charity projects, and the pawns of political ambition. To use the poor for the sake of Christian ministry or leftist ideology is again to make capital out of their suffering. We have seen too much of religious and political radicals building their personal careers on the oppression of the poor.

Poor people are best served by those who desire to be their friends. We identify with the poor not to save ourselves, but so that we might better identify with Christ. He is already among the suffering and forgotten ones and invites us to join him there. He has taught us to love and serve him by sharing his special passion for those who are loved the least.

Our actions of protest can become an idol. The Scriptures tell us that love and truth show themselves in action and not merely in words. Direct action in the public arena has become a central means for bearing faithful witness, for making peace, and for seeking social justice. Those actions bring to light what is dangerous and wrong and point to a better way.

However, there is an inherent danger in public protest. Critical tests of any public action or campaign are: What or whom is being made known and visible? Is the truth being made more clear? Or is a person, a group, an institution, or a movement being made more prominent?

All our public actions must be rooted in the power of love and truth. We act for the purpose of making that power known, not for the purpose of making ourselves known. Our motivation must be to open people's eyes to the truth, not to show ourselves as right and them as wrong.

Whenever our protest becomes an effort to "prove ourselves," we are in serious danger. Our best actions are those that admit our complicity in the evil we protest and are marked by a spirit of genuine repentance and humility. Our worst actions are those that seek to demonstrate our own righteousness, our purity, our freedom from complicity. When our pride overtakes our protest, we may simply be repeating, in political form, the self-righteous judgment of the fundamentalists: "I'm saved, and you're not."

A Christian friend wrote to me:

> I have seen so much of the "heresy of good works" in the religious Left, a belief that is based on the arrogance that we have to save the world, and a very real denial (if not in words, then in actions) that the world has *already* been saved. And believe me, it is very tiresome to go around feeling like the fate of the world rests on your words and on your deeds. . . . Sometimes I think that numbers of arrests have replaced indulgences in the "new church," and that is *not* spiritual progress.

Our actions do not have the power to save us. Instead, they can have the power to make the truth known. Although the actions we undertake will never substitute for grace, they can indeed be witnesses of God's grace. Since they lack the capacity to justify us, a better purpose for our actions would be communication.

Because communication is so basic to public action, the nature of what we say and do becomes very important. Actions that mostly communicate a threatening and desperate spirit should be carefully questioned. Free and open evaluation of all public action is necessary to protect the health and character of our protest. The quality and integrity of what we communicate will be its most crucial element.

Action done in public will always carry with it the great danger of presumption. We ought to act with the awareness of how risky it is to claim to be making the truth known. The ever-present threat is to identify the truth with ourselves, instead of the other way around. Because of the inherent presumption of public protest, it should always reflect a spirit of confession, humility, and invitation.

Judgment, arrogance, and exclusiveness are signs of spiritual immaturity. Protest characterized by such things will have the effect of hardening hearts, confirming people's fears, and convincing them of their present opinions. Public action has sometimes done more harm than good. It can drive people away from the very things we are trying to say. It can perpetuate, as well as dispel, public blindness.

Our principle of nonviolence can become an idol. Never has the absolute need for nonviolence been greater in a world full of bloody conflict. But even our position on nonviolence can be self-serving and hide deeper motives.

Nonviolence aims for truth and not for power. Its chief weapon is the application of spiritual force, not the use of coercion. A very serious problem in nonviolent movements is the hidden aggression, the manipulation, the assertive ego, and the desire for provocation that can lurk beneath the surface of repetitive platitudes about the commitment to nonviolence. The rhetorical cloak of nonviolence can be used to hide the will to power, which is the very foundation of violence. The desire to win over others, to defeat one's enemies, and to humiliate the opposition are all characteristics of violence and are too painfully evident in much of what is called nonviolent action.

The infighting, media grabbing, and intense competition of the peace movement are hardly an evidence that the will to power has been overcome. Some of the worst tyrannies have been hidden behind anarchist principles and the myth of leaderless groups and communities.

We should know by now that all violence is of a piece. If that is true, then the violence of dissent is directly linked to the violence of the established order. It is, in fact, a mirror reflection of it. Therefore, the violence present in the peace movement can be said to be part of the violence that fuels the world's violence. We can no longer justify the "excesses" of the peace movement by appealing to the greater violence of the war system. The urgency of our situation calls for more, not less, care in the actions we undertake.

Nonviolence does not try to overcome the adversary by defeating him, but by convincing him. It turns an adversary into a friend, not by winning over her, but by winning her over. Knowing that today's enemy may become tomorrow's friend should cause us to examine our treatment of opponents more closely. It is interesting how military and business leaders who "defect" to the peace movement are transformed from demons into saints overnight.

Patience is central to nonviolence. Nonviolence is based on the kind of love the Bible speaks of as "enduring all things." Thomas Merton taught us that the root of war is fear. If that is true, we must become much more understanding of the fears people have. The most effective peacemakers are those who have experienced the healing of their own fears and can now help lead others out of theirs. There is still too much fear in the peace movement to heal the fears of a nation. How can we be peacemakers when we are still afraid of one another? Our hope is in the deepening of our experience of the "perfect love that casts out fear."

Our prophetic identity can become an idol. The prophetic vocation is deeply biblical and highly dangerous. It is a calling most necessary for our time, but one that requires the most intense scrutiny.

Prophets have always challenged idolatry. The people of God forget who they are and to whom they belong. Before long, their forgetfulness causes them to fall into the false worship of idols. Prophets are then raised up to name the idolatries, to speak the word of the Lord, to lead the people out of their false worship, and to bring them back to God.

The need in our day is for clear words of God's judgment and mercy. The prophetic vocation is to faithfully communicate that judgment and mercy in a way people can bear and understand. A genuinely prophetic message will never show selectivity, partiality, or parochial interest. A prophet in the biblical tradition will not challenge some idols and leave others untouched. He or she will not rage against injustice and violence in some places and be strangely silent about oppression elsewhere.

It is painfully apparent that radical Christians have not always been true to the whole counsel of God's judgment. An ideological selectivity intrudes, a political bias that undermines the credibility and power of prophetic witness. The idolatries of the establishment are attacked while the idols of the antiestablishment receive less critical treatment. The evils of the majority culture are assailed but the sins of the counterculture are often passed over. The political prisoners of right-wing dictatorships seem to generate more interest than those languishing in the jails of leftist regimes.

Political orthodoxy is anathema to prophetic integrity. The maintenance of the party line describes propaganda, not prophecy. Prophecy is, in fact, profoundly anti-ideological. Karl Barth once wrote these words:

> The Christian Church must be guided by the Word of God and by it alone. It must not forget for an instant that all political systems, right and left alike, are the work of [people].It must hold itself free to carry out its own mission and to work out a possibly quite new form of obedience or resistance. It must not sell this birthright for any conservative or revolutionary mess of pottage.

Politicized theology is no substitute for prophetic witness. Radical proof-texting is no better than fundamentalist proof-texting. We are keenly aware of the conservative, militarist, patriotic, racist, and sexist distortions of the Bible. Likewise, there can be neither a leftist agenda in reading the Scriptures, nor anarchist, nor pacifist, nor communitarian, nor any other bias, for that matter. The Word of God is intended to judge all our priorities, to overturn all our biases, to correct all our perceptions.

If the prophetic vocation is to bring the judgment of God to bear, then the prophet must be the first to be placed under that judgment. The prophetic calling must be, by definition, an extremely troubling one. It must be as troubling to ourselves as it is to those who bear the brunt of our prophetic pronouncements – or more so.

Smugness and complacency are the prophet's worst enemies. The hardest words of judgment must always be reserved for our own group. God's word must be allowed to confront the idolatries closest to us before it will destroy those furthest away. Pride, alienation, and bitterness are the worst sources of prophetic zeal and will corrupt and distort our witness.

The biblical prophets loved the people, were a part of the people, and claimed them as their own. Therefore the disobedience and sin of the people hurt the prophets, and their first response to faithlessness was grief, not indignation. The prophets were the ones who spoke the hard words. But they spoke with a broken heart.

The prophets would not conform to the people, but they never lost their relationship to them. Jesus, in the tradition of the prophets, showed just such a capacity to love the people without conforming to their sinful ways. In our desire not to be conformed to the sins of the nation, we could lose the capacity to identify with the people that is so basic to the prophetic calling.

Those who would avow a prophetic vocation to the church must ask themselves a question: Do you love the church? Or do you hate it? God will not entrust us with a prophetic ministry merely to cloak our own rage and judgment. But if we love the church, if we love the people, if our hearts ache when we see their folly, then God may trust us to be vehicles of divine rage and judgment, to express God's purposes for the people.

The most basic question for the prophet is to whom he or she is accountable. Prophets not accountable to anyone but themselves are a dangerous and destructive lot. The worst things in history have been done out of prophetic zeal.

Grace saves the prophetic vocation. The knowledge and experience of grace can ease the seriousness with which we tend to take ourselves. Grace can restore our humility, our sense of humor, and our ability to laugh at ourselves. All are regularly needed by prophets. Only sinners make good prophets.

Our biggest idol is ourselves. Radical Christians, like all creatures, tend to boast most of all of themselves. To trust in our lifestyle, our commitment to the poor, our actions, our nonviolence, or our prophetic identity is, in the end, to trust in ourselves. It is to trust in our work, our principles, our causes, and our self-images.

Idolatry is the worship of anything other than God. And an idol is simply an image. When we worship an idol, we are worshiping an image. How important our images are to us! Our lives can so easily become exercises in image building.

We reject the prestige society offers only to find prestige through our radical status. We eschew success in the world, then pursue it through "alternative" channels. We snicker at the system's professionals while establishing a career in the movement. We leave worldly fame behind but enjoy the special status this society grants to its radicals and prophets. We rail against the power structure and build a power base of our own.

As the Bible says, "There is none righteous, no, not one." Grace can overcome the greatest temptation of radical Christians: to believe that we are better than those who need convincing and converting. Grace imparts to us the capacity to forgive because we know that we have been forgiven. The marks of grace are gentleness, hope, and faith. The most dependable sign of its presence is joy.

To trust grace is to know that the world has already been saved by Jesus Christ. It is to know that we cannot save the world any more than we can save ourselves. All our work is done only in response to Christ's work. To receive the gift of grace is to let go of self-sufficiency and to act out of a spirit of gratitude.

We must seek not a successful strategy but a deeper faith. Only then will we have the assurance of salvation, not because of what we have accomplished, but because we have allowed God's grace and mercy to flow through our lives.

33

Spiritual Comrades

GERHARD WEHR

❖

Dear Richard Rohr,

When I think of the immense intellectual and spiritual range en-
compassed by all those who send you greetings in this book, I feel
encouraged to make the following statement. I would like to introduce
you to, and make part of your circle of friends, a man with whom you
perhaps aren't yet acquainted. True, he's no longer alive, but we have
more than just an ecumene in the horizontal sense; we also have it in
the vertical sense – the brothers and sisters of the celestial brigade.
I'm thinking of Jakob Böhme, who died in Görlitz at age forty-nine in
1624. To be sure he wasn't the sort of "wild man" you have written
about, but he *was* a man of the spirit, a Lutheran Christian with an
unmistakably Franciscan outlook. The Francis I mean is the author of
the "Canticle of the Sun," a person who looked on the world's creatures as his brothers and sisters and lived on intimate terms with them.
For me Böhme is something like the younger brother of Hildegard of
Bingen. Because he too was a special sort of visionary. A meadow in
bloom, a tree, a clod of earth could become transparent evidence to
him of the creative, continually active hand of God. He was a cosmic
Christian, the very model of a mystic, that is. And thus he begins his
first work, *Aurora*, which is overflowing with obscurities and jolts of
enlightenment:

> But if you want to speak to God, you must busily weigh the forces in
> nature, and along with that, all of creation, heaven and earth, as well as
> the holy angels, devils and humans, heaven and hell too.

Yes, Richard, you read that right: Heaven and hell, angels and devils
belong in Böhme's view of reality. The realm of darkness is not left
out; it's part and parcel of the whole. Or to use Böhme's language:
God's light shines out of the fury of God's wrathful fire. And so this
man, who supported himself and his family as a simple shoemaker,
describes in violent images and symbols the destinies of God, the
world, and humankind. Böhme tells how the deity, which emerges

194

from its silence and its dark places, straining toward revelation, creates the universe. Then comes the tragic fall of the human race and finally its healing and returning home through Christ.

But that's still not enough, because there is also Sophia, divine wisdom: "This virgin of God's wisdom has stood in the Mysterium and in her God's spirit has looked upon the creatures, for she is what has been expressed by God, what God the Father utters out of the Word of the Deity with the Holy Spirit."

In ever new attempts Böhme circles around the wonders of this divine Sophia. How extraordinary that a Lutheran could put such a thing down on paper in the early seventeenth century, in the days when the "rabies theologica," the rabid fury of the theologians, was raging unchecked. Not surprisingly the manuscript of *Aurora* struck the *pastor primarius* of Görlitz as pure heresy, so that he publicly reprimanded his faithful parishioner, had the voluminous manuscript confiscated, and issued a prohibition against his writing any more. All of us, whether we live in Rio or Toronto, in Oakland or Schwarzenbruck (like me), will know from personal experience the machinations of these bureaucrats plotting against the Spirit. And their victims maintain their composure, no less aware of their mission than the Görlitz master, whose *Aurora* could be confiscated, but who would not be reduced to silence. His cause went on and still does. Indeed for him the mindless antagonist was even "God's embossing hammer," because this sort of resistance could not hinder his work. God uses the mighty to convict them of their powerlessness. The Marxist Ernst Bloch was right when he realized the dialectic in the writings of the simple shoemaker and "Philosophus teutonicus," and so wrote of him: "This kind of thing hadn't been heard since Heraclitus."

What made Böhme so sure of himself and turned him into a writer and a source of inspiration for countless others? It was no mere academic doctrine or bookish knowledge, but a breakthrough experience that surprised him when he was about twenty-five years old, after he had struggled for many years with the basic problems of human life, with the question of the origin of evil and injustice on earth. At this point I flip open the nineteenth chapter of *Aurora*, where Jakob Böhme, his hand still trembling, wrote of what happened to him. He says:

> But when in affliction and trouble I elevated my spirit . . . I earnestly raised it up into God, as with a great storm or onset, wrapping up my whole heart and mind, as also all my thoughts and whole will and resolution, incessantly to wrestle with the love and mercy of God, and not to give over, until he blessed me, that is, until he enlightened me with his holy spirit, whereby I might understand his will, and be rid

of my sadness. And then my spirit did break through... Suddenly, after some violent storms... my spirit did break through the gates of hell, even into the innermost birth... of the Deity, and there I was embraced by love, as a bridegroom embraces his dearly beloved bride. But the greatness of the triumphing that was in the spirit I cannot express, either in speaking or writing; neither can it be compared to anything but to that wherein life is generated in the midst of death, and it is like the resurrection from the dead. (*Aurora,* trans. John Sparrow [London: James Clarke, 1960], 487–88)

No doubt about it, here Böhme lets kindred spirits look into his heart. His report has become the document of a shattering, blissful inner experience. Even in translation it makes the reader feel what a breakthrough in knowledge and a personal turnaround has been sketched here. What need of any more words? There are certainties that one can't get for oneself but that we are given and that no one can take away from us, not even the lords — as Böhme would call them — of the stone heaps. And thus our author writes in his later meditation, *Christosophia,* the following words, which invite us to reflect: The true Christian "has his church *within him,* since inside he hears and teaches (or learns), but Babel has the heap of stones.... The Holy Spirit preaches to him through all creatures.... A true Christian brings his holy church with him into the community. His heart is the true church, where one should worship God.... If I don't have Christ *in me,* then everything is false and useless trash."

That is why I wanted to acquaint you — and any others who read these pages — with this Jakob Böhme. Given the need for brevity, of course, much had to be left unsaid, for example, about the evolution of Böhme's theosophy, his "cosmosophy," and "anthroposophy" (on the masculine-feminine totality of the person), or about the influence he had on philosophers like Hegel and Schelling, Soloviev and Berdyayev, and in our time Paul Tillich, on poets like Wilhelm Tieck, Novalis, Coleridge, or Blake, on Christians and Marxists, "anthroposophists" and depth psychologists of the Jungian school.

German and English colonists brought Böhme with them to the United States, where, I hear, they now have a Jakob Böhme Society. Admittedly, Böhme's fellow countrymen have long forgotten what spiritual treasures lie hidden in the works of the master from Görlitz, who, I might mention, was translated early on into English (J. Sparrow, 1656, cited above), Dutch, French, and Russian. But now Jakob Böhme is being rediscovered, with his *Aurora,* his *Christosophia,* his *Theological Epistles,* along with other works from his busy pen. So why should I hesitate to introduce you, my dear Richard Rohr, to this great man. Give him a friendly reception. I feel a fraternal bond with him — and with you.

Contributors

Daniel Berrigan, May 9, 1921, grew up in Syracuse, N.Y.; ordained a Jesuit June 21, 1952; poet, author, and lecturer and an active resister against war and its technologies. His next book, *Minor Prophets, Major Issues,* is due to be published in 1993.

Werner Binder, Feb. 15, 1945, Zurich, Switzerland; trained as a psychologist, founder of SEBIL, a center for spiritual work in Zurich.

Patricia C. Brockman, March 7, 1929, Cincinnati; Ursuline of Brown County, doctorate in community psychology, Union Institute, Cincinnati; instructor and writer on spirituality; preparing a book on the tribal dreams of Christian communities.

Catherine Brunner-Dubay, Sept. 23, 1960, Fribourg, Switzerland; nurse, director of the Friedensgasse Community in Basel and its ministries.

Pierre Brunner-Dubay, March 2, 1956, Wettingen, Switzerland; training in business, theater arts, youth work; director of the Friedensgasse Community in Basel and its ministries.

Thomas Buchter, July 1, 1960, Schaffhausen, Switzerland; car mechanic, social worker, poet, currently living in Switzerland.

Dom Helder Camara, Feb. 7, 1909, Fortaleza, Brazil; ordained priest Aug. 15, 1931, and consecrated bishop April 20, 1952; retired as bishop of Recife and Olinda in 1985; author of *The Desert Is Fertile, Into Your Hands Lord,* and *Hoping Against All Hope.*

Teddy Carney, Nov. 21, 1927, Memphis; rancher, occasional journalist; lives alternatively on two ranches in California and Wyoming.

Joan Chittister, April 26, 1936, Dubois, Pa.; doctorate in communications and art; member of the Benedictine Sisters of Erie; author and international lecturer (peace, justice, and women's issues).

Ed Colina, June 26, 1954, Cincinnati; father of four, former member of New Jerusalem Community, serving in liturgical and peace ministries.

Avis Crowe, Nov. 27, 1938, Dallas; professional performer, producer of television commercials, and arts administrator; active in the Quaker community; spent five years at Pendle Hill as a student then as a facilitator of journal-writing classes and retreat leader.

Andreas Ebert, March 12, 1952, Berlin, Germany; training in theological studies, founder of the base community "Lorenzer Laden" in Nuremberg; author (*Discovering the Enneagram* with Richard Rohr) and translator; assistant director of the Institute for Parish Development of the United Lutheran Church of Germany.

Felix Felix, Feb. 18, 1957, Wettingen, Switzerland; theological studies; Swiss reformed pastor in Basel, developing an alternative city church ministry.

Matthew Fox, 1940; ordained a Dominican in 1967; advanced studies in philosophy and theology; founder and director of the Institute for Culture and Creation Spirituality in Oakland, Calif.; author of *A Spirituality Named Compassion, Original Blessing,* and *The Coming of the Cosmic Christ.*

Knut Grønvik, Sept. 19, 1953, Oslo, Norway; theological studies and leader of the Fredens Bolig Community; art director for a Christian public relations office; works for a Christian daily newspaper.

John Herdtner, Oct. 10, 1952, Loveland, Ohio; husband and father of four; former member of New Jerusalem Community serving in liturgical and peace ministries; currently working in housing the poor.

Raymond E. Hunthausen, Aug. 21, 1921, Anaconda, Montana; theological studies, priest, bishop; from 1975 archbishop of Seattle; peace activist; since 1982 has refused to pay 50 percent of his income tax to protest nuclear armament; retired since 1991.

Inge Kanitz, Aug. 10, 1911, Schulau/Holstein, Germany; nurse, voluntary parish worker; works with children from Vietnam who are war victims.

Joachim Kanitz, March 28, 1910, Altraden/Posen, Germany; theological studies, pastors' seminary of the Confessing Church, Finkenwalde (director: Dietrich Bonhoeffer); pastor, soldier, prisoner of war in France, clinic pastor, board member of the Christian Peace Conference.

Margaret Frings Keyes, Aug. 8, 1929, Butte, Montana; psychiatric social worker, Gestalt therapy (with Fritz Perls), transaction analysis (with Eric Berne); Enneagram teacher, Jungian psychotherapist in San Francisco; author of *Out of the Shadow* and other works.

Dietrich Koller, Oct. 27, 1931, Neuendettelsau, Germany; theological studies, Lutheran pastor in Lower Saxony and Bavaria, teacher at the Institute for Integrative Gestalt Therapy, pastor for the Lutheran-Benedictine Sister Community "Casteller Ring" at Schwanberg Castle in Bavaria.

Lucia Koller, Sept. 22, 1930, Nuremberg, Germany; rhythmics teacher; works with base communities in Santiago, Chile; lives in Schwanberg Castle, Bavaria.

Marion Küstenmacher, July 3, 1956, Würzburg, Germany; active with an ecumenical base community; degree in German studies and theology; editor; has given many papers and workshops on the Enneagram.

Werner Küstenmacher, August 9, 1953, Munich, Germany; Lutheran pastor and journalist, originated a weekly religious television program broadcast in Bavaria; also active as a writer about computers and a cartoonist.

Bill Lonneman, Nov. 24, 1957, Covington, Ky.; a registered nurse, married and father of two children; member of New Jerusalem Community where he was active in the leadership, pastoring, and justice ministries; currently active as a nurse and in the hospice ministry.

Frank Lorenz, Nov. 2, 1965, Velden/Vils, Germany; training in theological studies, radio, and theater arts; nurse at the Lighthouse, an AIDS hospice.

Anne Martina, July 12, 1955, Cincinnati; a founding member of the New Jerusalem Community; wife and mother of three; nurse.

Gerald May, June 12, 1940, Hillsdale, Mich.; M.D. from Wayne State University, Detroit; director for research and program development, Shalem Institute, Washington, D.C.; author of *Addiction and Grace* and other works.

Peter Meis, April 30, 1953, Leipzig, Germany; theological studies; youth pastor in Dresden, professor and dean of the College of Parish Deaconate and Religious Education in Moritzburg/Saxony.

Rita Meis, April 19, 1954, Limbach-Oberfrohna, Germany; pediatric nurse and social worker in Dresden.

Christa Mulack, Oct. 10, 1943; theological degree; edited a volume of feminist theology and has written books on Mary and Jesus.

Ched Myers, Feb. 1, 1955, Pasadena, Calif.; theology and New Testament studies; cofounder of the Bartimeus Community in San

Francisco; program director of the American Friends Service Committee for the Pacific Southwest; author of *Binding the Strong Man,* a commentary on the Gospel of Mark.

Helen Palmer, Nov. 24, 1937, New York; psychology teacher, director of an institute for the Enneagram and Inner Life, author of several publications on the Enneagram.

John Quigley, Feb. 20, 1945, London, Ontario; attended Duns Scotus College in Detroit; member of the Order of Friars Minor; ordained Dec. 21, 1972; presently director of the International OFM Office of Peace and Justice; editor of *Mustard Seed.*

Andreas Richter-Böhne, May 21, 1954, Konigshofen/Bavaria, Germany; theological studies; peace activist and pastor of the Lorenzer Laden base community in Nuremberg.

Pat Flatley Simmons, July 23, 1938, Erie, Pa.; worked in social services administration and child advocacy for fifteen years before coming to the Center for Action and Contemplation as codirector in 1988; involved in justice and peace ministries; master's level training in clinical psychology; widowed, the mother of four and grandmother of two.

Christina Spahn, Dec. 12, 1945, Seattle; codirector of the Center of Action and Contemplation since 1988; formerly the director of religious education for the archdiocese of Santa Fe; author of a high school text on ministry and three adult education texts.

Jim Wallis, June 2, 1948, Detroit; student leader of the late 1960s, theological studies in Chicago, founder of *Sojourners* magazine and community, peace activist; lives in Washington, D.C.; author of *Agenda for a Biblical People, Call to Conversion,* and *Revive Us Again.*

Gerhard Wehr, Sept. 26, 1931, Schweinfurt/Bavaria, Germany; deacon and author of several books including a biography of Carl Gustav Jung.